Having A Heart For God Devotional

365 Days of the
One Minute Bible Study

Tracy Baumer Fox

Layout design: Cheryl Perez

Cover design: Nicole Lyons

This Book is dedicated to two people

My Mom, The Reverend, Judith T. Baumer,

who gave me my very first Bible

and

Robin Minton who encouraged me to open it

and meditate on God's Word for myself

"AND YOU SHALL LOVE THE LORD YOUR GOD WITH ALL YOUR HEART, AND WITH ALL YOUR SOUL, AND WITH ALL YOUR MIND, AND WITH ALL YOUR STRENGTH."

Mark 12:30

Welcome to the Having A Heart For God, One Minute Bible Study, Devotional - affectionately known by readers all over the world as simply the OMBS. I created the <u>One Minute Bible Study</u> because I believe that all the answers for how to live a successful, happy, productive and meaningful life are clearly stated in the Bible.

However, most of us neither have the time nor the belief that we can interpret the Bible on our own. It seems complicated and not relevant to our modern 21st century life.

The goal of the OMBS is to educate men and women on the biblical principles and strategies that can be used daily. Each study is thoughtfully researched and broken down into bite-size, inspirational and applicable biblical truth.

The Bible has withstood the test of time because it is simply the greatest book ever written. It is enriching, uplifting, and always transformational because it connects you to the most powerful resource in the world – God, Himself.

What sets the OMBS apart is that you will be both educated about the Bible and inspired by God's Word daily. Readers tell me the OMBS is the "best minute of their day".

I sincerely pray that this devotional will result in you enjoying more peace, more purpose and more connection to God's will for your life.

I would love to hear from you. Please visit our website at <u>www.havingaheartforgod.com</u>

Sincerely

Tracy Fox

P.S. There are many people to thank who encouraged, supported, motivated and believed in the dream of getting this book in print. Mark, Maribeth, Pam, Marnie, Susan, Jake, Kim, just to name a few. However special appreciation goes to Nicole Lyons my beautiful friend and brilliantly talented cover artist.

Hi, Tracy. I LOVE OMBS! I have been a 'student' of the Bible all my life on an ecumenical basis. Your insights and declarations are right to the point and inspirational as well. Thank you and bless you!"

— *Kathleen, Orlando, Florida*

"Ok, Tracy, ALL of your lessons are outstanding, but today's was particularly amazing."

— *Haynes, Darien, Conn.*

"I just forwarded this to my three girls. It is so timely for me given that I will be sending off my youngest to college in a few short weeks."

— *Nancy, Rowayton, Conn.*

"Beautiful, poignant, personal. Your OMBS is a must-have devotional, Tracy. Thank you."

— *Susan, Minneapolis, Minn.*

"You have no idea how these bless me, especially this one! I run to my computer in the a.m. and then share it with my Bible study group!"

— *Louise, New Canaan, Conn.*

"Tracy, I feel as though I am just discovering the Bible and am absorbing your words. ... I cannot tell you how much these words mean to me ... they set me right in the morning, ground my day and have changed me for the better. Thank you so much."

— *Carmel, New York, N.Y.*

"Thank you, Tracy! Your messages always inspire me. God bless you."

— *Christopher, 22, student, East Africa*"

"Hi, Tracy! I have LOVED receiving your daily devotional. God bless you and thank you for bringing Scripture and provoking thought and practice of my faith."

— *Jenna, 55, Cary, S.C.*

"Tracy Fox, your OMBS has helped me at a very important time in my life when I was ready to raise my consciousness to a higher level in order to connect more closely with God."

— *Steve, Stamford, Conn.*

"I love these messages – I started every session with my group of abused girls in Kenya by having them sing 'This is the day ---.' Many blessings,"

— *Marilyn, Kenya, Africa*

The Bible Will Change Your Life

2 Timothy 3:16-17

"All Scripture is God-breathed and is useful for teaching, rebuking, correcting and training in righteousness, so that the servant of God may be thoroughly equipped for every good work."

Understanding the Bible and the power it has to transform our lives is the most amazing and eternally important venture we can ever undertake.

In our passage today, we discover the clue to why God's Word has the power to alter our destiny. We learn that Scripture is God-breathed and useful for teaching, rebuking, correcting and training in righteousness so that we can be equipped for every good work in God's kingdom.

The Bible is a personal love letter from God to His people. He spells out His character, His purpose and His principles so that we can live joy-filled, successful lives.

The word "Bible" comes from the Latin and Greek words meaning, "book". The Bible is a collection of sixty-six books written over many years by at least forty different authors. These writers were kings, fishermen, farmers, shepherds and doctors. You will find every kind of writing in the Bible - love letters, songs, historical records, diaries, visions, genealogies and stories. The Bible is divided into two main sections. The Old Testament (39 books) focuses on God's creation and His interaction with the nation of Israel. The New Testament (27 books) written later, focuses on Jesus and His early followers, called Christians.

The entire Bible points to God's intention to save the people He created and His desire to have perfect fellowship with mankind. Leviticus 26:12 states God avowing, *"I will walk among you and be your God, and you will be my people."* The Bible is written from God's perspective and explains to us how we can enjoy life here on earth and the life to come in Heaven for eternity thereafter.

One Minute Reflection
Do you believe the Bible is an accurate record of what God said?

"For the essential theme of the whole Bible from beginning to end is that God's historical purpose is to call out a people for Himself."
(John Stott)

Knowing Jesus Christ

<u>John 14:6-7</u>
"Jesus answered, "I am the way and the truth and the life. No one comes to the Father except through me. If you really know me, you will know my Father as well. From now on, you do know Him and have seen Him."

Here in John 14:6-7, Jesus tells us that He is in fact God. Jesus says: *"If you really know me, you will know my Father as well."*

It is important to deeply understand who Christ is and why He deserves our total allegiance.

What do we know about Jesus?
First, He claimed to be the fulfillment of the Old Testament Scriptures.
Second, He claimed to be the Son of God.
Third, He claimed to be the Savior and Judge of the world.

There is overwhelming evidence to Christ's divinity, power and authority. He taught the multitudes, He healed the sick, He governed nature, He had power over death, He performed miracles and He forgave sins.

We need to pay special attention to what Jesus Christ said about Himself. In our passage today, He refers to Himself as *"the way, the truth and the life"*. Jesus puts Himself forward as the one true God in whom we should place our faith and He then invites us to follow Him.

As Christians, our entire destiny is to conform to the likeness of Christ and in doing so we will be creating eternal, intimate fellowship with the God of the universe.

Knowing Christ is about relationship not religion.

<u>One Minute Reflection</u>
Do you truly believe that Jesus Christ is the Son of God?

"Instinctively, we do not class Him with others. Jesus is not one of the world's greatest - Jesus is apart. He is beyond our analysis. He confounds our canons of human nature. He compels our criticism and over leaps it. He awes our spirit. He said of Himself, "I AM." He assumed His uniqueness and did not draw attention to it. Jesus was sinless because He was selfless, and selflessness is love."
(Carnegie Simpson)

Be Still

Psalm 46:10
"Be Still and Know that I AM GOD."

One of the most effective ways to know God more deeply is simply to be still.

To be still means:
"not moving or making a sound; deep silence and calm".

That may sound like an outdated concept in our busy, noisy, distracted, 21st century lives, however we are told in Psalm 46 above, that if we want to know God, we must be still.

When was the last time we felt the profound presence of God in our life? What we need to be in search of is not just an intellectual connection but also a deep, abiding awareness that God is with us at the deepest heart and soul level.

Knowing God and experiencing His peace, wisdom and eternal love is one of the most profound ways to discover God's will for our life.

How to get still
Today, sit for 5 minutes in complete silence.
Find a place away from the daily distractions and invite God to join you.
Do not ask for anything; do not say anything.
Simply bask in the glory of God.
If your mind wanders, go back to surrendering all your thoughts to God.
When you are done, write down what you believe God wanted to impress upon you.

You Will Be Amazed!!

One Minute Reflection
Will you commit to more "stillness" in your life?

"One's action ought to come out of an achieved stillness:
not to be mere rushing on."
(D.H. Lawrence)

Discipline Of Prayer

<u>1 John 5:14-15</u>
"And this is the confidence which we have before Him, that, if we ask anything according to His will, He hears us. And if we know that He hears us in whatever we ask, we know that we have the requests which we have asked from Him."

Prayer is a discipline that completely transforms our lives!

<u>Why?</u>
The more we understand the heart of God, the more we are taught to see things from God's point of view and not just our own.

When we plug back into our Creator, He gives us the answers we seek.

Most of the serious iconoclasts of Christianity have viewed prayer as the primary business of their lives. Jesus, Moses, David and the Apostles invested a regular part of their day in prayer. Other great inspirational leaders such as Martin Luther, John Wesley, Charles Stanley, and Billy Graham - all have proclaimed the discipline of prayer as the most important of spiritual disciplines.

Prayer is something we learn and cultivate over time. The more time we spend in prayer, the better we get at it. The Bible teaches that prayer makes a difference in the events and situations of our lives.

Prayer is so important that it is mentioned over 250 times in Scripture.

In 1 John 5 above we are reminded of several things:
Prayer gives us an opportunity to share all aspects of our lives with God
Prayer gives us the chance to express our gratitude for the things God provides
Prayer provides the platform for confessing our sin and asking for help
Prayer is an act of worship to acknowledge that God is really in control of our lives
During prayer, we find communion with God

<u>One Minute Reflection</u>
How much more time could you dedicate to prayer this week?

"Fight all your battles on your knees."
(Charles Stanley)

The Sermon On The Mount

Matthew 5:1-2

"Now when Jesus saw the crowds, He went up on a mountainside and sat down. His disciples came to Him, and He began to teach them."

The Sermon on the Mount is considered the manifesto of Christ's teachings. Found in the Gospel of Matthew (chapters 5, 6 and 7). This sermon takes place relatively early in the ministry of Jesus after He has been baptized by John the Baptist and preached in Galilee.

What we know is that Jesus went up to a mountain, sat down and started to teach. In attendance were His twelve, newly appointed inner circle, other disciples, and then, the crowds. Even though Jesus' words were directed to His disciples at that time in history, they are also meant to speak personally to all of us who follow Christ today.

This sermon is the longest piece of teaching from Jesus in the New Testament and includes some of the best-known Scripture such as the Beatitudes and the Lord's Prayer. The sermon addresses both inward motives and outward conduct too.

Jesus' Sermon on the Mount is about a new kingdom, where Jesus rules as king. So when Jesus teaches, He is not just advocating rules or giving advice, He is describing a new life that can only be accessed by having faith in Him and obeying His words.

If we want to really call ourselves Christians then we need to follow Christ.
Investing time reading the Sermon on the Mount will give us a better understanding of Christ's teachings and how to apply them to our modern lives.
When we follow Christ, He promises a life full of love, grace, wisdom and deep connection to our source and Creator.

One Minute Reflection
Have you read the Sermon on the Mount for yourself?

"Our lives should always be the first things to speak; and if our lips speak more than our lives, it will avail very little. So often the tragedy has been that people proclaim the gospel in words, but their whole life and demeanor has been a denial of it. We need to study and learn from the Sermon on the Mount."
(Martyn Lloyd-Jones)

Blessed Are

Matthew 5:3-4
*"Blessed are the poor in spirit, for theirs is the kingdom of Heaven.
Blessed are those who mourn, for they will be comforted."*

The Sermon on the Mount is the most famous teaching Jesus ever gave because it describes what human life and human community looks like under the rule of God. It describes a "kingdom" that Jesus spoke of often.

You may know today's passage of Scripture from Matthew 5 by heart. It is the start of the Beatitudes. Here Jesus states several blessings each beginning with the phrase, "Blessed are". Each saying speaks of a blessing or "divine favor" bestowed upon a person resulting from the possession of a certain character quality.

The word "beatitude" comes from the Latin *beatitudo*, meaning "blessedness". The phrase "Blessed are" in each of the beatitudes implies a current state of happiness or well being. In other words, Jesus was saying that divinely happy and fortunate are those who possess these inward qualities.

If you read all of the beatitudes, several qualities of the blessed are:
"the poor in spirit"
"those who mourn"
"the meek"
"the righteous"
"the merciful"
"the pure in heart"
and
"the peacemakers"

Jesus tells us the place to start if we want to be blessed is to be "poor in spirit" or humble before God and to "mourn" over our own sin. This is a place of complete humility and repentance, a place where we are dependent upon God and a place where we find fellowship with God is the very foundation of true happiness.

One Minute Reflection
Which quality of Christ will you reflect today?

"I am not lucky, I am blessed."
(Terry Laughlin)

Money Is A Spiritual Issue

<u>Matthew 19:24</u>
"Again I tell you, it is easier for a camel to go through the eye of a needle than for someone who is rich to enter the kingdom of God."

Money is a daily reality in our lives. How much we earn, how much we spend, and how much we give away are questions that are always on our minds.

We may not want to examine our issues surrounding money, but make no mistake; the Bible declares that money is a spiritual issue.

One of Christ's most potent warnings about money is stated in the passage above from Matthew 19:24.

Jesus uses a hyperbole to explain His teaching. He tells us that it will be easier for a camel to go through the eye of a needle than for a rich man to enter the Kingdom of Heaven. In other words, it will be impossible.

Jesus was contradicting the rabbinical teaching of the time that rich people were blessed by God and therefore more likely candidates for entry into Heaven. Jesus is destroying that line of thinking and reminding His disciples that no man can save himself. In fact, the pursuit of material wealth often becomes a stumbling block to our own righteousness.

Why?
Because slowly but surely, the pursuit of money can take first place in our lives while God becomes a distant second concern. We start to gain more confidence in our earthly treasures than in our allegiance to God for all things.

As we follow Christ we need to consistently check our motives and discipline ourselves to ensure that money does not become a primary idol in our lives.

<u>One Minute Reflection</u>
How would you rate your own love of money?

"If a person gets his attitude toward money straight, it will help straighten out almost every other area in his life."
(Billy Graham)

Audience Of One

Matthew 6:1
"Be careful not to practice your righteousness in front of others to be seen by them. If you do, you will have no reward from your Father in Heaven."

Most of us, whether we are aware of it or not, do things to please an audience. This has become increasingly true in our modern, publicity seeking, popularity-concerned, reality-television based society.

The question is not whether we have an audience but which audience we have.

As followers of Jesus Christ, we should only be concerned with God being our number one fan. When we take this pursuit seriously almost all of our endeavors are transformed.

God has designed each of His commands for our benefit: to protect us from harm and help us develop a foundational contentment, regardless of circumstance.

Jesus makes it very clear in our passage today that we are not to practice our righteousness in front of others because if we do, we will receive no reward from our Father in Heaven. When we live only for God's praise, we realize that His commands are actually blessings in disguise.

If we want to create a tangible difference in our own call as Christians, we need to grow in our awareness that only one opinion ultimately matters.

Our desire should be to please God alone.

One Minute Reflection
What audience do you care about and why?

"I have only one audience. Before you I have nothing to prove, nothing to gain, nothing to lose."
(Winston Churchill)

What Do You Think?

<u>Proverbs 23:7</u>
"For as He thinks in His heart, so is He."

Today we are looking at our thinking. A lot of modern philosophers take credit for the wisdom of Proverbs 23 but of course God said it first in the Bible in no uncertain terms.

As we think - so shall we be!
What we think about matters. The people who are the happiest and most fulfilled with their lives are the people who focus on the Word of God and His promises. They are intentional about maintaining joy and gratitude as they honor God with their lives.
And we can experience the same thing!
If we want to be happy and joyful, we must mentally affirm and reaffirm all good things so that it becomes our second nature to emit joy!

Here Are Some Suggestions For A Happy and Successful Mindset

1) Start your day with Scripture: *"This is the day the Lord hath made - let me rejoice and be glad it in" (Psalm 118:24)*

2) Do not speak negative words about other people, situations, or feelings

3) Thank God for everything in your life - both the good and the bad. Then remind yourself that God has a better plan in mind when we place our trust in Him

4) Expect only the best and then go get it

5) Be very careful what you think about:
As Philippians 4:8 reminds us, *"Finally, brethren, whatsoever things are true, whatsoever things are honorable, whatsoever things are just, whatsoever things are pure, whatsoever things are lovely, whatsoever things are of good report; if there be any virtue, and if there be any praise, think on these things."*

<u>One Minute Reflection</u>
What do you think about all day long?

"Whether you think you can, or you think you can't, you are always right." (Henry Ford)

Joy, Prayer, And Thanks

1Thessalonians 5:16-18
"Be joyful always; pray continually; give thanks in all circumstances,
for this is God's will for you in Christ Jesus."

The Bible is filled with life principles!
A principle is a fundamental truth or proposition that serves as the
foundation for a system of belief that governs one's personal behavior.
1 Thessalonians was the first letter Paul wrote to a group of new
believers who lived in the capital city of Thessalonica in the Roman
province of Macedonia. It is a short letter filled with extensive wisdom
on how to live the committed Christian life.

The Apostle Paul shares a three-step principle for a successful life

Be Joyful Always
Being joyful always might seem like a tall order but not as far as God is
concerned. We serve an awesome, all loving, all powerful, all sacrificing
God who desires nothing more than deep and intimate fellowship with
the men and women He created. The reason we can be joyful always is
that our joy is not self-manufactured. Instead, it comes from the Holy
Spirit that God gave to us the moment we put our faith in Jesus Christ.

Pray Continually
The primary tool for communication with God is prayer. He tells us to
bring the big requests and the tiny details too. Prayer is not reserved
only for a Sunday morning church service. God wants all of us, every
minute of every day.

Give Thanks In All Circumstances
By thanking God for whatever lays before us - the promotion or the
demotion, the friendship or the betrayal, the prosperity or the poverty,
we are acknowledging God has it covered. Our gratitude demonstrates
true faith.

One Minute Reflection
**Can you commit to being joyful, praying continually and giving
thanks in everything?**

"It is not how much we have, but how much we enjoy, that makes
happiness."
(Charles Spurgeon)

God's Wisdom

James 1:5
"If any of you lacks wisdom, you should ask God, who gives generously to all without finding fault, and it will be given to you."

Most scholars believe the book of James was written around 45 A.D. making it the first (or one of the first books) of the New Testament. James was the half-brother of Jesus and if we study the book of James carefully, we will find striking similarities to the teaching of Jesus in the Gospels.

The central message of James is very practical; namely that genuine faith in Christ will be reflected in a life of obedience to His teaching.

James was often referred to as "camel knees" because of his devotion to prayer. James developed a humble recognition that the wisdom of God is far better than the world's strategies for enjoying a purpose-driven life. James encourages us to trust in God above all other endeavors.

How do we discover God's wisdom?
James tell us in the Scripture passage above from Chapter 1:5.

1) Know that God is the source for all wisdom.

2) Know that God reveals His wisdom to anyone that asks.

3) Know that God gives generously and without finding fault to everyone that asks Him in faith.

One Minute Reflection
How will you seek God's wisdom over worldly strategies this week?

"Wisdom in Scripture is, broadly speaking, the knowledge of God's world and the knack of fitting oneself into it."
(Cornelius Plantinga)

Taming Of The Tongue

James 3:3-5

"When we put bits into the mouths of horses to make them obey us, we can turn the whole animal. Or take ships as an example. Although they are so large and are driven by strong winds, they are steered by a very small rudder wherever the pilot wants to go. Likewise the tongue is a small part of the body, but it makes great boasts."

The average person will spend one fifth of their life talking. James reminds us that the tongue is a powerful instrument. It can destroy relationships. It can wreck a marriage. It can devastate a family. It can divide a nation. It can lead to violence, death and war. On the other hand, a tongue can build up. It can create love, encouragement, comfort, peace, and joy. It can save a family, a friendship or even a life. James is telling us in our passage that the tongue is a powerful tool and he is emphasizing that if we get a hold of it and control it, we can control the rest of us as well including our behavior, our spiritual growth, and our destiny.

To help us understand this, James gives us two illustrations.

A horse.
We control a horse by controlling his tongue. We put a piece of metal in a horse's mouth called a "bit" which lies on his tongue. By controlling the horse's tongue we control the horse's movements.

The ships.
Although ships are huge and driven by strong winds, they are maneuvered with a very small rudder.

James suggests that if we want to bring our whole spiritual life under control, we need to work on our tongue. The discipline of the tongue is both a means to spiritual maturity and evidence that we are growing into the people God calls us to be.

<u>One Minute Reflection</u>
Do your words reflect your own spiritual growth?

"Throughout the ages the church has understood that the most significant manifestation of true faith is love. Faith without love is not faith, only speculation or knowledge or mere intellectual assent. The fruit of authentic faith is always love."
(R.C. Sproul)

True Humility Before God

<u>James 4:10</u>
"Humble yourself in the sight of the Lord and He will lift you up."

In this passage from the book of James we learn that the most expedient way to be exalted by God is to humble ourselves in His presence.

What is true humility?
It means seeing God as the gracious giver of everything and seeing ourselves as sinful and needy in His presence.

Ultimately we need to get the focus off our own abilities and trust totally in God, so that He gets all the glory and our own light is merely a reflection of all He has done.

How do we keep our humility in check?

1) Routinely confess our sin to God
2) Always keep God's Grace in view
3) Remember that all we have comes from God
4) Invite God to search and expose places where pride has taken root
5) Get on our knees as an act of humility before God in prayer

True humility is a place where our pride is abandoned and our hope is lifted.
It is when we admit our need and claim our dependence upon Almighty God.

<u>One Minute Reflection</u>
What area of your life could you demonstrate more humility?

"The true way to be humble, is not to stoop until you are smaller than yourself, but to stand at your real height against some higher nature."
(Philip Brooks)

Patience And Reward

James 5:7
"Be patient, then, brothers, until the Lord's coming. See how the farmer waits for the land to yield its valuable crop and how patient he is for the autumn and spring rains."

James 5:7 teaches us about patience and its reward.
A great lesson in our hurried and fast paced modern life.

James describes a familiar scene of farm life to help us learn the virtue of patience. The farmer can prepare the soil, plant the seed and keep the field weeded but what he cannot do is make the seed grow. The farmer is completely dependent on God for the timing of that.

We also notice that the farmer has to wait through both a late autumn and a spring rain, until the crop grows to maturity. We are being reminded that there is no hurrying God's perfect timing.

A valuable lesson for us!

We must also be patient when waiting on God for something important. We may be facing hardships, trials, unmet needs, strained relationships, sickness, fear, uncertainty, anxiety, discouragement or a diagnosis. On the other hand, we might be waiting for a promotion, an important deal, a contract, a raise or a great inheritance.

Regardless of circumstance, we can count on God's grace and good timing. We must do everything to protect it, nourish it, grow it and sustain it just like the farmer does with his seed.

When we live by faith, we look toward the future reward, knowing that it will come.

One Minute Reflection
What day of "harvest" are you looking toward?

"Adopt the pace of nature: her secret is patience."
(Ralph Waldo Emerson)

For The Love Of God

"Whoever does not love does not know God, because God is love."

Why do we need to study and understand the love of God?

Arthur Walkington Pink (1 April 1886 - 15 July 1952), an English Christian evangelist and biblical scholar, explained it best when he penned these famous words:
"There are many who talk about the love of God, who are total strangers to the God of love. The divine love is commonly regarded as a species of amiable weakness, a sort of good-natured indulgence; it is reduced to a mere sickly sentiment, patterned after human emotion. The truth is that on this, as on everything else, our thoughts need to be formed and regulated by what is revealed in Scripture. The better we are acquainted with His love-its character, fullness, blessedness-the more our hearts will be drawn out in love to Him."

If you and I are going to testify to God's love and explain it to a searching world, we need to be careful not to distort the truth of it. God is the One who defines love and we must accept His definition and then express it clearly to those in need.

Scripture tells us
God's Love is Infinite, Limitless, Unfathomable
God's Love is Eternal
God's Love is Immutable and Changeless
God's Love is Holy
God's Love is Sacrificial
God's Love is Personal and Individual
God's Love is the Source of Human Love
God's Love is Expressed and Experienced in Christ
God's Love is Proven in the Forgiveness of Sins

As 1 John 4:8 above reminds us,
We only know love, because God is love.

One Minute Reflection
What do you know for sure about God's love?

"On the whole, God's love for us is a much safer subject to think about than our love for Him."
(C.S. Lewis)

It's Personal

1 Peter 5:7
"Cast all your anxiety on Him because He cares for you."

One of the hardest things for people to come to terms with is that God's love is personal and individual. We sometimes think that even almighty God doesn't have the time or energy to deal with the details of our lives. Luckily the Bible makes it very clear that God is a God who expresses the deepest intimacy and concern for us.

In 1 Peter 5:7 above, Peter tells us, *"God cares for you"*. These are significant words that come from Simon Peter who was an early Christian leader and one of the twelve apostles of Jesus Christ. Peter is featured prominently in the New Testament Gospels and the Acts of the Apostles and is venerated as a saint.

We know from reading the Bible that Peter was a worrier like many of us. He had many questions as well as nagging doubts. And so when Peter tells us that we can cast all our anxiety upon God because He cares for us, those words have a special meaning because they come from a man in search of the truth himself.

Peter makes it clear that God cares for us.

Jesus also spoke of the individual care and concern of God in Matthew 10:29-3. He said, *"Are not two sparrows sold for a penny? Yet not one of them will fall to the ground apart from the will of your Father. And even the very hairs of your head are all numbered. So don't be afraid; you are worth more than many sparrows"*.

This reminds us that every detail is within God's reach and He gives us a permanent reassurance that we are never alone. Every messy detail of our lives has purpose and meaning to God.

One Minute Reflection
Have you "casted" all your cares upon God?

"In almost everything that touches our everyday life on earth, God is pleased when we're pleased. He wills that we be as free as birds to soar and sing our maker's praise without anxiety."
(A.W. Tozer)

Some Things Never Change

<u>James 1:17</u>
"Every good thing bestowed and every perfect gift is from above, coming down from the Father of lights, with whom there is no variation, or shifting shadow."

Today we discover that God's love never changes. This fact distinguishes God from all His creatures. Human beings are very emotional and our love toward someone or something can quickly and illogically change at a moment's notice. We, ourselves, may have experienced a fluctuation in how we love and who we love but God is not like that. His love is unchanging.

What we know from Scripture is God is immutable in His essence. His nature and being are infinite. All that He is today, He has ever been, and will ever be.

And since God is always perfect, we can count on God's love.

James 1:17 above illustrates that every perfect thing comes from God and there is no "variation" or "shifting shadow". The Bible affirms that God is good and that He continually pours out His mercy upon mankind.

What does this mean for you and for me?

Whether we are searching for a promise of comfort, forgiveness, peace, wisdom, help with temptation, or relief from the pressure of daily life, God will deliver on His promises. He desires to give us every good thing because He loves us and that love can never change.

<u>One Minute Reflection</u>
What aspect of God's love do you need to count on?

"Philosophies change by the day while God never changes, simply because, being perfect, He does not have to change!"
(A.B. Simpson)

Experiencing God's Love

Ephesians 3:18-19
"And I pray that you, being rooted and established in love, may have power, together with all the Lord's Holy people, to grasp how wide and long and high and deep is the love of Christ, and to know this love that surpasses knowledge-that you may be filled to the measure of all the fullness of God."

Today's lesson is about how God's love is expressed and experienced in Christ. There may be no better experience than the one Paul is discussing in his letter to the Ephesian Church in our passage above. It is the experience of being *"filled to the measure of all the fullness of God".*

Paul is perhaps the most influential early Christian missionary and leader of the first generation of Christians. Almost half of the books of the New Testament are credited to his authorship. In Ephesians above, Paul is praying that the people of Ephesus can truly experience the love of God. He tells them that the fullest expression of God's love is experienced in Jesus Christ. We all experience God's love in varying degrees. So the question is how can we experience and grasp *"how wide and long and high and deep is the love of Christ".*

We need to know three things.

1)   Comprehending Christ's love does not come naturally, but supernaturally. We need to invite the Holy Spirit to fill us to the measure of all the fullness of God.

2) Knowing Christ's love is a never-ending process, because God's love is eternal.

3) We can know God's love through hearing His word and experiencing the revelation of His truth.

In other words, it is one thing to fall in love with God, but it's another thing to sustain it and cause it to grow deeper over the years. To fully experience God's love in all its riches and glory we must know Christ and then invite the Holy Spirit to fill us up until we overflow.

One Minute Reflection
Do you feel rooted and established in God's love?

"Intense love does not measure, it just gives."
(Mother Teresa)

A Spiritual Heritage

Isaiah 40:4-5
"Every valley shall be raised up, every mountain and hill made low; the rough ground shall become level, the rugged places a plain. And the glory of the Lord will be revealed, and all people will see it together. For the mouth of the Lord has spoken."

Today we celebrate the birthday of Martin Luther King Jr. Martin Luther King, Jr. (January 15, 1929 - April 4, 1968) was an American clergyman, activist, and prominent leader in the Civil Rights Movement. King also became the youngest recipient of the Nobel Peace Prize.

As we celebrate the life of the Rev. Dr. Martin Luther King Jr., we remember how important the Bible was to him and that he left all of us with a very special spiritual legacy. Dr. King's vision of racial justice was deeply rooted in the Judeo-Christian heritage. It was the Bible that led him to choose the way of love expressed by Christ and nonviolent protest over hatred and despair.

Dr. King's "I Have A Dream" speech expressed his desire for a day when American people came together and when freedom and justice would reign. His speech echoed the prophet Isaiah whose passage above states: *"every valley shall be raised up, every mountain and hill made low ... and the glory of the Lord will be revealed, and all people will see it together."*
Dr. King delivered his last speech on April 3rd, 1968 called, "I've Been to the Mountaintop", and it is also full of prophetic, biblical references. He was assassinated the next day.

This is what Dr. King said:
"I just want to do God's will. And He's allowed me to go up to the mountain. And I've looked over. And I've seen the Promised Land. I may not get there with you. But I want you to know tonight, that we, as a people, will get to the Promised Land. So I'm happy, tonight. I'm not worried about anything. I'm not fearing any man. Mine eyes have seen the glory of the coming of the Lord".

One Minute Reflection
What will your spiritual legacy be?

"I have decided to stick with love. Hate is too great a burden to bear."
(Martin Luther King, Jr.)

A New Command

John 13:34
"A new command I give you: Love one another. As I have loved you, so you must love one another. By this all men will know that you are my disciples, if you love one another."

The "new commandment" of Jesus found in John 13:34 above *("love one another as I have loved you")* is part of the final instructions given to His disciples after the Last Supper had ended. It is found in the Gospel of John, which was written around 80 A.D.

John was one of Jesus' closest companions and was included in His "inner circle" which is reflected in the fact that John never referred to himself by name but called himself "the disciple whom Jesus loved".

Loving each other is clearly not a new command. It was already spelled out in the Old Testament Book of Leviticus 19:18 which stated, *"You shall love your neighbor as yourself"*. The newness of the command is found in the second half of the Scripture passage in the words - *"as I have loved you."*
Jesus now sets the pattern by which we are to live out our love.

We learn two significant lessons.

One
We are to love our neighbor as ourselves, but we are also to love our neighbor as Christ loved us, and that is often far more than we love ourselves.

Two
We are to use God's supernatural power found in the Holy Spirit to show deep abiding love of Jesus to others. We don't have to depend on our own limited ability or strength to love others. Jesus tells us that if we demonstrate this new command of love, the world will know we are truly disciples of Him.

One Minute Reflection
In what way will you love others as Christ loved you today?

"Learning how to love your neighbor requires a willingness to draw on the strength of Jesus Christ as you die to self and live for Him. Living in this manner allows you to practice biblical love for others in spite of adverse circumstances or your feelings to the contrary."
(John C. Broger)

Practical Love

1 John 4:7
"Dear friends, let us love one another, for love comes from God. Everyone who loves has been born of God and knows God."

Today's lesson is about love in action.

John is teaching us in the passage above about a very simple fact. God is love. Not just that God can love or does love but that He defines love by His very nature.
We are invited to understand God's love and then live it out in our daily life.

We can live out God's love in three practical ways.

Forgive One Another
The ultimate example of forgiveness was displayed when Jesus hung on the Cross and cried out for those who were crucifying Him: *"Father, forgive them, for they do not know what they are doing"* (Luke 23:34).
We should forgive others even when they don't deserve it or ask for it.
We can forgive others as Christ forgave us.

Accept One Another
To truly love someone, we must not judge him or her because the Bible teaches that true love keeps no record of wrongs. To demonstrate God's love is to be patient and kind, even when someone does not meet our expectations,
We can accept others as Christ accepts us.

Honor One another
To honor someone means, "to esteem someone as highly valuable". We need to treat others as though they are the unique handiwork of God, special in every way because God created them in His image. When we value others above ourselves, we are emulating the attitude of Christ,
We can honor others as God honors us.

One Minute Reflection
Can you accept and honor everyone you meet today?

"If I take offense easily; if I am content to continue in cold unfriendliness, though friendship be possible, then I know nothing of Calvary love."
(Amy Carmichael)

Love Is Patient

1 Corinthians 13:4
"Love is patient, love is kind."

There is a Peanuts cartoon showing Lucy standing with her arms folded and a stern expression on her face. Charlie Brown pleads, "Lucy, you must be more loving. This world really needs love. You have to let yourself love to make this world a better place." Lucy angrily whirls around and knocks Charlie Brown to the ground. She screams at him, "Look, Blockhead, the world I love, it's the people I can't stand."

Loving in the abstract is easy, but loving in reality can often be quite hard.
The Apostle Paul tells us in our passage today that there are two important aspects to love that we need to embody in our own lives.

1) Love is Patient
The word for patience used here is derived from the word, makrothumeo which is made up of two words, makros, meaning "long" and, humos, meaning "passion, anger, rage." The word literally means long tempered or long-suffering. The word denotes a long waiting time while we endure another's shortcomings because we are not without faults of our own. Patient love will endure because it is willing to put up with the inadequacies of others.

2) Love is Kind
The love of kindness is demonstrated by seeking to do good. It cares about the welfare of others. Christ spent a great portion of His life simply helping people and we can emulate that kind of love in our own life. We can be kind with an encouraging word, a gentle hug, an open door, an unexpected invitation, a hot meal, an apology, a phone call, a hand up, or a way out. Being kind denotes the willingness to put oneself at the service of others.

One Minute Reflection
How will you demonstrate patience and kindness today?

"This year, or this month, or, more likely, this very day, we have failed to practice ourselves the kind of behavior we expect from other people."
(C. S. Lewis)

Romantic/Marital Love

<u>Song of Solomon 6:3</u>
"I am my beloved's and my beloved is mine, He who pastures his flock among the lilies."

The Song of Solomon is found in the Old Testament.
Today's passage is part of a ballad regarding the romantic love between a man and a woman.

Written by King Solomon, this beautiful poem literally depicts his courtship and wedding to a shepherdess along with the joys and heartbreaks of relational love.
On a deeper level, marital love also depicts God's love of His people.

Solomon has several themes here.

1) We can learn to express ourselves gently and poetically
Our love for God and our love for our spouse should be of the same highest order expressed in tender and profound words. We can learn to speak a gentler language, full of support, intention and devotion.

2) We are incomplete without each other and without God
Men and women were made in the image of God for the delight of each other and for deep intimate fellowship with their Creator.

3) God authored biblical, marital love
Loving one's spouse is both a choice, and a command of God.
Be proud of your union and celebrate it. God chose marriage as something to be "set apart". This is why marriage is called "Holy Matrimony". We can honor that love with commitment and joy.

<u>One Minute Reflection</u>
How can your romantic life reflect God's love?

"When a man and a woman give themselves to each other in an act of marital love, they can know the love of Christ as no one else can know it."
(Vernon McGee)

Jonah And The Whale

Jonah 1:3
"But Jonah ran away from the Lord and headed for Tarshish. He went down to Joppa, where he found a ship bound for that port. After paying the fare, he went aboard and sailed for Tarshish to flee from the Lord."

Jonah was a prophet from Galilee and his story takes place somewhere between 780 B.C and 760 B.C. During this period of history, Assyria was a powerful, evil nation and Israel's most dreaded enemy. The Lord spoke to Jonah and told him to go to the capital city of Nineveh, but clearly Jonah did not want to go. He tried numerous plans to escape God's plan and eventually ends up swallowed by a whale.

For three days and nights Jonah remained alive inside the whale. This gives him time to think about God and how he had ultimately disobeyed Him. Finally Jonah cried out to God, which causes the whale to open his mouth and deliver Jonah safely on dry land.

What is particularly interesting about this story is that Jesus, Himself, mentions it in Matthew 12:39-41 and Luke 11:29-30. He said, *"For as Jonah was three days and three nights in the whale's belly so shall the Son of man be three days and three nights in the heart of the earth."*

What are the lessons for us?

God is everywhere - there is no fleeing from His commands
There are consequences to disobeying God
God's plan is always better than anything we can devise
God never turns away from a repentant heart
God uses trials not to punish us but to bring us back to Him
God will pursue us to the ends of the earth
When we cry out to God, He delivers us

One Minute Reflection
What lesson you can take from the story of Jonah and the Whale?

"The remarkable thing about God is that when you fear God, you fear nothing else, whereas if you do not fear God, you fear everything else."
(Oswald Chambers)

I Am The Bread Of Life

John 6:35

"Then Jesus declared, 'I am the bread of life. Whoever comes to me will never go hungry, and whoever believes in me will never be thirsty.'"

John Chapter 6 opens with Jesus crossing over to the far side of the Sea of Galilee. A large group of people was following Him after they had witnessed His miraculous healing of the sick. Jesus, seeing the great crowd, asked His disciples where they might find enough bread to feed all the hungry people. He eventually takes five loaves and two fish, blesses them, gives thanks and feeds the crowd. It could be argued that this is the most significant miracle Jesus performed, since it's the only one recorded in all four Gospels. Right after the feeding of the 5,000, Jesus made the first of the "I AM" statements recorded above. He declared, *"I am the bread of life."*

The context is significant
The crowd following Jesus wanted literal bread to satisfy their physical hunger; but Jesus is spiritual bread, to give and sustain spiritual life; He doesn't give the bread, He is the bread.

Why is this important for us to know?
The truth is that we are still hungry for spiritual bread today. We fill up on all sorts of things to satiate our appetite including drugs, alcohol, food, shopping, sex, fame, and money. St. Augustine observed that every single person has a God-shaped hole in his or her soul. We can attempt to fill up on a host of other things, but ultimately nothing satisfies our hunger except Jesus and His Gospel message.

What does this Scripture ultimately mean for us?
When we are willing to surrender our insufficient resources and abilities (as in five loaves and two fish) to Jesus to use as He pleases, He exchanges His sufficiency for our insufficiency.

One Minute Reflection
What does "I am the bread of life" mean to you personally?

"Nothing makes God more supreme and more central in worship than when a people are utterly persuaded that nothing - not money or prestige or leisure or family or job or health or sports or toys or friends - nothing is going to bring satisfaction to their sinful, guilty, aching hearts besides God."
(John Piper)

I Am The Light Of The World

<u>John 8:12</u>
"When Jesus spoke again to the people, He said, 'I am the light of the world. Whoever follows me will never walk in darkness, but will have the light of life.'"

Today we are examining Jesus' claim that He is the light of the world. Darkness and light are familiar metaphors in Scripture. Jesus brings spiritual illumination into each believer, enabling us to have "the light of life".

The context for this revelation by Jesus is significant. John hints that Jesus probably declared Himself to be the light of the world during the celebration of the Feast of Tabernacles in Jerusalem which recalled the wandering (in darkness) of Israel in the desert before their occupation of the Promised Land.

There are four truths concerning Jesus being "light" from our passage today.

1) Jesus is declaring to us that He came into the world to manifest the very glory of God. Jesus shines with the full brilliance and nature of God.

2) Light in Scripture stands for all, which is morally pure, and without sin. Jesus is the manifestation of all that is perfect.

3) Light also stands for truth and guidance. When we trust completely in Christ, we will have direction for our lives. We will no longer be stumbling around in the dark trying to figure out the best path for our daily life. Christ gives us answers.

4) Jesus is the source of spiritual life. Jesus promises to shine light on the dark areas of our life. When we follow Him, we are convicted of our sin and need for a Savior.

<u>One Minute Reflection</u>
How is Christ the "light of the world" to you?

"What right do we have to make God out to be someone other than who He really is in order to make people like Him more? Honor God by declaring the truth about Him."
(Jim Elliff)

I Am The Gate For The Sheep

John 10-7-9
"Therefore Jesus said again, 'Very truly I tell you, I am the gate for the sheep. All who have come before me are thieves and robbers, but the sheep have not listened to them. I am the gate; whoever enters through me will be saved.'"

Here in John 10, Jesus declares, *"I am the gate for the sheep"*. Jesus' metaphor would be familiar to the people of His day, since they understood historical customs, as we do not. The sheep pen had only one gate; there was only one way for the sheep to get in and one way to get out.

Jesus chooses this metaphor on purpose. We are the sheep and He is the gate. When He says, *"I am the gate"*, we are to understand that He is the only gate by which the sheep (us) may make their way into the pen. Moreover, once the sheep are safely inside the pen, the Shepherd will use Himself as the gate to protect His flock.

So what kind of gate is Jesus?

Jesus is an inviting gate
Christ forces no one to enter but He does invite us to come.

Jesus is a saving gate
Jesus says that anyone who enters will be saved. We can be saved from sin, saved from ourselves, saved from the wrath of God, and saved from *"thieves and robbers"* who will try to lead us astray.

Jesus is a provisional gate
Jesus promises that once we enter through Him, the gate, we will find His full provision for everything we need.

One Minute Reflection
Is Christ the gate you will enter by today?

"Do not look to your hope, but to Christ, the source of your hope."
(C.H. Spurgeon)

He Can Empathize

<u>Hebrews 4:15</u>
"For we do not have a high priest who is unable to empathize with our weaknesses, but we have one who has been tempted in every way, just as we are - yet He did not sin."

Empathy is the ability to mutually experience the thoughts, emotions, and direct experience of others. It goes beyond sympathy, which is a feeling of care and understanding for the suffering of others. Both words have similar usage but differ in their emotional meaning.

We all wish there was someone who could empathize with our specific situation. We want to surrender our burdens to someone who has been through the same experience we have been through. We are in search of someone who can understand the challenges we face at any given moment and the depth of feeling that pulls at our heart.

Hebrews 4:15 above claims that Jesus is able to empathize with our weaknesses because He, Himself, has been tempted in every way.

Jesus has been tempted with every danger, every sorrow, every trial, every addiction that human life can inflict. He was exposed to all of them and He endured triumphantly every form of testing that a man could possibly encounter.

Jesus knows our battles. He understands and empathizes with us and He also provides a way through our trials and heartaches. All we have to do is surrender our burdens to Him and He will grant us a peace that surpasses all understanding.

Jesus offers us forgiveness for our past sins and a saving power to overcome any additional temptation in the future,

One Minute Reflection
Is there something you are being tempted with today?

"Every temptation, directly or indirectly, is the temptation to doubt and distrust God."
(John MacArthur)

Heavenly Calling

<u>Hebrews 3:1</u>
"Therefore, Holy brothers and sisters, who share in the heavenly calling, fix your thoughts on Jesus, whom we acknowledge as our apostle and high priest."

The Bible tells us that as Christians we share in a *"heavenly calling"*. What exactly does that mean? Our passage gives us insight into four specific points and they all have to do with our identity in Christ.

First
Notice that this passage is addressed to "*Holy brothers and sisters*". This is anyone who has placed his/her trust in Jesus Christ as their Lord and Savior. The word "Holy" means that because of our faith in Christ, we have been sanctified and therefore "set apart" as sacred in the eyes of God. When we start to identify ourselves as sacred, our behavior has a corresponding transformation. We want to please God.

Second
To be *"partakers of the heavenly calling"* conveys that although we reside here on earth, our home is actually in Heaven. This is clearly explained in John 18:36, *"Jesus answered, My kingdom is not of this world."*

Third
Our passage makes a distinction about the dual nature of Jesus. He is both an "Apostle" signifying that Jesus represents the full manifestation of God to us. And He is also a "High Priest" signifying that Jesus intercedes for us to God. We can think of Jesus as the bridge between man and God.

Finally
We are asked to "consider" Jesus Christ. To do this seriously, we must spend time, not only reading the Bible about Christ, but also meditating on whom He is and what His mission was on earth. Our heavenly calling is to know Christ, to love Christ and to ultimately emulate Christ.

<u>One Minute Reflection</u>
Do you know what your heavenly calling is?

"Nothing makes God more supreme and more central in worship than when a people are utterly persuaded that nothing - not money or prestige or leisure or family or job or health or sports or toys or friends - nothing is going to bring satisfaction to their sinful, guilty, aching hearts besides God." (John Piper)

Abraham Sacrifices His Son

Genesis 22:1-2

"Some time later God tested Abraham. He said to him, "Abraham!" "Here I am," he replied. Then God said, "Take your son, your only son, whom you love-Isaac-and go to the region of Moriah. Sacrifice him there as a burnt offering on a mountain I will show you."

Abraham, the founding father of the Jewish nation of Israel, was a man of great faith and obedience to the will of God. He was born in 2165 B.C. and we can find his story in the first book of the Bible, Genesis. Abraham in Hebrew means "father of a multitude." Originally called Abram, or "exalted father," the Lord changed his name to Abraham as a symbol of the covenant promise to multiply his descendants into a great nation that God would call His own.

In Genesis 22 above we witness the unthinkable. God commands Abraham to sacrifice his own son, Isaac. We know Abraham obeyed God. He was fully prepared to slay his son, while trusting God to either resurrect Isaac from the dead, or provide a substitutionary sacrifice. This is probably the most strikingly dramatic example of faith and trust in God found in the entire Bible.

How does this story apply to us today?

One
God can use us for great things in spite of ourselves.

Two
Faith is not really tested until God asks us to consider what seems unbearable; to do what seems unreasonable, and to question what seems impossible.

Three
God reveals Himself when we demonstrate faith. Abraham came to the full realization of God's purpose and promise every time he chose to obey God's commands.

One Minute Reflection
Is God asking you to step out in faith today?

"God does not so much want us to do things as to let people see what He can do for us."
(A.B. Simpson)

David And Goliath

1 Samuel 17:45
"David said to the Philistine, "You come against me with sword and spear and javelin, but I come against you in the name of the Lord Almighty, the God of the armies of Israel, whom you have defied."

The story of David and Goliath can be found in the Old Testament in 1 Samuel. The Philistine army had gathered for war against Israel and the two armies faced each other, camped for battle on opposite sides of a steep valley. A Philistine giant measuring over nine feet tall and wearing full armor came out each day for forty days, mocking and challenging the Israelites to fight. His name was Goliath. Saul, the King of Israel, and the whole army were terrified of Goliath.

A young David volunteered to fight Goliath. We know from the passage above that
David responded with these prophetic words: *"You come against me with sword and spear and javelin, but I come against you in the name of the Lord Almighty, the God of the armies of Israel".*

What can we learn from this story?
David's faith in God caused him to look at the giant from a different perspective. David looked at the battle from God's point of view. If we look at giant problems and impossible situations from God's perspective, we realize we have nothing to fear because we are relying on God and not just our own abilities.

There is nothing more powerful than the name of Almighty God.
Remember with God - all things are possible.

One Minute Reflection
What Goliath are you facing in your own life today?

"I took my power in my hand
And went against the world
'Twas not so much as David had
But I was twice as bold
I aimed my pebble but myself
Was all the one that fell
Was it Goliath was too large
Or was myself too small?"
(Emily Dickinson)

God's Gifts

1 Corinthians 12:4-5
"There are different kinds of gifts, but the same Spirit distributes them. There are different kinds of service, but the same Lord. There are different kinds of working, but in all of them and in everyone it is the same God at work."

Spiritual Gifts are one of the most important tools God employs. We know that spiritual gifts are given to God's people, by the Holy Spirit, according to God's sovereign will. The term "spiritual gifts" comes from the Greek words charismata (gifts) and pneumatika (spirits). Most Bible scholars classify these gifts into three categories:

Ministry gifts
The ministry gifts serve to reveal the plan of God.
They are characteristic of a full-time office or calling, Pastors, Evangelists, Ministers and Teachers have ministry gifts.

Manifestation gifts
The manifestation gifts serve to reveal the power of God.
These gifts are supernatural in nature. Prophecy, Healing, Speaking in Tongues are all good examples.

Motivational gifts
The motivational gifts serve to reveal the character of God.
These gifts are practical in nature and most of us possess several of these. We experience them in Leadership, Hospitality, Giving, Service and Administration.

It is important to reflect on what your special spiritual gifts are and how you can use them to build up people around you. Gifts are not for a few special people but for everybody. It is the supreme joy of life to discover your spiritual gifts and to be used by God to bring hope and faith to a needy world.

One Minute Reflection
Can you name out loud one spiritual gift you possess?

"God's gifts are not given capriciously; neither are they given in such a way that the option for their use is left with us. As the gifts are discovered they are to be developed and used to the full in His service and to His glory. God distributes His gifts for His purposes and for the good of His people."
(Jay Adams)

The Supremacy Of Knowledge

Romans 11:33
"Oh, the depth of the riches of the wisdom and knowledge of God! How unsearchable His judgments, and His paths beyond tracing out!"

Knowledge is a supreme subject in Scripture.
Remember the Bible starts with the tree of knowledge in the Garden of Eden. God never intended for knowledge to be an end in itself. He desires application of this knowledge to be woven into our daily lives so that it becomes wisdom for a lifetime. Today we are examining how knowledge of Scripture, God and Christ will affect our lives in four distinct areas. Our passage from Romans 11:33 gives us a good starting place.

Worship
Knowledge first and foremost leads to devotion.
The more we know God, the more we want to praise and worship Him. As we begin to grasp the unsearchable riches of God's character, we desire to honor and worship God with our lives.

Faith
Knowledge makes faith reasonable. We are no longer wishing on a star or hoping for a happy ending. We have real security in a God who we know and understand. The God presented in the Bible is a God who has a proven track record. We have faith in a God who sent His own son to die so we could live fully.

Holiness
Knowledge leads to a transformation in our behavior. God is Holy and He calls us to Holy living as well. Our entire destiny is now shaped by a mission to conform to the likeness of Christ.

Love
The more we know God, the more we understand the love of God. Our lives change in dramatic, poignant and positive ways when we love ourselves the way God loves us and then we share that love with our fellow man.

ne Minute Reflection
What riches of God's knowledge do you need to search out?

"Christianity distinguishes itself from other religions; it contains doctrine. It comes to men with definite, positive teaching; it claims to be the truth, it bases religion on knowledge. A knowledge, which is only attainable under moral conditions." (James Orr)

In Christ

2 Corinthians 5:17-18

"Therefore, if anyone is in Christ, he is a new creation; the old has gone, the new has come! All this is from God, who reconciled us to Himself through Christ and gave us the ministry of reconciliation."

One of the most significant realizations is that in Christ we are a new creation.
This means that you and I have access to all of the power and glory of the risen Christ when we put our faith in Him.

Christ's resurrection proves that He was from God and spoke the truth about everything He said. The resurrection not only confirms the past value of Christ's earthly life and work on the cross, but it also demonstrates His ministry in Heaven for us as our advocate, intercessor, and the sender of the Holy Spirit.

2 Corinthians 5:17 tells us that because of Christ, the old has gone and the new has come. Christ now "indwells" us with His Holy Spirit and enables us to do great things in His name that we could never accomplish by our own strength.

In Christ we find redemption from sin and peace with God
In Christ we enjoy personal fellowship with God
In Christ we now have the power of the Holy Spirit working for us
In Christ we have a new heart and new nature

The Grace of God in Christ should make such a profound change in our soul. It does not mean we never sin but it does mean that old things begin to pass away; old thoughts, old principles, and old behaviors and they become replaced with a Christ centered life.

This is incredible news for us because we get a fresh start in our life and it is all possible because of Christ.

One Minute Reflection
Name one change you could make as a "new" person in Christ?

"The message of the Resurrection is that God's new world has been unveiled in Jesus Christ and that you're now invited to belong to it."
(N.T. Wright)

All Is Good

1 Timothy 4:4
"For everything God created is good, and nothing is to be rejected if it is received with thanksgiving, because it is consecrated by the word of God and prayer."

Everything God created is good.
What an amazing and refreshing truth of life when it's received from God's point of view. One shining example of this is the great composer Ludwig van Beethoven (1770-1827) who lived much of his life in fear of deafness. He was deeply concerned because he felt the sense of hearing was essential to creating music of lasting value. Beethoven's letters and diaries contain dozens of devout references to God, giving evidence of a deeply personal conviction to make sense out of life's unfairness.

To everyone's astonishment, Beethoven wrote some of his most brilliant music after he became totally deaf. Beethoven's 5th Symphony is perhaps the most universally recognized song in the world. With all distractions shut out, creativity flooded in. His deafness became his greatest asset.

This is a valuable lesson for us
God always has a plan. We just need to believe in His ability to create good out of anything we surrender to Him with thanksgiving. We need to know that the God we serve is a God of miracles and possibilities.

Everything God created is good.
We need to get the focus off our own abilities and surrender to God's power.

We can consecrate all things with the Word of God and then be thankful as God uses it for His good purposes.

One Minute Reflection
What recent trial or tribulation can you surrender to God?

"Yes, give thanks for "all things" for, as it has been well said
our disappointments are but His appointments."
(A.W. Pink)

I Can Do All Things

<u>Philippians 4:13</u>
"I can do all things through Christ who strengthens me."

Philippians 4:13 is a very uplifting verse.
But it may surprise you to know that the apostle Paul wrote to the Philippians from a dirty, miserable, first-century jail cell. He was at one of the lowest points of his ministry.

Paul was speaking as a man who wanted to do the will of God but knows he is too weak and sinful to do it, so he holds onto Christ's power to do what he believes he cannot do by his own strength.

Notice the verb "can" is present tense in our verse today, meaning, God is continually, day-by-day, infusing us with strength as we serve Him. We can ask for the provisions needed to get through any situation and count on Christ to grant us the perfect response.

This verse helps us remember and celebrate the greatness of Christ, when all is well, and life is going favorably but also when things are the hardest and life is a continual challenge.

A useful exercise is to memorize this verse and call on it daily:
"I can do ALL things through Christ who strengthens me."

Whatever our needs and regardless of our situation, we can learn to trust in Jesus and know that He will give us the strength to continue on and eventually succeed in victory.

<u>One Minute Reflection</u>
Is there something you need Christ's strength for today?

"The man or woman who is wholly or joyously surrendered to Christ can't make a wrong choice - any choice will be the right one."
(A.W. Tozer)

Power From Above

John 4:16
"And I will pray to the Father, and He shall give you another a Comforter, that He may abide with you forever."

One of the greatest promises Christ gave to each of us is the indwelling power of the Holy Spirit. Here in John 4:16, Jesus tells His disciples that He will pray to the Father, and He will send a Comforter that will abide with them forever.

The Holy Spirit abides with us forever too.

Jesus assured His disciples during His earthly ministry that although He must leave them; He would not leave them alone or comfortless. He promised that He would come to them through the work of the Holy Spirit for fellowship, guidance, comfort, and strength.

We learn in the Bible that Jesus appeared to some of the disciples after His death to illustrate this point.

This is an important revelation for us today.
Christ showing Himself alive after His death gives evidence of His victory as the resurrected and glorified Savior to the world.

Christ's appearances teach us the truth of His availability and companionship even though He is physically absent. Christ sent the Holy Spirit as an inexhaustible source of love, revelation, guidance, and power that resides in our hearts just as it did for the disciples thousands of years ago.

Jesus said those who receive the Holy Spirit, receive power.
Jesus was talking about power for living, power for witness, power for prayer, power to perform miracles, power to love, and power to change the hearts and minds of a broken world.

One Minute Reflection
Do you need the power of the Holy Spirit for some task today?

"Faith is a steady and certain knowledge of the Divine benevolence towards us, which being founded on the truth of the gratuitous promise in Christ, is both revealed to our minds, and confirmed to our hearts, by the Holy Spirit"
(John Calvin)

May Your Joy Be Full

<u>John 15:11</u>
"These things I have spoken to you, that my joy may be in you, and that your joy may be full."

Sixteen centuries ago, Augustine observed,
"I am not alone in this desire for happiness, nor are there only a few who share it with me: without exception we all long for happiness. They may all search for it in different ways, but all try their hardest to reach the same goal, that is, joy"
In other words – we all desire authentic joy.

Jesus' aim in all He taught was the joy of His people.

Above in John 15:11, Jesus shares a very profound statement with His disciples. He is preparing them for His eventual death on the cross and the earthly ministry they will have to pursue without Him. He speaks of joy.

The Bible mentions seeking joy in many places and at the same time reminds us to always seek it in the right places. God Himself is the source of all joy and gladness. If we seek joy in God, we will find an eternal satisfaction that is discovered separate from the circumstances of our life.

Jesus is our prime example of how to live continually with joy.

Jesus could weep, and yet have the fullness of joy, even as He faced the cross because He knew He was living His purpose with complete obedience to God and that His eventual outcome would be one of victory.

Glorifying God is the Christian's highest endeavor and therefore finding joy and satisfaction in God must be our intentional lifelong pursuit.

The joy is discovered in three places:

1) Experiencing God's presence
2) Conforming to God's holiness
3) Enjoying the promise of God's eternal home in Heaven

<u>One Minute Reflection</u>
Can you find joy in a life devoted to Jesus?

"The Lord gives His people perpetual joy when they walk in obedience to Him." (D.L. Moody)

Enemies Into Friends

<u>Colossians 3:13</u>
"Bear with each other and forgive one another if any of you has a grievance against someone. Forgive as the Lord forgave you."

The Bible is replete with statements and teachings on forgiveness. The primary Greek term forgive (i.e., aphiami) occurs 142 times in the New Testament and it means to "send sin away from; to acquit to let go; to remove guilt or obligation of punishment".

The Christian statement on forgiveness is best demonstrated in the Gospel message itself, namely that God the Father, chose to forgive mankind not because of our own merit, but by His unmerited Grace.

A Christian's forgiveness is given by God because of Christ's sacrifice, and cannot be obtained by any works done by us. In other words, it is not about how good we are, because we can never be good enough. Forgiveness is offered because of what God has done.

When God forgives us, He does so because of Grace. A nice way to remember Grace is "God's Riches at Christ's Expense". God does not offer us "performance based" forgiveness. We don't have to do one thing to earn this forgiveness. It is a free gift given by God because He loves us.

When we consider forgiving another person who has betrayed us, we do it not because the offender deserves it but because Christ forgave us and He has asked us to offer that Grace to our fellow man.

<u>One Minute Reflection</u>
Is there someone you could forgive today?

"We need lots of love to forgive, and we need lots of humility to forget. Humility completes forgiveness, before we forgive somebody we need to know that we too need forgiveness, and it is here that humility of the heart comes in."
(Mother Teresa)

Deeper Prayer

<u>Luke 11:9-11</u>
"And so I tell you, keep on asking, and you will receive what you ask for.
Keep on seeking, and you will find. Keep on knocking, and the door will be
opened to you. For everyone who asks, receives. Everyone who seeks, finds.
And to everyone who knocks, the door will be opened."

Ask, Seek, Knock are some of the most famous and remembered words
that Jesus ever spoke on the subject of prayer.

Ask, Seek, Knock are not only commands but they are also instructions
that offer us a reward. We are told to ask and keep on asking to receive;
to seek and keep on seeking to find; and to knock and keep on knocking
so that the door will be opened to us.

Asking
We start by asking God for what we need because we know at a heart
and soul level only God can provide what we are truly searching for at
any given time.

Seeking
Seeking is a deeper level of prayer than just asking. Here we commit to
getting to know God and seeking His will for our life instead of our own.

Knocking
The knocking here suggests a demand to get in. This is the most
intimate level of prayer. We are knocking to enter into Christ's Holy
presence. Intimacy with Christ ultimately becomes the only thing we
desire.

Jesus found time for serious prayer every day away from the daily
distractions of life. Seeking His Father's will was His first priority. This
should be our first priority as well. God wants deep, personal prayer and
us on our knees before Him in humility, devotion.

<u>One Minute Reflection</u>
Are you asking, seeking or knocking today?

"I have been driven many times upon my knees by the overwhelming
conviction that I had nowhere else to go. My own wisdom and that of all
about me seemed insufficient for that day."
(Abraham Lincoln)

Renewing Of Your Mind

<u>Romans 12:2</u>
*"And do not be conformed to this world, but be transformed by the
renewing of your mind, that you may prove what is the good and
acceptable and perfect will of God."*

Romans 12:2 above gives us very clear instructions to
not be conformed to the prevailing culture so that we can prove the
perfect will of God. This is a very difficult thing to do because a barrage
of seductive, worldly messages surrounds us. Magazines tell us beauty is
essential and thin is in.
Reality television boasts that instant fame will bring happiness. And we
learn
greed is good, truth is relative and everything goes.

**However the apostle Paul is reminding us in our passage today that
the world's standard and God's standard are incompatible.**

Paul implores us to not conform to the world but instead to commit
to the transformation of our own conduct and character into the image
of Christ Himself. Then we can *"prove what is the good and acceptable
and perfect will of God".*

Romans 12:2 conveys three solid points
1) The process of transformation is a lifelong work of God
for which we are also responsible.

2) The means of transformation is through the renewing of our minds.

3) The result of transformation is that we will test and approve in
practical ways what is the good, acceptable, and perfect will of God. This
will lead to holiness and joy.

<u>One Minute Reflection</u>
How will you renew your mind today?

"The same Jesus who turned water into wine can transform your home,
your life, your family, and your future. He is still in the miracle-working
business, and His business is the business of transformation."⬚
(Adrian Rogers)

Seek God First

Matthew 6:33
*"But seek first His kingdom and His righteousness,
and all these things will be given to you as well."*

Today we are given a very simple promise.
Seek God's kingdom and righteousness FIRST and all things will be given to us as well.

What exactly is Jesus talking about?

Below is a good illustration of how one man put the teaching in Matthew 6:33 to practical use.

In the late 19th century John Wanamaker opened a department store in Philadelphia. Within a few years that enterprise had become one of the most successful businesses in the country. But operating his store wasn't Wanamaker's only responsibility. He was named Postmaster General of the United States, he was president of the YMCA and he served as superintendent for the largest Sunday school in the world at Bethany Presbyterian Church. Wanamaker was a very religious man. When someone asked him how he could hold all those positions at once, he explained. "Early in life I read, 'Seek ye first the kingdom of God, and His righteousness, and all these things shall be added unto you.' The Sunday school is my business, all the rest are the things."

Evidence of Wanamaker's desire to keep the Lord's work first in his life was a specially constructed soundproof room in his store. Every day he spent 30 minutes there praying and meditating upon God's Word. He had his priorities straight!

We need to trust God enough to put Him first and bank on His promise that all things will be given to us as well. We may not have the same level of earthly success as Mr. Wanamaker but God will take care of all our needs in His perfect timing.

One Minute Reflection
How will you see God's righteousness FIRST today?

"Let us more and more insist on raising funds of love, of kindness, of understanding, of peace. Money will come if we seek first the Kingdom of God - the rest will be given."
(Mother Theresa)

Children Are A Heritage

Psalm 127:3

"Behold, children are a heritage from the LORD, the fruit of the womb a reward."

Most things come with an instruction book. Our car has a manual. Our class has a study guide. Our appliances come with a set of directions. But when we become a parent, no one sends us home with a book of how to raise children well. As Christians we can look to the Bible for a full set of instructions on how to be parents that will honor God. It starts with realizing that *"children are a heritage from the Lord"*.

The Bible tells us to be alert in three areas concerning raising successful kids.

A Reward of Love

Our children are gifts from God, and because they really belong to God, they are only on loan to us for this lifetime. We have both the privilege and the responsibility of raising them to become healthy adults who love and serve God.

Instruction

The Bible has a great deal to say about the way we can successfully raise our children and the first thing it says to do is teach them the truth about God's Word.

Modeling Behavior

Our children are looking for trustworthy role models and as their parents this should be our primary concern. We should model with integrity so that our words and actions align with a Godly character.

One Minute Reflection
How will you honor God through your parenting today?

"God gives your children a mind that will receive impressions like moist clay. He gives them a disposition at the starting-point of life to believe what you tell them, and to take for granted what you advise them, and to trust your word rather than a stranger's. He gives you, in short, a golden opportunity of doing them good. See that you do not neglect such an opportunity."
(J.C. Ryle)

Protection From Harm

Psalm 121:7
*"The Lord will keep you from all harm, He will watch over your life;
the Lord will watch over your coming and going both now and
forevermore."*

All we have to do is turn on the evening news or pick up a newspaper to realize how scary a place the world has become. Mass shootings, wild fires, terrorist plots, disease, political unrest and war all seem to dominate our headlines. People suffer every day from crime, accidents, health issues, natural disasters, and more. So how can we possibly protect our families from harm?

**Our Psalm today tells us:
We must claim the protection of God.**

First of all, we need to interpret Psalm 121:7 and its promise of physical safety in the context of the Old Testament Covenant. God promised Israel many material and earthly blessings, as they were obedient to the Mosaic covenant. However we no longer live under the Old Covenant. We live under the New Covenant in Christ that promises us spiritual protection. God promises to provide us with the strength, peace, and perseverance we need to make it through any circumstance we may have to face.

This means that although there are many times when God will shield us from tragedy, injury or loss, He does not always grant it. He knows we are strengthened by the trials that come our way, and in each physical trial, He assures us of His spiritual protection.

One of the best ways to protect our family is to pray over each person as they go out into the world each day. We must claim the promise that the Lord will watch over them both now and forever more.

One Minute Reflection
In what way will you pray for protection daily?

"God knows what each one of us is dealing with.
He knows our pressures. He knows our conflicts. And He has made a provision for each and every one of them. That provision is Himself in the person of the Holy Spirit, indwelling us and empowering us to respond rightly."
(Kay Arthur)

Happy Valentine's Day

Ephesians 5:31-33

"For this reason a man will leave his father and mother and be united to his wife, and the two will become one flesh. This is a profound mystery-but I am talking about Christ and the church. However, each one of you also must love his wife as he loves himself, and the wife must respect her husband."

Today we are examining Eros, or romantic, sexual love between a man and a woman. God created man and woman in His image and gave us romantic love for the most intimate part of a union. If we study the Scripture from Ephesians above, we realize that love in a marriage is meant to reflect how Christ loved the church. We must be willing to lay down our lives for our spouse, love them as much as we love ourselves and proceed with respect.

"Two will become ONE flesh," God declared.
"However, each one of you also must love his wife as he loves himself, and the wife must respect her husband."

Thousands of years since those words were written, modern couples agree. In a recent gallop poll, it was noted that women want love above all else, demonstrated through communication, emotional and financial security as well as family leadership from their husbands. Men desired respect above all else, along with sexual affection, and time spent enjoying recreational fun with their wives.

How can we operate as "one" entity in marriage?
The term "one flesh" means that just as our bodies are one whole being and cannot be divided, so God intended it to be with the marriage relationship. There are no longer two entities (two individuals), but now there is one entity (a married couple).

Our "oneness" can be manifested physically, emotionally, spiritually, intellectually, financially, and in all ways to build up the family unit. It should be the wife's imperative to serve the highest calling of her husband and it should be the husband's imperative to serve the highest calling of his wife.

One Minute Reflection
How could you serve your spouse today?

"The job of love is to realize the potential in others. If both of you [in a relationship] are doing this, you'll get places."
(Bono)

No Longer Lost

<u>Matthew 18:12-14</u>
"What do you think? If a man has a hundred sheep, and one of them goes astray, does he not leave the ninety-nine and go to the mountains to seek the one that is straying? And if he should find it, assuredly, I say to you, he rejoices more over that sheep than over the ninety-nine that did not go astray. Even so it is not the will of your Father who is in Heaven that one of these little ones should perish."

Here in Matthew 18, Jesus tells His disciples the story of the Lost Sheep. When a man who owns a hundred sheep discovers that he has one missing, he leaves the ninety-nine behind and goes in search of the one that became lost. And when he finds the lost sheep that wandered off, he brings it back to the fold in celebration.

Of course Jesus is really using a metaphor to explain how much God loves us. Remember, He referred to Himself as the Good Shepherd. This story is a poignant illustration of how God cares for all of His children and how He will actively seek and rescue anyone who, for what ever reason, becomes separated or lost. We learn several significant points about God's love in this story:

God's love is individual and intimate
There is one sheep gone out of a hundred, and when the shepherd realizes it is missing, he doesn't rest until he brings it home. Every individual person matters to God.

God's love is persistent
God searches and waits patiently to bring back every lost soul into His fold. When we go astray, God will keep searching until He finds us.

God's love is celebratory
There's no guilt, there is no condemnation and there is no lecture for being lost. God rejoices when we repent and return to Him no matter what mess we might have found ourselves in or how many mistakes we have made along the way.

<u>One Minute Reflection</u>
God is searching for you; do you want to be found?

"Experience has taught me that the Shepherd is far more willing to show His sheep the path than the sheep are to follow. He is endlessly merciful, patient, tender, and loving." (Elisabeth Elliott)

What Rules Your Life

Matthew 19:16 &21 - 22

"Just then a man came up to Jesus and asked, 'Teacher, what good thing must I do to get eternal life?' Jesus answered, 'If you want to be perfect, go, sell your possessions and give to the poor, and you will have treasure in Heaven. Then come, follow me.' When the young man heard this, he went away sad, because he had great wealth."

Today we look at a very personal encounter with a man who asks Jesus what he must do to inherit eternal life. This encounter is not really about money but about commitment. Webster's Dictionary defines commitment as "to speak or act in such a manner as to bind oneself to a certain line of conduct."

Commitment to Jesus Christ is more than one definition: it requires our life, our soul, and our everything. But too often we find ourselves lingering between being committed and being uncommitted.

We often falter in commitment because we are afraid that God might ask us to give up something for His sake. He illustrates this in our story today of the rich, young ruler, who was seeking eternal life and is asked to sell all his possessions.

Jesus knows every person's heart. He knew how much the young man loved being rich. Jesus knew that the young man trusted his money more than he trusted God. Jesus wasn't merely telling this man to give up his riches; Jesus was revealing the condition of this man's heart. The ruler really loved the almighty dollar more than he loved Almighty God.

Jesus helps us understand that money will not last and that possessions cannot buy peace or joy and it certainly will never secure a place in God's eternal kingdom.
Jesus hopes that ultimately all of us will choose a commitment to God over devotion to money or any other earthly thing.

One Minute Reflection
What is blocking your commitment to a deep relationship with Christ?

"God's agenda for our lives may be far different from our own. He cares more about our character and condition of our soul than our convenience, comfort or cash."
(Joseph M. Stowell)

Consider The Lilies

Luke 12:27-28

"Who of you by worrying can add a single hour to his life? Since you cannot do this very little thing, why do you worry about the rest? Consider how the lilies grow. They do not labor or spin. Yet I tell you, not even Solomon in all his splendor was dressed like one of these."

It makes sense that the Bible would be replete with teaching references having to do with earth and soil, vines and branches, sowing and reaping, seeds and plants, along with everything having its season. After all human existence did start in the Garden of Eden. In today's passage from the Gospel of Luke, we are asked to *"consider how the lilies grow"*.

What can the lily teach us about life itself?

1. Majestic beauty
A flower is perfectly designed by God bursting with color and fragrance. They are delicate to the touch yet possess power in their loveliness. Jesus tells us *"not even Solomon in all his splendor was dressed as well as these"*.

2. Complete dependence
A flower gives us the picture of something that is completely dependent on someone to plant it, water it, and keep the weeds from growing in too close. The flower needs tender loving care that only God can provide.

3. Peace
A flower simply blooms where it is planted. Its purpose is inherent in its existence. The flower does not "labor" or "spin". It does not try to be anything except what it was created to be. It is in this context that Jesus asks a simple question,
"Who of you by worrying can add a single hour to his life?"

We know the answer. Worry accomplishes nothing except perhaps more worry. It is a futile, emotional investment that yields nothing. We should not let worry hijack our faith; instead we can surrender to God and live the life of a lily.

One Minute Reflection
What does Jesus' illustration teach you?

"Oh, how great peace and quietness would he possess who should cut off all vain anxiety and place all his confidence in God." (Thomas a Kempis)

Ash Wednesday

Mark 1:11-12

"Then a voice came from Heaven, 'You are My beloved Son, in whom I am well pleased.' Immediately the Spirit drove Him into the wilderness. And He was there in the wilderness forty days, tempted by Satan, and was with the wild beasts; and the angels ministered to Him."

Ash Wednesday is the first day of Lent and it occurs 46 days before Easter. The Bible does not mention Ash Wednesday or the custom of Lent. However, Lent is a time to prepare for the greatest events in human history: God's offering of His Son on the Cross for our sins, and Jesus' resurrection from the dead, destroying death and restoring life for those of us who have faith in Christ.

Lent is a time when many Christians prepare for Easter by observing a period of fasting, repentance, moderation and spiritual discipline in recognition and appreciation of Christ's suffering so that they can be back in right relationship with a Holy God.

Ash Wednesday derives its name because at some Church services, the minister will rub the sign of the cross with ashes onto the foreheads of worshipers as a symbol of mourning and repentance to God. The ashes used are typically gathered after the palms from the previous year's Palm Sunday are burned. We can think of Lent as a "time-out" period of personal reflection, renewal, and recommitment to Christ.

Fasting, meditation, prayer, solitude, service, confession, and worship are just some of the ways we can celebrate and encounter the true meaning of Lent.
We need to remember, that as we draw close to God,
God will draw close to us.

<u>One Minute Reflection</u>
Will you celebrate Ash Wednesday?

"Ash Wednesday is for people who know what it means for their soul to be logged with these icy waters: all of us are such people, if only we can realize it." (Thomas Merton)

Closer To God

<u>Matthew 4:4</u>
"Jesus answered, 'It is written: 'Man does not live on bread alone, but on every word that comes from the mouth of God.'"

The word "Lent" is derived from the Anglo-Saxon word *lencten*, meaning "Spring". Lent is a time when many Christians prepare for Easter by observing a period of fasting, repentance, moderation and spiritual discipline in recognition and appreciation of Christ's suffering.

We can also use Lent as a season of recommitting ourselves to Christ and realigning ourselves to His core values and exemplary conduct.

One of the most obvious ways that Christians do this is by fasting. When people fast, the purpose is to be completely sustained by God alone and keep our focus solely on Him. Jesus states above in Matthew 4:4, *"It is written, Man shall not live by bread alone but by every word of God"*. This is a reminder that it is God who ultimately sustains us.

However if fasting from food is something that we are not willing to try, we can remember there are many other things we can fast from also.

We can fast from:
Hatred and Gossip
An Unforgiving Heart
Pride and Busyness
Greed and Arguing
Toxic Relationships
Unkind Thoughts
Overspending
Arrogance or Anxiety
Lent is a time to reconnect to the person God wants us to be!

<u>One Minute Reflection</u>
What one thing can you commit to "fasting" from during Lent?

"Lent is not about fasting or self-denial; it's about serious participation-here and now-in God's divine forgiveness with all his people. It doesn't change God, it changes us."
(Fr. Ken Tanner)

Solitary Refinement

Mark 1:35
"Very early in the morning, while it was still dark, Jesus got up, left the house and went off to a solitary place, where He prayed."

Solitude is a very critical element of the process of finding intimacy with God.

The difference between loneliness and solitude is that loneliness is an anxious feeling of longing for a personal connection and solitude is a deliberate choice to spend time alone in search of an experience of God. Loneliness is something we flee away from and solitude is something we can run towards.

As we see in the Scripture above from Mark, Jesus spent time in solitude as He searched to reconnect with His Heavenly Father. He did this often during His public ministry and could never have accomplished the significant work He was called to do without spending time alone with God. Neither can we.
We can receive much inner strength, wisdom and power when we set aside time in silence waiting upon a God who not only reveals Himself but also transforms us in the process.

One of the key components to solitude is silence. It is during silence that we often hear from God. An increasingly noisy, distracted world filled with televisions, car radios, smart phones, computers, and IPods, are contributing to our separation from God.

If you are in search of solitude - try the following:
Set aside a special place where you can withdraw from others
Try an entire day without speaking
Go on a mini retreat with just yourself to re-prioritize
Stop by a church during the week and sit alone with God
Enter into solitude during daily chores with an expectant heart

Be intentional during Lent to practice solitude and remember that loneliness is inner emptiness but solitude is inner fulfillment.

One Minute Reflection
How will you make time for solitude this week?

"Settle yourself in solitude and you will come upon Him in yourself."
(Teresa of Avila)

Small Things, Great Service

Matthew 20:28
"Just as the Son of Man did not come to be served, but to serve, and to give His life as a ransom for many."

Nothing is more important than the act of service if we want to align with Christ because He was the greatest servant of all. Take a look at what He said in Matthew 20:28 above.

The discipline of service is more than a "to do" list of good endeavors. It is not about seeking applause from others, calculating results, or expecting external rewards. The discipline of service is about humility.

In our current fame-seeking society, we are often attracted to the "big service" opportunities. However the discipline of "small service" is the place where we seek no credit.

St. Francis of Assisi gives us a wonderful example of service in his simple prayer.

Lord, make me an instrument of Your peace.
Where there is hatred, let me sow love;
where there is injury, pardon;
where there is doubt, faith;
where there is despair, hope;
where there is darkness, light;
and where there is sadness, joy.
O Divine Master, grant that I may not so much seek
to be consoled as to console;
to be understood as to understand;
to be loved as to love.
For it is in giving that we receive;
it is in pardoning that we are pardoned;
and it is in dying that we are born to eternal life. Amen.

One Minute Reflection
What small service will you invest in today?

"We can do no great things, only small things with great love."
(Mother Teresa)

Christian Meditation

<u>Joshua 1:8</u>
"Keep this Book of the Law always on your lips; meditate on it day and night, so that you may be careful to do everything written in it. Then you will be prosperous and successful."

If you read the Scripture above, you will recognize that this instruction from the Old Testament Book of Joshua tells us that when we mediate on the Bible day and night and do everything written in it that we will be prosperous and successful.

Christian meditation is the ability to study God's word and obey it. Meditation allows us to enter into the presence of the living God. This is of paramount importance because change does not take place by "doing" more to please God as much as it happens by "being" in the presence of God and responding to His infinite Holiness and love.

God instructs us for our own good.
We need to deeply consider what God wants us to know and that only happens when we study God's laws allowing them to descend from our heads down into our hearts.

How to meditate?
There is no place, posture or position necessary. All you need is an open heart, focused mind, calm body and your spirit centered completely on Christ. The idea of *"meditating on His laws"* means we find a passage of Scripture that speaks to us, and then internalize and personalize what God is saying.
We must listen to God and then obey Him.

Meditation is not a single act, but a lifetime of creating fellowship with God. We will never be as blessed as when we are sitting in the presence of the Almighty, Eternal, Omniscient, and Loving God of the Universe.

<u>One Minute Reflection</u>
What passage of Scripture will you meditate on today?

"Give yourself to prayer, to reading and meditation on divine truths: strive to penetrate to the bottom of them and never be content with a superficial knowledge."
(David Brainerd)

An Encounter With God

<u>Jeremiah 7:23</u>
"Listen to and obey My voice, and I will be your God and you will be My people; and walk in the whole way that I command you, that it may be well with you."

We all want to have an encounter with God.
Encounters with God are not just limited to pastors or biblical figures. God wants to communicate intimately with all of us.
However our busy, noisy, modern lifestyle can often get in the way.

What is an encounter with God?
Although God wants to converse with us daily, there are times when He has something important to convey and He will step into our life in a more supernatural fashion.

What will we experience with an encounter with God?
There will be an overwhelming awareness of His presence.
God will usually ask something of us and we need to respond.

How can we create opportunities to encounter God?
Encounters with God are always initiated by Him and usually come as a surprise to us. However we can prepare for them by cultivating a deeper relationship with Him. We can do this by the following actions:

Be Available
Be Silent
Spend Time Praying
Attune to God's Voice
Read Scripture
Ask God to Speak to us
Listen

What to do when we encounter God?
Jeremiah 7:23 above tells us: *"Listen and Obey His Voice. Walk in His whole way...that it may be well with you".*

<u>One Minute Reflection</u>
How can you prepare for an encounter with God today?

"Expect great things from God; attempt great things for God."
(William Carey)

A Lesson From Moses

<u>Exodus 3:3-4</u>
"So Moses thought, 'I will go over and see this strange sight-why the bush does not burn up.' When the Lord saw that he had gone over to look, God called to him from within the bush, 'Moses! Moses!' And Moses said, 'Here I am.'"

One of the things that is so spectacular about the story of Moses and the burning bush is that Moses did not anticipate the presence of God!

For forty years this well-educated man had taken on the personality and the dress of a desert sheepherder, but God knew where he was and wanted to use him for a very specific purpose!

In God's perfect timing, He lit a bush and called Moses by name!

Why should we care?
Because God is preparing a special encounter just for us as well.

There are numerous Bible characters that also had encounters with God they were not expecting! Throughout the Bible the story repeats itself: Noah wasn't looking for an encounter with God, but God called him to build an Ark.
Abraham wasn't looking for an encounter with God, but God called him to build a nation. David wasn't looking for an encounter with God, but God called him to build a kingdom.

Encounters with God are designed for a reason. We don't want to miss the best God has for us and so we need to always be prepared to meet God when He calls us.

<u>One Minute Reflection</u>
Will you be prepared when God calls you?

"We need to find God, and He cannot be found in noise and restlessness. God is the friend of silence. See how nature - trees, flowers, grass- grows in silence; see the stars, the moon and the sun, how they move in silence. We need silence to be able to touch souls."
(Mother Teresa)

Authentic Worship

<u>1 Colossians 1:10</u>
"Then you will live a life that honors the Lord, and you will always please Him by doing good deeds. You will come to know God even better."

Worship is one of the best places to encounter God.
By definition, worship is: "To pay great honor and respect to."

In the First Book of Colossians, verse 10 above,
Paul explains that worship and intimacy are bound together. He says, *"live a life that honors the Lord (worship) and you will come to know God even better (intimacy)."*

True worship leads to knowing God better at a transformational level.

Today's church culture suggests that worship is predominantly something related to music. This is not what is meant by praise and worship in the Bible, at least not in the New Testament. The word 'worship' is never used in the Bible in the context of Christians meeting together. Fundamentally, authentic worship is about pursuing that which pleases God.

How can we authentically worship God?
Worship is not primarily what we do in church; instead it encompasses every moment of a believer's life. Worship is living our lives every moment of the day to please God by our obedience to His Spirit. God wants us to live a life of love and mercy to those around us, and a life of love, respect and obedience towards Him. We honor God and show that we love Him by following the example that Jesus set.

<u>One Minute Reflection</u>
How can you worship God each and every day of the week?

"God is most glorified in us, when we are most satisfied in Him."
(John Piper)

The Gospel Of John

<u>John 1:1</u>
"In the beginning was the Word, and the Word was with God, and the Word was God."

John, the author of the 4th Gospel was one of Jesus' closest companions. Out of His followers, Jesus chose twelve to be with Him as disciples. Within the twelve, three men, Peter, John and James, were invited by Jesus to go with Him for times of prayer and special insight.

John wrote the Gospel to convince his readers that Jesus was, in fact, God. John points to astonishing miracles and amazing teachings in order to convey the Gospel truth which is that Jesus is the eternal God who became fully human and lived here on earth where many could see Him and all could be forgiven for their sins and have eternal life.

**If you want to see God, says John, look to Jesus.
If you want to hear God, listen to Jesus.
If you want to truly know God, know Jesus.**

John's title for Jesus is "the Word".
Jesus is the tangible expression of all that is God including His character and His majesty.

John tells us that Jesus is:
The Word - the full expression of who God is
The One who was in the beginning with God
The One who is Himself God
The Creator of all things
The Word who became flesh
The One who made God known to us

**<u>One Minute Reflection</u>
How is Jesus the "Word" to you?**

"You must make your choice. Either this man was, and is, the Son of God: or else a madman or something worse. You can shut Him up for a fool; you can spit at Him and kill Him for a demon; or you can fall at His feet and call Him Lord and God. But let us not come with any patronizing nonsense about His being a great human teacher. He has not left that open to us. He did not intend to."
(C.S. Lewis)

Washing The Feet

*"After that, He poured water into a basin and began to wash His disciples'
feet, drying them with the towel that was wrapped around Him."*

Today, we are looking at the story of Jesus washing His disciples' feet. It
is one of the most memorable incidents in the Bible and can be found in
John 13:5 above.
It was the night before Jesus' betrayal and crucifixion and while His
public ministry had ended Jesus was now fully engaged with His
disciples.

In the culture of that day, it was a common courtesy for the host to have
his slave wash the guest's feet as they entered the house.

**Jesus is making several bold statements with this one act of
washing of the feet.**

One - Jesus is teaching us that as His followers we should serve others.
If Jesus would choose to lower Himself to do the job of the least
important servant by washing His friends' feet, then we should always
be willing to serve others as well.

Two - Unwashed feet is a picture of carrying along the dirt of sin. Jesus
washing His disciples' feet is an illustration that we all need daily
cleansing through forgiveness that can only be found in a personal
relationship with Jesus Christ.

Three – Jesus performed a task, which someone else could have
done. We need to be willing to undertake the most unpopular task, care
for the most despised person, and stand up for any rejected Christian
stance because Christ has invited us to do so.

Four - Never miss an opportunity to show Christ to a hurting
world. Jesus' act does not appear to be very significant and yet look at
the impact it has had for centuries. We never know when we will make
a lasting impression with our most menial task.

One Minute Reflection
Would you be willing to wash someone's feet for Christ's sake?

"God did not save you to be a sensation. He saved you to be a servant."
(John E. Hunter)

Work To Do

John 17:4
"I have brought You glory on earth by finishing the work You gave me to do."

We hear a lot about glory in the Bible and it is essential to understand its definition. There is no better role model for glory revealed than Jesus Christ Himself.
If you read the passage from John 17:4 above very carefully you will notice that Jesus refers to glory as, *"Finishing the work that You gave me to do".*

Jesus' work was doing everything that God, His Father, sent Him to earth to do. It was preaching, teaching, and performing miracles, healing, caring for the poor and intentionally going to the cross to die for the sins of the entire world.

Christ Himself refers to bringing glory to God through "work".
We know that work is significant to God. This concept goes all the way back to the very beginning of the Bible to Genesis 2:15 which states, *"The Lord God took the man and put him in the Garden of Eden to __work__ it and take care of it."*

Work is where Jesus' glory was revealed and where our glory is revealed also.

God is concerned with fruitfulness. Being fruitful means to bring out what is on the inside of us: to expose the hidden glory. We can be productive with our lives doing the work that God created us to do with our individual gifts all while bringing glory to God in that area.

The Apostle Paul also reminds us of the work that God prepared for us in advance for us to do. He said in Ephesians 2:10, *"For we are God's handiwork, created in Christ Jesus to do good works, which God prepared in advance for us to do."*

One Minute Reflection
What work is God calling you to do?

"It is our best work that God wants, not the dregs of our exhaustion. I think He must prefer quality to quantity."
(George MacDonald)

Reveal God's Glory

Isaiah 43:7
"Everyone who is called by my name, whom I created for my glory, whom I formed and made."

What is glory and why is it so important to God?
Glory is used to denote the manifestation of God's presence in its most focused, radiant, and beautiful display. Overall, the glory of God is used in a variety of ways in Scripture. It can refer to God's greatness, His honor, His beauty, His power, and His light. In every case, the glory of God acknowledges the Lord's supreme being and our need to both acknowledge and serve Him.

Divine glory is an important motif throughout Christian theology, as God is regarded as the most glorious being ever. Since we are created in the image of God, human beings can share in divine glory as image-bearers.

We reflect God's glory in all we do.

We can bring glory to parenting, preaching, teaching, coaching, befriending, witnessing, caring, feeding, loving, praying, nursing, motivating, or any number of other opportunities to serve others. We can manifest God's glory while dancing, singing, painting, gardening, building, inventing, drawing, or cooking. And we can be a glory image bearer while working in a bank, a factory or in a field.

Whatever it is...we can display the glory of God for the entire world to see.

One Minute Reflection
How will you go about revealing God's glory today?

"You are a child of God. Your playing small does not serve the world. There is nothing enlightened about shrinking so that other people won't feel insecure about you. We were born to manifest the glory of God that is within us."
(Marianne Williamson)

Prayer And Persecution

"You have heard that it was said, 'Love your neighbors and hate your enemy.' But I tell you, love your enemies and pray for those who persecute you."

Today we are covering the one topic that many people find hard to address which is the command to love our enemies and pray for those who persecute us.

"Persecute" means to pursue with harmful intentions. It might include very severe hostility like the rejection Jesus faced. Or it might simply be an act of ridicule by friends and neighbors for our faith.

Jesus reminds us to respond to our enemies with love and to acknowledge our persecutors with prayer as we reflect the character of Christ in everything we do.

Christ came to save not to condemn.

John Piper explains it this way:
"The command to love our enemies and pray for those that persecute us is not an isolated ethical teaching. It rises up out of a great foundation of grace in the life and ministry of Jesus." In other words, *prayer* for our enemies is one of the deepest forms of love. We can pray for our enemies conversion or that they would be awakened to the hatred in their hearts. We can pray that they themselves would be able to enjoy the peace that only Christ offers.

One Minute Reflection
Is there an enemy you could love or pray for today?

"The apostles went away rejoicing that they were counted worthy to suffer shame for the name of Christ, that they were graced so far as to be disgraced for the name of Christ!"
(Thomas Watson)

Be Holy

1 Peter 1:15-16
"But as He who called you is Holy, you also be Holy in all your conduct, since it is written, "You shall be Holy, for I am Holy."

In 1 Peter 1:15-16 above, Peter, who was one of Jesus' closest companions and often a leader of the twelve disciples, quotes a passage from Leviticus found in the Old Testament. Peter asserts that God calls men of faith to be Holy because God is Holy.

What does that mean?
The Lord has an amazing plan for the life of every person, and it can be summed up in a single word: sanctification. In its verb form, sanctify means "to make Holy" or "to separate." So when something is sanctified, it is separated from a common use to a sacred one.

God is in the "sanctification" business. He set apart the Sabbath as a Holy Day to be honored, He set apart marriage as Holy Matrimony, He sets apart His word as the Holy Bible, and He sets apart Christians to be Holy as well.

The Lord still sanctifies people every single day.
As members of God's family we are expected to reflect His glory. This does not mean we live sinless lives but with God's help through the Holy Spirit we live a life consistent with the God we represent. In other words, we are sanctified as we follow Jesus Christ. Sanctification is a matter of the heart but a changed heart bears evidence of changed behavior.

In every situation, we can ask ourselves, what would Jesus do?
Would Jesus walk by a homeless person?
Would Jesus tell a racist joke?
Would Jesus criticize their spouse?
Would Jesus get behind the wheel of a car drunk?
Would Jesus pray for guidance?
Would Jesus forgive His enemies?

One Minute Reflection
Are there areas of your life that need sanctification?

"God has one destined end for mankind - holiness! His one aim is the production of saints. God is not an eternal blessing- machine for men. He did not come to save men out of pity. He came to save men because He had created them to be Holy."
(Oswald Chambers)

Keep In Step

Galatians 5:22-25

"But the fruit of the Spirit is love, joy, peace, forbearance, kindness, goodness, faithfulness, gentleness and self-control. Against such things there is no law. Those who belong to Christ Jesus have crucified the flesh with its passions and desires. Since we live by the Spirit, let us keep in step with the Spirit."

In this passage from Galatians above, Paul, the author of this letter, is emphasizing that once we develop a relationship with Jesus Christ, our life is no longer held captive by a list of rules and regulations. Instead, we are guided by the Holy Spirit who lives inside of us. The demonstration of a Christian life well lived is the "fruit" of that Spirit being displayed daily.

What is the Fruit of the Spirit?

"Fruit of the Spirit" is a biblical term that sums up the nine visible attributes of a true Christian life. Using the NIV version of Galatians 5:22-23, these attributes are: love, joy, peace, forbearance, kindness, goodness, faithfulness, gentleness and self-control. We learn from scripture that these are not individual "fruits" from which we pick and choose. Rather, the fruit of the Spirit is one nine-fold "fruit" that characterizes all who truly walk in the Holy Spirit.

How to keep in step with the Spirit

Be joyful in every situation
Exhibit more kindness to a hurting world
Offer patience when it comes to family and friends
Silence our tongue when we are tempted to gossip
Spend extra time in prayer instead of rushing on

One Minute Reflection
Which of the nine-fold fruit will you exhibit today?

"Fruit is always the miraculous, the created; it is never the result of willing, but always a growth. The fruit of the Spirit is a gift of God, and only He can produce it. They who bear it know as little about it as the tree knows of its fruit. They know only the power of Him on whom their life depends."
(Dietrich Bonheoffer)

God First

Matthew 22:36-37
"Teacher, which is the great commandment in the law?"
Jesus said to him, "You shall love the Lord your God with all your heart,
with all your soul, and with all your mind."

Here in Matthew 22, Jesus is answering the question of which is the greatest commandment in the Law. And no surprise, Jesus answers with a reference to The First Commandment, which is written in Old Testament Scripture.

We find the original First Commandment in Exodus 20:1 and then written again in Deuteronomy 5:6; *"And God spoke all these words, saying, I am the LORD thy God, who have brought thee out of the land of Egypt, out of the house of bondage. Thou shalt have no other gods before me".*

The First Commandment summons man to believe in God, to hope in Him, and to love Him above all else. It is God's demand for exclusive worship that calls us to respond with allegiance to the one true and living God.

We worship many things in modern life. God is not often at the top of the list. Fame, fortune, celebrity, ambition, popularity, excellence, wealth, prestige all seem to have pushed God out of first place. None of these are wrong in and of themselves, however when they become an "idol", God is offended.

We need to be careful not to exalt the creation over the creator.
We should love, honor and respect God so much that He alone is the supreme authority and model in our lives.

How do we love God above all else?
Jesus proclaims, *"with all your heart, with all your soul and with all your mind".*

One Minute Reflection
What claims first place in your life today?

"Following Christ has nothing to do with success as the world sees success. It has to do with love."
(Madeleine L'Engle)

Forgive, Forgive, Forgive

Matthew 18:21-22
"Then Peter came to Jesus and asked, 'Lord, how many times shall I forgive my brother or sister who sins against me? Up to seven times?' Jesus answered, 'I tell you, not seven times, but seventy-seven times.'"

In today's passage, the disciple, Peter, asks the question we all want the answer to. How many time are we supposed to forgive people who have betrayed us, hurt us, ignored or abused us?

Peter asks; *how many times shall I forgive my brother or sister?" Jesus answers "I tell you not seven times but, seventy- seven times. "*

In other words, Jesus avows that we must forgive over and over and over again.

Why are we called to forgive?

1) God commands us to forgive because forgiveness is a Christian's duty. Jesus said, *"If you love me, you will obey me."* Part of obeying God is forgiving others.

2) Christ has forgiven us out of love, and we need to offer that same forgiveness to someone else who does not deserve it either. This has nothing to do with our feelings. We can forgive because we love God more than we hate the offender.

3) As Christians - we must conform to the likeness of Christ. The entire purpose of our lives is to become more "Christ-like". We are no longer meant to behave like the rest of the world. Forgiveness is part of God's plan for our life.

Colossians 3:12-13 summarizes this well.
"Therefore, as God's chosen people, Holy and dearly loved, clothe yourselves with compassion, kindness, humility, gentleness and patience. Bear with each other and forgive whatever grievances you may have against one another. Forgive as the Lord forgave you. "

One Minute Reflection
Who will you forgive today?

"To err is human, to forgive divine."
(Alexander Pope)

Divine Healing

Luke 17:19
"Then Jesus said to him, 'Get up and go. Your faith has made you well.'"

The Bible speaks often of miraculous healings through the work of Jesus
Christ and through faith in God.

Out of all the verses in the four New Testament
Gospels, 484 relate specifically to the healing of physical and mental
Illnesses. During His earthly ministry, Jesus Christ touched and
transformed countless lives both physically and spiritually.

In our story today from Luke 17, Jesus encounters ten lepers and cures
all of them of their disease. Leprosy is one of the oldest diseases in
recorded history. It is a chronic, progressive, bacterial infection that
causes severe disfigurement and disability.

Jesus cures all ten lepers but there is one man that returns to thank and
praise Him. Jesus tells this man in verse 19 above, *"Get up and go, your
faith has made you well".*

**All of the men are "cured" of leprosy but not all "are made well" or
healed.**
What is significant to note here is that Jesus is emphasizing
a relationship between healing and salvation; and a distinction between
a healing and a cure.

Four people in the Gospel of Luke hear from Jesus the same powerful
words, *"Your faith has made you well."* Each is, in her or his own way, an
outcast: the woman of questionable reputation, washing Jesus' feet; the
woman with the twelve-year flow of blood; the Samaritan leper; and the
blind man.

It is Jesus who redeems them socially, physically and spiritually. It is
their faith in Him that ultimately saves each of them and makes them
well.

One Minute Reflection
How can you experience divine healing this week?

"Health is a good thing; but sickness is far better, if it leads us to God."
(J.C. Ryle)

The Power We Need

Acts 2:38-39

"Peter replied, 'Repent and be baptized, every one of you, in the name of Jesus Christ for the forgiveness of your sins. And you will receive the gift of the Holy Spirit. The promise is for you and your children and for all who are far off-for all whom the Lord our God will call.'"

In our passage today from Acts, we find the disciples alone and wondering how they are going to continue without Jesus Christ here on earth. Peter reminds them if they repent and are baptized they will receive the promise of Jesus Christ in the gift of the Holy Spirit. The Holy Spirit is the One who will take care of the disciples and allow them to ignite the early church. The Holy Spirit will strengthen them, and lead them in the way they should go.

Why is this important to you and me?

Because what was true of the disciples is also true of us. We are also given the Holy Spirit as a promise written in Acts 2:39 above, *"For the promise is to you and to your children, and to all who are far off, as many as the Lord our God will call."*

The Holy Spirit will strengthen us, encourage us, lead us, and guide us. Often when we try to live this challenging life by our own strength, we find ourselves depleted and discouraged. However, as surely as the Holy Spirit had been sent to the early disciples, He has also been sent to us.

The Holy Spirit indwells every believer when they give their heart and allegiance to Jesus Christ. The Holy Spirit is a dynamic Third Person of the Trinity working in our lives daily.

How does the Holy Spirit help us?

Our task might be encouraging a friend, seeking deeper prayer, caring for a loved one, understanding Scripture, having the courage to give a testimony, or forgiving someone that has betrayed us. We should invite The Holy Spirit to give us supernatural strength to carry out any endeavor.

One Minute Reflection
What do you need the power of the Holy Spirit for today?

"Do not pray for more of the Holy Spirit. The Holy Spirit is the Third Person of the Trinity and is not in pieces. Every child of God has all of Him, but does He have all of us" (F.B. Meyer)

A Prayer Of Intercession

<u>1 Timothy 2:1</u>
"I urge, then, first of all, that petitions, prayers, intercession and thanksgiving be made for all people."

Scripture repeatedly emphasizes the importance of prayer.
We are meant to be a "praying" people.

We often pray for our families and ourselves. However, the Bible clearly calls us to a life of prayer that includes praying for others, also referred to as "intercessory" prayer.
An intercessor is one who takes the place of another or pleads another person's case. We can define intercession as "Holy, believing, persevering prayer whereby someone pleads with God on behalf of another or others who desperately need God's intervention."

Jesus Christ is our model for intercessory prayer.
Jesus stands before God and pleads our case. We know this because in The Letter to the Hebrews we are told that because Jesus' priesthood is eternal, *"He is able for all time to save those who draw near to God through him, since he always lives to make intercession for them" (7:25).*

At this moment, whether you know it or not, Jesus is in heaven interceding for you, even as He intercedes for the entire world. We are called to do the same.

Is there someone for whom you pray for regularly in Christ's name?
A person in the military serving our country
A friend experiencing loss or sickness
A husband battling depression or discouragement
A homeless woman you saw on the street

Start praying for someone today and stick with it daily.
God calls us to pray for others and promises that He will intervene on their behalf.

<u>One Minute Reflection</u>
Who could you intercede for today?

"How different the world would look, how different the state of our nation would be, if there were more sanctified priestly souls! These are souls who have the power to bless, for they intercede with sanctified hearts in the act of intercessory." (Basilea Schlink)

A Great Conversion

Acts 9:3-6
"As he neared Damascus on his journey, suddenly a light from Heaven flashed around him. He fell to the ground and heard a voice say to him, 'Saul, Saul, why do you persecute me?' 'Who are You, Lord?' Saul asked. 'I am Jesus, whom you are persecuting,' He replied."

One of the most notable and powerful stories in the entire Bible happens in the book of Acts. It is the conversion of Saul, a Jewish leader who was intent on stopping the spread of Christianity through persecution and murder.

As we see in Acts 9:3-6 above,
Saul has an encounter with the risen Lord on his way to Damascus.

We know that must get the attention of the student before we can teach him/her anything. God had to get Saul's attention and He used adversity to do it. Jesus sent Saul crashing to the ground with a blazing light, which blinded him. He then told Saul to enter the city and wait for further instructions.

God had Saul just where He wanted him; humbled, fearful, waiting for answers and turning back to God for help. Within just a few days a true transformation had taken place as Saul was proclaiming Jesus in the synagogues instead of persecuting Christians. Saul was later renamed Paul and becomes the most prolific writer of the New Testament as well as the strongest advocate for Christianity and its future.

Why is the Saul/Paul story important for us to know?
Because God is always on the lookout for helpers to further His kingdom's purposes. If He has to use trials and tribulations to get our attention, He will. Next time you face an uncertain situation, ask God how He can use you. Often what seems like a negative event can be one of the most profound spiritual encounters of our life.

One Minute Reflection
Is there some trial you are facing that God could use for His purposes?

"Brokenness is God's requirement for maximum usefulness."
(Charles Stanley)

A Psalm Of Encouragement

Psalm 23
"The Lord is my Shepherd."

The Book of Psalms is perhaps the most widely read and used book in the Bible. People reach for psalms to understand a whole range of human emotions and experiences. The Book of Psalms is in fact a collection of 150 songs, prayers and poetry that run in themes from creation to jubilation, worship, judgment, prophecy, praise and lament. Each psalm is a stand-alone work emphasizing a particular topic.

One the most beloved of all the psalms is Psalm 23.
It speaks to us at a heart and soul level and gives us encouragement when the world seems a particularly dark place.

David, the author of this poem, is a shepherd, the son of a shepherd and is known as the "shepherd king". David became the second King of Israel. In Psalm 23, David shows us the world from God's perspective; a place of provision, beauty and majesty all under the protection of God, the Good Shepherd.

Today we are simply looking at the first line of Psalm 23, "The Lord is my Shepherd".

What do these words mean to us?
God is near
God is real
God will not leave us or forsake us
God knows us intimately as a Shepherd knows his sheep
God watches over us, protecting, feeding and guiding us
God will see us through the worst of times
Christ referred to Himself as "the Good Shepherd"
Christ reminds us that the Good Shepherd lays down His life for His sheep
Christ lays down His life for each of us

One Minute Reflection
What other ways do you render God as your personal Shepherd?

"The Lord is my Shepherd." In these words, the believer is taught to express his satisfaction in the care of the great Pastor of the universe, the Redeemer and Preserver of men. With joy he reflects that he has a shepherd, and that shepherd is Jehovah." (Matthew Henry)

I Shall Not Want

"The Lord is my Shepherd, I shall not want. He makes me lie down in green pastures, He leads me besides still waters, He restores my soul."

Today we are looking at the first three promises found in Psalm 23.

"I shall not want"
What a wonderful, bold and comforting statement.
Why does Psalm 23 tell us we will not want for anything?
Because we are in the Good Shepherd's care. Yes, we might find trials and tribulations along the journey of life, but God has promised us that if we entrust our lives to Him, He will care for us and we shall not want for anything.

"He makes me lie down in green pastures, He leads me besides still waters"
Green pastures did not just appear on the horizon. The shepherd with skill and lots of hard work cultivated them. The analogy is soothing to us. God who is the ultimate Good Shepherd will manage all the details of our own "green pastures", if we just surrender our life to Him with complete faith and trust.

"He restores my soul"
Clearly, we are all in need of soul restoration. Life is challenging. It could be the loss of a job, the loss of a relationship, the loss of a dream, the loss of a loved one that has us down and out. However, David assures us that God will restore our souls.
Jesus Christ reminded us of this so beautifully in Matthew 11:28-29:
"Come to me, all you who are weary and burdened, and I will give you rest. Take my yoke upon you and learn from me, for I am gentle and humble in heart, and you will find rest for your souls."

One Minute Reflection
Do you need to surrender your life to the Good Shepherd's care?

"If you have a special need today, focus your full attention on the goodness and greatness of your Father rather than on the size of your need. Your need is tiny compared to His ability to meet it."
(Bill Patterson)

For You Are With Me

Psalm 23:3-4
"He guides me in the paths of righteousness For His name's sake.
Even though I walk through the valley of the shadow of death,
I fear no evil, for You are with me; Your rod and Your staff, they
comfort me."

Promises abound in Psalm 23.

"He guides me in the paths of righteousness For His name's sake."
God desires to lead us into greater righteousness in our lives and He
does it for His own name's sake. In other words, it is for the sake of the
glory and reputation of God's own name and honor. God wants to show
the world that if we allow Him to guide us, He is faithful to provide a
Holy life satisfying to us and pleasing to Him.

"Even though I walk through the valley of the shadow of death,
I fear no evil, for You are with me;"
The Good Shepherd does not provide contentment by keeping us from
trials, but rather by providing His presence in the midst of our pain and
heartache. We are being told in no uncertain terms that nothing can
separate us from the love and protection of God. Therefore, ultimately
there is nothing to fear even in "the valley of the shadow of death"
because God is with us.

"Your rod and Your staff, they comfort me"
The rod was a symbol of authority, used to ward off predators and to
discipline wayward sheep. It is a comfort to know that God is in charge.
Just like the sheep, knowing that God's rod and staff will be used for our
ultimate protection can soothe us.

One Minute Reflection
Which of these promises will bring you peace today?

"The little world within us, like the great world without, is full of
confusion and strife; but when Jesus enters it, and whispers peace be
unto you, there is a calm, yea, a rapture of bliss."
(C.H. Spurgeon)

In The House Of The Lord Forever

Psalm 23:5-8
"You prepare a table before me in the presence of my enemies;
You anoint my head with oil, my cup overflows.
Surely goodness and mercy shall follow me all the days of my life,
and I shall dwell in the house of the Lord
forever."

"You prepare a table before me in the presence of my enemies"
For us, "enemies" come in many forms; from people, addictions, bad choices, anxiety, negative thinking, despair, and yes even satanic forces. Yet, God prepares a table for us in the midst of this. The communion table comes to mind. Here we are invited to dine with Christ Himself, intimately and abundantly.

"You anoint my head with oil; my cup overflows"
Shepherds anointed sheep with oil to heal their wounds and to keep the flies and bugs away from them. This is a radical illustration of the sheep going from frenzy to a peaceful calm when they are bathed in oil. Once settled, they can receive all that the Good Shepherd offers until their cup overflows. We can too.

"Surely goodness and mercy shall follow me all the days of my life, and I shall dwell in the house of the Lord forever."
The house of the Lord is not just a saying but also an actual place. Jesus describes Heaven as a real location that He goes to prepare for each of us. Jesus describes it fully in John 14, *"My Father's house has many rooms; if that were not so, would I have told you that I am going there to prepare a place for you? And if I go and prepare a place for you, I will come back and take you to be with me that you also may be where I am."*

The final lines of Psalm 23 leave us with majestic reassurance. Heaven is a beautiful, thoughtful, appointed place that God Himself has prepared for us. And we get to dwell there forever!

<u>One-Minute Reflection</u>
Can you experience God's goodness and mercy today?

"If we want to prepare for our final destination, we should begin to worship God here on earth. Our arrival in Heaven will only be a continuation of what we have already begun. Praise is the language of Heaven and the language of the faithful on earth."
(Erwin Luther)

A Divine Calling

<u>Ephesians 2:10</u>
"For we are God's handiwork, created in Christ Jesus to do good works,
which God prepared in advance for us to do."

A calling is defined as "a strong inner impulse toward a particular
course of action especially when accompanied by conviction of divine
influence".
In today's modern, fast-paced culture, people tend to believe they are
the ones to make things happen. Or as the infamous words go of W. E.
Henley, in his well-known *Invites*, "I am the master of my fate; I am the
captain of my soul."

However, we know as students of the Bible, that God is really the one in
charge and He is doing the calling. We can examine Scripture for well-
known examples. Moses was called to lead Israel out of Egypt, Mary was
called to be the mother of God and the disciples were all called with a
direct invitation by Jesus to follow Him. Abraham, Isaac, Jacob, Joseph
(via dream), and Joshua, Gideon, Samuel, David, Solomon, Elisha, Isaiah,
and Jeremiah were all called, as was Paul, author of most of the New
Testament Epistles.

Ephesians 2:10 above tells us that *"we are God's handiwork, created in*
Christ Jesus to do good works". God has a purpose and a plan for each of
us. If we want to hone our calling, we can do the following:

Be available
Be ready and willing to do the work of God. God is in search of people
who are not "too busy" to meet the needs of those around them.

Demonstrate Humility
God is opposed to the proud. He is looking for those who will give Him
the glory.

Have A Pure Heart
Pure people still sin but they confess often, repent immediately, and
forgive easily.

<u>One Minute Reflection</u>
Are you ready to be called?

"The place God calls you to is the place where your deepest gladness and
the world's deep hunger meet." (Frederick Buechner)

Potter's Clay

Isaiah 64:8
"But now, O Lord, You are our Father; we are the clay, and You our potter; and all we are the work of Your hand."

One of the most powerful analogies in the Bible is that of the potter and the clay. The Bible says that God is the Potter and we are the clay. It is up to God to mold, transform, and sanctify us as we journey through this earthly life.

The potter's wheel was one of mankind's earliest inventions and has changed surprisingly little in the last 6,000 years. It is an illustration that makes sense to generations of people.

Isaiah 64:8 above boldly proclaims, *"we are all the work of your hand."* In other words, we are like a lump of ordinary clay. The potter has an end product in mind, a vessel that will be useful and ultimately bring glory to the potter's craftsmanship. The potter labors over the clay forming and shaping until the final product is realized.

God does the same thing with us. He is continuously molding and shaping us into the people He has called us to be.

Ultimately, we are being shaped into the perfect container for the residence of the Holy Spirit. The clay vessel is not nearly as important as the treasure it was designed to contain and to reveal.

2 Corinthians 4:7 explains it this way: *"But we have this treasure in jars of clay to show that this all-surpassing power is from God and not from us."*

We may be like vessels made of common muddy clay - fragile and easily broken yet God has entrusted the invaluable treasure of Himself to reside within us.

One Minute Reflection
What kind of clay are you?

"The reason why many are still troubled, still seeking, still making little forward progress is because they haven't yet come to the end of themselves. We're still trying to give orders, and interfering with God's work within us."
(A.W. Tozer)

The Goal Of Love

<u>1 Timothy 1:5</u>
"But the goal of our instruction is love, from a pure heart and a good conscience and a sincere faith."

When we discover the will of God for our lives, it provides the greatest sense of fulfillment and joy we will ever know. In the passage above from 1 Timothy, the Apostle Paul imparts wisdom on this subject. We can learn a lot from this exchange.

Paul explains that the goal of our instruction from God is love in three areas.

1) Love from a Pure Heart
When Paul references a "pure heart," he is speaking about the aim or focus of one's life. Our heart is meant to emulate Christ. We can do this in thought, word and deed.

2) Love from a Good Conscience
In Biblical terms the word conscience has to do with the intention of the individual to seek and do good. Our actions matter to God. We need to always be intentional about showing God's love to those around us.

3) Love from a Sincere Faith
God desires that we never abandon our faith.
This is about believing that God is who He says He is and that His promises are true.

Jesus Christ was deeply concerned about love. He spoke of it often and declared that love was the first supreme command. We must love God and consequently manifest that love to each other.

If we want to be used by God, any goal we set should be in accordance with the will of God. And the will of God starts and ends in love.

<u>One Minute Reflection</u>
In what way can you demonstrate the goal of love today?

"We cannot become what we need by remaining what we are."
(John C. Maxwell)

A Purpose That Prevails

<u>Proverbs 19:21</u>
"Many are the plans in a person's heart,
but it is the Lord's purpose that prevails."

We all eventually ask ourselves the same question:
What is the purpose of our life?

When God created mankind, He had a purpose in mind. Purpose therefore is the original intent in the mind of the Creator that motivated Him to create you and me in the first place.

Proverbs 19:21 above clarifies this perfectly.
"Many are the plans in a person's heart, but it is the Lord's purpose that prevails."

If we want to experience life at its absolute best then we need to figure out God's purpose for our life and be less concerned with our own plans. Everything in creation has a God-given purpose and if we want to know the purpose, we should not ask the thing but instead ask the Creator of that thing.

So how do we find our purpose?

Ask God. We are meant to be in relationship with our Creator. We can do three things to deepen our insight into purpose.

1. We need to meditate on His word
2. Pray for His wisdom
3. Seek His will through the discernment of His Holy Spirit

How often and how long do we need to do these three things?
Until we know for sure that everything we do is in alignment with God's will and purpose for our lives.

<u>One Minute Reflection</u>
Do you know the God given purpose of your life?

"The Spirit-filled life is not a special, deluxe edition of Christianity. It is part and parcel of the total plan of God for His people."
(A.W. Tozer)

The Parables Of Christ

<u>Mark 4:9-12</u>
"Then Jesus said, 'Whoever has ears to hear, let them hear.' When He was alone, the Twelve and the others around Him asked Him about the parables. He told them, 'The secret of the kingdom of God has been given to you. But to those on the outside everything is said in parables so that they may be ever seeing but never perceiving, and ever hearing but never understanding; otherwise they might turn and be forgiven!'"

What is a parable?
A parable is a story designed to teach a lesson through comparison. Jesus' parables are seemingly simple and memorable stories, often with imagery that convey a message of truth. The messages which parables convey are deep and central to the teachings of Jesus.

In the passage above from the Gospel of Mark, Jesus teaches His disciples why He uses parables. He tells them that parables are often hard to understand but are composed that way intentionally so that the listener has to invest oneself fully to know more. In other words – the listener is dependent on Christ to find out the whole truth.

The deeper we search for meaning, the closer we become to Christ. That is why most parables are linked with the saying, "whoever has ears to hear, let him hear".

And this is exactly what Christ desires...ardent followers!
Those that don't really care about God's truth *will "be ever seeing but never perceiving, and ever hearing but never understanding"*; Jesus is explaining that understanding the kingdom of God is not merely academic pursuit but a matter of the heart.

Parables are told to make a point. They answer a question or deal with a problem. Ultimately, however a parable is meant to prompt us to ask ourselves:
What is the central truth of Jesus' message?

<u>One Minute Reflection</u>
What is one new thing you learned about a parable today?

"With Jesus, however, the device of parabolic utterance is used not to explain things to people's satisfaction but to call attention to the dissatisfaction of all their previous explanations and understandings."
(Robert Farrar Capon)

Be A Wise Builder

Matthew 7:24-27

"Everyone therefore who hears these words of mine, and does them, I will liken him to a wise man, who built his house on a rock. The rain came down, the floods came, and the winds blew, and beat on that house; and it didn't fall, for it was founded on the rock. Everyone who hears these words of mine, and doesn't do them will be like a foolish man, who built his house on the sand. The rain came down, the floods came, and the winds blew, and beat on that house; and it fell-and great was its fall."

The Parable of the Wise Builder can be found in two of the gospels and you can read one of them above from Matthew 7. The most notable thing about today's passage is that it is found at the end of the Sermon on the Mount. In this parable we are given a story about two builders who are constructing a house.
The "house" Jesus refers to is our life.

Foolish Builder

Many of us are like the foolish builder. We are people who build our lives on shifting sand. We live by preferences instead of principles. We do what feels right, what feels good or what might impress our peers. We often ignore God's wisdom while we alternate our allegiances daily.

Wise Builder

The wise builder, on the other hand, carefully plans his house. He listens to the master carpenter and follows His instructions as if his very life depends on it. This parable emphasizes the need to put Jesus' teachings into practice, relying on the Word of God. If we do this, Jesus tells us that our house is going to stand strong regardless of life's circumstances. Whether "rain" or "floods," or "winds," Christ is expressing metaphorically the calamities and afflictions that befall all of us.

The wonderful thing about the teaching of Christ is that we are constantly urged not to do things by our own strength. Jesus invites us to build our life on the foundation and wisdom of God. The result will be true security here on earth and into eternity forever after.

One Minute Reflection
What foundation are you building your life on?

"The ultimate measure of a man is not where he stands in moments of comfort and convenience, but where he stands at times of challenge and controversy." (Martin Luther King Jr.)

A Mustard Seed

<u>Luke 13:18-19</u>
"What is the Kingdom of God like? To what shall I compare it? It is like a grain of mustard seed, which a man took, and put in his own garden. It grew, and became a large tree, and the birds of the sky lodged in its branches."

The parable of the Mustard Seed is one of the shorter parables but also one of the most memorable. It can be found in three of the four gospels. Jesus was very concerned with people knowing the truth of who God was, what God was like, and what life was like in God's kingdom and so He compares it to a mustard seed.
The mustard seed is one of the smallest seeds but it eventually grows to a tree of up to 12 feet tall.

How is a mustard seed like the kingdom of God?

First, Jesus is demonstrating that the beginning of Christianity appeared small like a seed during His ministry with only a handful of disciples. However it would grow exponentially into something very large. Like a tree, Christ's kingdom has become firmly rooted in the world and has become a source of food, rest, and shelter for generations to come.

Secondly, like a mustard seed, God's kingdom grows in the life of each believer. When a person puts his trust in Jesus, the Holy Spirit comes to live inside of him. This is similar to the mustard seed being planted in the ground. No one can see it from the outside, but it is definitely there.

If we can have even the tiniest seed-amount of faith in God, then He will meet us where we are, grow our faith, and boldly bring us to the place we need to be. He will invite us into the Kingdom of God.

<u>One Minute Reflection</u>
In what way does the image of a mustard seed strengthen your faith?

"So never lose an opportunity of urging a practical beginning, however small, for it is wonderful how often in such matters the mustard-seed germinates and roots itself."
(Florence Nightingale)

Let Your Light Shine

<u>Luke 8:16-17</u>
"No one lights a lamp and hides it in a clay jar or puts it under a bed. Instead, they put it on a stand, so that those who come in can see the light. For there is nothing hidden that will not be disclosed, and nothing concealed that will not be known or brought out into the open."

Today we are studying the parable of the Hidden Lamp.

The use of parables can be a very effective teaching technique. The Greek word for "parable" is derived from two other Greek words, para meaning "beside" and ballo meaning "to throw." Literally, then, a parable is an illustrative story that is "thrown alongside" a similar or comparative concept.

As He always does in His parables, Jesus uses common objects to illustrate a point. In the passage above He is speaking of a lamp, like we each have in our own homes.   However, the parallel story is really about how God's light is reflected in our home, neighborhood, community and out into the world.

Here's the question Jesus poses:
Is a lamp brought into a house to be set under a clay jar?
Or should it be put on a stand so that that light may shine brightly for the benefit of everyone?

In other words, we glorify God when we provide witness to the world about the greatest light of all, Jesus Christ Himself. We learn several things from this parable.

1. God's truth cannot be concealed.
2. Attempting to hide our Christianity betrays God's trust.
3. Our life is viewed and judged by others, we make God proud when we shine a light on all that He is doing!
4. Be the light that God has called us to be.

<u>One Minute Reflection</u>
What is one way you could let your light shine for God today?

"Jesus Christ is the Light that cannot be hidden, the Truth that cannot be denied, the Word that cannot be silenced, the Mystery that cannot be concealed, the King who cannot be defeated."
(James Fowler)

Cursing Of The Fig Tree

Matthew 21:18-19
"Early in the morning as He was on His way back into the city, He was hungry. Seeing a fig tree by the road, He went up to it but found nothing on it except leaves. Then He said to it, 'May you never bear fruit again!' Immediately the tree withered."

This is a very interesting passage of Scripture we are reading today becausewe encounter Jesus unlike we normally view Him. He is angry and is cursing a fig tree.

Why?
This scene is really a parable of Jesus acted out for His disciples and a wonderful lesson for us to learn today.

The time was Holy week, which in 33 A.D. was the last week of March. During this time of year, the presence of leaves on fig trees indicates there should be fruit on the tree as well. However on this particular tree, there was no fruit.

Jesus' action of cursing the tree was symbolic.
The leaves on the tree advertised that there were figs there as well, but it was a false advertisement. Jesus used this tree to teach a memorable lesson: the tree was cursed not just because it was not bearing fruit, but also because it was making a show of its outward life that promised fruit and then delivered none.

Jesus does not tolerate hypocrites.
Jesus is warning us that those of us who act religious but, in fact, are spiritually barren will be cursed. Jesus expects us to produce evidence of a genuine spiritual life.

A more modern translation might be:
Just don't "talk the walk", but "walk the walk", following Jesus every step of the way.

One Minute Reflection
Is religion trumping your real relationship with Jesus Christ?

"Everybody thinks of changing humanity,
but nobody thinks of changing himself."
(Leo Tolstoy)

Which Soil Are You?

Matthew 13:3-8

"Then he told them many things in parables, saying: 'A farmer went out to sow his seed. As he was scattering the seed, some fell along the path, and the birds came and ate it up. Some fell on rocky places, where it did not have much soil. It sprang up quickly, because the soil was shallow. But when the sun came up, the plants were scorched, and they withered because they had no root. Other seed fell among thorns, which grew up and choked the plants. Still other seed fell on good soil, where it produced a crop-a hundred, sixty or thirty times what was sown.'"

Today we are reviewing one of the most well known parables that Jesus tells to His disciples regarding the Word of God. He compares the sowing of that Word to how a farmer sows his seed. The farmer is like Jesus. He sows the seed of good news regarding the Kingdom of God. The farmer sows the seed in many different places and with many varying results. It is the same with the Word of God. It has a good result in the lives of some people, and it has a little or no result in the lives of others.

But what makes the difference?
Jesus' emphasis is not on the sower; rather His focus is on the soil types. Jesus explained that the four soil types represent man's capacity to understand His Word.

The first person allows the devil, the world, or daily distractions, to snatch away the Word before it can take root in their lives.

Another allows tribulation to prevent any real spiritual growth. We know plenty of people who don't believe in God because pain has hardened their hearts.

Others permit the immediate pursuit of riches and pleasures to make the Word unproductive. They have no time to invest in God.

Finally there are some that accept and nourish the Word, producing *"a crop-a hundred, sixty or thirty times what was sown."*

One Minute Reflection
What type of soil are you?

"The true contemplative is one who remains empty because he knows that he can never expect to anticipate the Word that will transform his darkness into light." (Thomas Merton)

Due Season

<u>Galatians 6:9</u>
"And let us not grow weary of doing good, for in due season we will reap, if we do not give up."

Today's passage comes from the Book of Galatians found in the New Testament. This is probably one of the first books that Paul ever wrote and is considered to be his most passionate letter. If you want to get re-excited about the Bible, the Book of Galatians is a great place to start. Paul's words are filled with genuine pleas for the church to protect and defend the truth of Jesus Christ and His message.

The line of Scripture we are studying today has to do with sowing and reaping but more importantly understanding God's timing in this process.

The best analogy Jesus used for a life of faith was that of a seed.
Not only does a gardener need to plant their seed in fertile soil, he also has to water it, weed it and allow the sunlight to nourish it.
Then he has to wait to reap the harvest.

We as Christians need to operate in the same way.
Watering might mean praying, reading, and meditating.
Weeding might be working on bad habits, toxic relationships or sin.
Sunlight might mean worship, fellowship, or communion.
Then we too need to wait to reap our harvest also.

We often forget that God works in the eternal realm and has declared,
"For everything there is a season, a time for every purpose under heaven".

We must learn to do our part and then wait on God to do His; trusting in His promise that all things will work for good in *"due season".* This is why Paul encourages us in this passage to *"not grow weary of doing good"* and to *"not give up".*

<u>One Minute Reflection</u>
Are you willing to trust God for a full harvest?

"Waiting has four purposes. It practices the patience of faith. It gives time for preparation for the coming gift. It makes the blessing the sweeter when it arrives. And it shows the sovereignty of God - to give just when and just as He pleases."
(James Vaughan)

Declaring God's Glory

Psalm 19:1-2
"The heavens declare the glory of God;
The skies proclaim the work of His hands.
Day after day they pour forth speech;
night after night they reveal knowledge."

Psalm 19 above illustrates that "*The heavens declare the glory of God*".
If we stop to look lovingly upon this amazing earth or spend a moment
gazing at the night sky, we will always discover splendor; and splendor
is God's expression of Himself.
We are told that the skies *"pour forth speech"* and *"reveal knowledge"*.

God speaks to us through:
Twinkling Stars
Shining Sun
Babbling Brooks
Windswept Mountaintops
Singing Birds
Crashing Waves
Blooming Flowers
Fluttering Butterflies

Psalm 19 has been called one of the noblest examples of Hebrew poetry
in existence and C.S. Lewis called Psalm 19 "the greatest poem in the
Bible."

God warns us to pay attention to nature and the world He created for us
to enjoy. He tells us that we can know Him by appreciating His creation.
Romans 1:20 states it this way: *"For since the creation of the world God's*
invisible qualities-His eternal power and divine nature-have been clearly
seen, being understood from what has been made, so that people are
without excuse."

It is not merely glory that the heavens declare, but the "glory of God"
that they reveal. Nature is God's revelation of Himself.

One Minute Reflection
What is God revealing to you as you study creation?

"The more I study nature, the more I am amazed at the Creator."
(Louis Pasteur)

Brother's Keeper

Genesis 4:9
"Then the LORD said to Cain, 'Where is your brother Abel?' 'I don't know,'
he replied. 'Am I my brother's keeper?'"

When God created humans, He designed us to live in families.
Family relationships, therefore, are important to God.
The Bible teaches that the institution of family is of divine origin and
purpose.

Clearly our "physical family" is important but just as noteworthy is the
new "spiritual family" that God has enabled through belief in Christ. This
is a family drawn *"from every nation, tribe, people and language".*
(Revelation 7:9)

Today we are looking at the question, "Am I my brother's keeper?"

The story of Cain and Abel is well known to many people including those
who never read the Bible. It can be found in Genesis Chapter 4.

As the story goes, Cain and Abel were brothers and the first two sons of
Adam and Eve. Abel was a shepherd and Cain was a farmer. Cain
offered a gift of fruit to God while Abel offered the firstborn of his
flock. God was more pleased with Abel's gift than Cain's because Abel
gave from his heart and Cain gave out of obligation. This made Cain
angry. So, while the two brothers were out in the field one day, Cain
killed his brother Abel. When God asks Cain about his brother, he
disavows any concern.

This story is important because it provokes us to consider who really is
our "brother" and what is our responsibility in being their keeper.

The Bible is clear that we all belong to God's family. Failure for us to be
our brother's keeper is an offense to God and a rejection of who God
created us to be both in our humanity and in our spirituality.

One Minute Reflection
Are you your brother's keeper?

"Injustice anywhere is a threat to justice everywhere. We are caught in
an inescapable network of mutuality, tied in a single garment of destiny.
Whatever affects one directly, affects all of us indirectly."
(Martin Luther King Jr.)

Honor Your Parents

Deuteronomy 5:16
"Honor your father and your mother, as the Lord your God has commanded you, so that you may live long and that it may go well with you in the land the Lord your God is giving you."

Nothing is more important to God when it comes to family than "honoring our father and mother". Honoring parents is a vitally important obligation, indicated by its inclusion in the Ten Commandments.

The word translated "honor" is a Hebrew word with a root meaning of "weight" or "heaviness." It is the same word often translated "glory" in reference to the Lord.
In other words, God is telling us to take our relationship with our parents very seriously, attending to it as we would attend to God. We should seek to honor our parents in much the same way we honor God in our thoughts, words, and deeds.

Granted, some of us have amazing parents who provide for us financially, spiritually, emotionally, and physically. Others of us have parents that have fallen woefully short of our expectations. However, God states no qualifier. He does not tell us to honor our parents only if they are honorable.

Why Should We Honor Our Parents?
By honoring parents, we honor God because He gave us this as a primary commandment. Obedience to God is learned by obedience to parents, which gives reverence to the family, the backbone of society.

An Additional Promise
If we look closely, the command given to honor our parents isn't a stand-alone mandate, but instead is linked to a very special promise: *"Honor your father and your mother, so that you may live long in the land the LORD your God is giving you".*

<u>One Minute Reflection</u>
Is there some way you could "honor" your parents today?

"To maintain a joyful family requires much from both the parents and the children. Each member of the family has to become, in a special way, the servant of the others."
(Pope John Paul II)

Thoughts On Palm Sunday

Matthew 11:7-8
"They brought the donkey and the colt and placed their cloaks on them for Jesus to sit on. A very large crowd spread their cloaks on the road, while others cut branches from the trees and spread them on the road."

Palm Sunday commemorates the triumphal entry of Jesus into Jerusalem to celebrate the Passover. The gospels record the arrival of Jesus riding into the city on a donkey, while the crowds spread their cloaks and palm branches on the street and shouted "Hosanna to the Son of David" and "Blessed is He who comes in the name of the Lord" to honor Him as their long-awaited Messiah and King. Palm Sunday highlights two important symbols.

The Donkey
The significance of Jesus riding a donkey and having His way paved with palm branches is a fulfillment of a prophecy spoken by the prophet Zechariah (Zechariah 9:9). In biblical times, the regional custom called for kings and nobles arriving in procession to ride on the back of a donkey. The donkey was a symbol of peace; those who rode upon them proclaimed peaceful intentions.

Palm Branches
The laying of palm branches historically indicated that a king or dignitary was arriving in victory or triumph. Then beginning in the fourth century in Jerusalem, Palm Sunday was marked by a procession of the faithful carrying palm branches, representing the Jews who celebrated Christ's entrance into Jerusalem. In different parts of the Christian world, particularly where palms were historically hard to obtain, branches of other bushes and trees were used, including olive, box elder, spruce, and various willows.

In the simplest of terms,
Palm Sunday is an occasion for reflecting on the final weeks of Jesus' life.

One Minute Reflection
Is it the majesty of Christ that strikes you or His humility?

"Palm Sunday tells us that it is the cross that is the true tree of life."
(Pope Benedict XVI)

Building Solid Families

Colossians 3:12 -14

"Put on then, as God's chosen ones, Holy and beloved, compassionate hearts, kindness, humility, meekness, and patience, bearing with one another and, if one has a complaint against another, forgiving each other; as the Lord has forgiven you, so you also must forgive. And above all these put on love, which binds everything together in perfect harmony."

Our passage today comes from Colossians 3:12-14. It discusses how to achieve perfect harmony within relationship to each other.

Family unity is under siege. We seem to be buckling under the pressure of divorce, parents who are absent, a breakdown of authority, less time spent together, financial pressures, the invasion of technology, and a host of other problems such as violence, drugs and toxic influences. This is not what God intended.

Today's passage helps us with family accountability

We are Holy and Beloved
We need to start behaving like the Christians God has called us to be. We are Holy and beloved and we can demonstrate compassion, kindness, and humility within the walls of our own home life.

Practice Patience and Forgiveness
We can start with spending more time together and be willing to put aside other obligations as we give priority to family life. We must be patient with each other offering forgiveness easily. The Lord forgives us; therefore, we can forgive each other.

Always Express Love and Gratitude
Everyone likes to feel appreciated and nurtured. We can affirm and validate each person's unique contribution to family life. It is crucial to intentionally demonstrate love to each member of the family. Our passage today concludes that love binds everything together in perfect harmony.

One Minute Reflection
How will you be more accountable to building a solid family life?

"An ideal Christian home ought to be a place where love rules. It ought to be beautiful, bright, joyous, full of tenderness and affection, a place in which all are growing happier and holier each day."
(J.R. Miller)

The Last Supper

Matthew 26:17-18
"On the first day of the Festival of Unleavened Bread, the disciples came to Jesus and asked, 'Where do You want us to make preparations for You to eat the Passover?' He replied, 'Go into the city to a certain man and tell him, The Teacher says: My appointed time is near. I am going to celebrate the Passover with my disciples at your house.'"

Today we are looking at The Last Supper, which took place hours before the Lord's crucifixion. The "Last Supper" was instituted by Jesus Christ to His Twelve Disciples in the upper room of a house in Jerusalem.

The Last Supper was a Seder (Passover observance). Previously, the feast's symbols had only pointed back to the Hebrews' redemption from Egypt. But that night, Jesus revealed the Messianic significance of two symbols: bread and wine.

In a Seder, a cloth bag with separate compartments holds three sheets of Matzo, or unleavened bread. The middle Matzo is removed and split. One half is broken and distributed; the other is wrapped in a napkin, hidden, and brought back after it is found. Breaking the bread, Jesus said, *"Take, eat; this is My body"* (Matt. 26:26). In Scripture, leaven symbolizes sin, so bread without yeast represents Holy God.

Wine, the other symbol that Jesus highlighted, is poured four times at a Seder. Scholars believe it is the third cup-known as the cup of redemption-that He called *"My blood of the covenant, which is poured out for many for forgiveness of sins"* (Matt. 26:27-28).

Every time we participate in Communion, we are to remember the deeper significance of all that Christ has done for us.

One Minute Reflection
What does Holy Communion mean to you?

"One of the most admirable effects of Holy Communion is to preserve the soul from sin, and to help those who fall through weakness to rise again. It is much more profitable, then, to approach this divine Sacrament with love, respect, and confidence, than to remain away through an excess of fear and scrupulosity."
(St. Ignatius of Loyola)

Easter & Resurrection

Revelation 1:17-18
*"I am the first and the last, and the Living one;
and I was dead, and behold, I am alive for evermore."*

In a few days, millions of people around the world celebrate "Easter", commemorating the resurrection of Jesus Christ on the third day after His crucifixion at Calvary as described in the New Testament.

The origin of this term is uncertain, though it is commonly thought to derive from Eastre, the name of a Teutonic spring goddess. In essence Christianity is really about Christ Himself, He is the core because without Christ, there is no Christianity.

Easter means several significant things for Christians

1. The resurrection is one of the major evidences that Jesus Christ is the Son of God.

2. Jesus' resurrection represents an assurance that we have forgiveness for our sins.

3. The resurrection tells the world that the kingdom of God is ruled by a living being. As noted in the passage above, Jesus appeared to John on the island of Patmos and said: *"I am the first and the last, and the Living one; and I was dead, and behold, I am alive for evermore".*

4. Jesus' resurrection proves that physical death is not the termination of human existence and that is good news for all of us who look forward to eternal life.

5. Finally, Easter conveys the fact that we can have a relationship with a living God. For Christianity is less about religion and more about a relationship with Jesus Christ.

One Minute Reflection
What does the resurrection mean to you?

"Our old history ends with the cross; our new history begins with the resurrection."
(Watchman Nee)

Raised With Christ

<u>Colossians 3:1-3</u>
"Since, then, you have been raised with Christ, set your hearts on things above, where Christ is, seated at the right hand of God. Set your minds on things above, not on earthly things. For you died, and your life is now hidden with Christ in God. When Christ, who is your life, appears, then you also will appear with him in glory."

Easter is about celebrating the resurrection of Christ. However, it is also about understanding that we ourselves have been *"raised with Christ"*, but what does that mean? The premise calls for action! If we are *"raised with Christ"* (baptized, joined to Christ), then there is a corresponding behavior we should engage in.

Our Scripture passage spells it out for us. It states,
"Set your mind on things above, not on earthly things for you died and your life is now hidden with Christ in God"

In other words since we have been raised with Christ, our heavenly priorities should be put into daily practice.

1) We are no longer simply a "believer" in Christ instead we must become a "follower" of Christ as well.

2) Creed and conduct are now synonymous. Faith in action is what is required. God is calling us to step out of the shadows and into the spotlight for His namesake.

3) Self-examination is always unpleasant but often necessary for growth. We need to look at our thoughts, words and deeds and align them with Christ's principles.

4) Finally, we can take into account that everything here on earth is temporary and God has declared that our new home is with Him in Heaven.

<u>One Minute Reflection</u>
How can you set your mind on things above?

"To know the Word of God, to live the Word of God, to preach the Word, to teach the Word, is the sum of all wisdom, the heart of all Christian service."
(Charles E. Fuller)

Get Some Rest

<u>Hebrews 4:9-10</u>
"There remains, then, a Sabbath-rest for the people of God; for anyone who enters God's rest also rests from their works, just as God did from his."

Rest is important to God. We know from Genesis 2:1-3, that God ordained the seventh day of creation as a day of rest. God is all knowing and all-powerful, so when God created the world in six days and sanctified the seventh day as a day of rest, it was to instruct us that spiritual rest is of the highest significance.

God also ordained rest as a commandment when He told us in Exodus 20:8 to *"Remember the Sabbath day, to keep it Holy. Six days you shall labor, and do all your work, but the seventh day is a Sabbath to the LORD your God. On it you shall not do any work."*

Why is rest important to God?

Rest is a necessity for all of God's creatures. Without proper rest the human body will break down and the human spirit will be depleted.

The Hebrew word "rest" is the root word for "Sabbath." It means to cease from busyness, toil, or strain. The rest God promises is both spiritual as well as physical.

Our passage today reminds us that just as God rested, we are required to rest as well. God has provided a model for our renewal and rejuvenation not just in abstaining from work but also more importantly in the incredible knowledge that we can rest in Him for all of our needs.

<u>One Minute Reflection</u>
What does Sabbath rest mean to you?

"God did not command men simply to keep holiday every seventh day, as if he delighted in their indolence; but rather that they, being released from all other business, might the more readily apply their minds to the Creator of the world."
(John Calvin)

Forgive Yourself?

Psalm 103:10-12
"He does not treat us as our sins deserve or repay us according to our iniquities. For as high as the heavens are above the earth, so great is His love for those who fear Him; as far as the east is from the west, so far has He removed our transgressions from us."

Today we are examining the need to forgive ourselves.

We all sin and we all need forgiveness. But often the hardest obstacle to overcome is forgiving ourselves. It may surprise you to hear that Scripture says absolutely nothing about forgiving yourself. There is not one word or verse or even description of anybody coming to terms with the struggle to forgive him or herself in the Bible. The Bible always presents forgiveness as a relational issue--something that takes place between God and man or between one person and another.

If we struggle to forgive ourselves it is because we don't fully understand biblical forgiveness. Our forgiveness comes from God, because ultimately it is God against whom we have sinned.

The issue should never be about forgiving ourselves.
The issue is always about whether or not God forgives us.

And we know, out of love, God sent His own Son to die on a cross to atone for the sins of mankind. When we don't forgive ourselves, the underlying message is that God may have forgiven me, but my own standards are higher than God's, and my standard is what really matters.

We need to realize that once God has forgiven us, we are forgiven.

If you are still struggling with the issue of self-forgiveness – try this simple prayer: "Thank you God on the basis of Your Word, and the act of Your Son, I can forgive myself because You have already forgiven me."

One Minute Reflection
Can you forgive yourself today?

"I think that if God forgives us we must forgive ourselves. Otherwise it is almost like setting up ourselves as a higher tribunal than Him."
(C.S.Lewis)

Easter Message

<u>Matthew 16:13-15</u>
"And He began to teach them that the Son of Man must suffer many things and be rejected by the elders and the chief priests and the scribes and be killed, and after three days rise again."

It is significant to highlight the extraordinary importance Christians put on the death of Christ. All other spiritual leaders are marked by their life not their death. Christians even chose the symbol of the cross to remember Jesus's death. For in essence Christianity is really about Christ Himself, He is the core and center of everything.

As we approach this Holy Day, it is a wonderful opportunity to contemplate again three very important questions:

Who is Jesus Christ?

Why did Jesus go voluntarily and deliberately to the Cross?

How is Christ on the Cross relevant to my 21st century life?

In the Christian faith, Easter has come to mean the celebration of the resurrection of Christ three days after His crucifixion. It is the oldest Christian holiday and the most important day of the church year because of the significance of the crucifixion and resurrection of Jesus Christ.

If we are going to call ourselves Christians, then it is our duty to understand who Christ proclaimed Himself to be, why His death is eternally significant and if His claims are worthy of our full allegiance.

<u>One Minute Reflection</u>
What does Easter really mean to you?

"One must keep on pointing out that Christianity is a statement which, if false, is of no importance, and if true, of infinite importance. The one thing it cannot be is moderately important."
(C.S. Lewis)

The Rest Of The Story

<u>Acts 1:8</u>
"But you will receive power when the Holy Spirit comes on you; and you will be my witnesses in Jerusalem, and in all Judea and Samaria, and to the ends of the earth."

After Easter has come and gone, it is important to ask what happens next.

The book of Acts answers that question.
The book of Acts picks up the story of Jesus and His followers where the Gospels leave off. In Acts 1:8 above, Jesus challenges His disciples to tell the whole world what He has done and to be His witnesses to the end of the earth.

Acts is in fact the transition book of the Bible.

When Acts opens men and women are still under the Law of Moses, they still worship in the temple in Jerusalem and they still operate under the Old Testament way of doing things. However when Acts closes, Christians no longer keep the regulation of the law, animal sacrifices are obsolete and people now gather in churches.

Today, we benefit from the freedom Christ offers.

In Acts, the Holy Spirit comes to rest on and empower the followers of Christ. The Holy Spirit equips disciples to carry out the calling of God. We learn how the Holy Spirit swept over Jesus' followers on the Jewish feast of Pentecost and how the apostles were then able to proclaim the message of Christ to all those people who had gathered in the city.

The Holy Spirit is available to each of us as well.

Christ challenges us to continue His ministry. Today, two thousand years after the book of Acts, growth of the Christian church is still in progress. Christ began His eternal ministry by dying on a cross and rising again in power. That is the Easter message. However Christ invites us to be witnesses that will take His message to the *"ends of the earth"*.

God has included us in His great plan of salvation

<u>One Minute Reflection</u>
What do you think Jesus meant by calling you to witness?

"I have found that there are three stages in every great work of God; first, it is impossible, then it is difficult, then it is done."
(Hudson Taylor)

Make Yourself Nothing

<u>Philippians 2:5-7</u>
"In your relationships with one another, have the same mindset as Christ Jesus: Who, being in very nature God, did not consider equality with God something to be used to His own advantage; rather, He made Himself nothing by taking the very nature of a servant, being made in human likeness."

There may be no greater mission of Jesus Christ than that of being a servant. In our passage today, Paul, who was the author of the Book of Philippians, takes every opportunity to convey that the road to spiritual maturity is paved with opportunities to care about others more than we care about ourselves. We are told, *"have the same mindset as Jesus Christ...who made Himself nothing by taking the very nature of a servant."*

What does being a servant look like?

1) Being a servant is the state, condition, or quality of one who lives as a servant.

2) A servant is one who is under submission to another. For Christians, this means under God first, and then each other.

3) A servant is one who seeks to meet the real needs of others and does whatever it takes to accomplish what is best for that person.

For inspiration, we must look to Christ

Paul presents Jesus as one who, although He existed in the form of God, voluntarily put aside all the rights and of His deity for our sake. Christ emptied Himself by taking on the form of a servant for mankind. Humility is the hallmark of Christian ministry. We can serve anyone, anywhere, at any time. All we need is a willing heart and Christ-like attitude. Once we make the decision *"to take on the nature of a servant"* we will find endless opportunities minister to the needs of a hurting world.

<u>One Minute Reflection</u>
Who will you serve today?

"Jesus' kind of service set an example. Thus He showed His followers how to serve, and He demanded no less of those who would carry on His work on earth. Jesus teaches all leaders for all time that greatness is not found in rank or position but in service."
(Ted Engstrom)

A Life Changing Verse

<u>Romans 8:28</u>
"And we know that in all things God works for the good of those who love Him, who have been called according to His purpose."

There are many life transforming verses of Scripture in the Bible and Romans 8:28 is a favorite of many. The Book of Romans is found in the New Testament and was written by the Apostle Paul to a group of Christians in Rome he had never met. The important thing to know about the Book of Romans is that it contains every foundational truth pertaining to the Christian Faith and is a must read for any serious student of the Bible.

Here Paul is sharing a promise of God to His people. God promises, *"in all things God works for the good of those who love Him and have been called according to His purposes."*
This means every trial, every tragedy, every hard choice, bad decision, wrong turn, thoughtless remark, or unexplainable predicament can be made for good when we surrender it to Christ.

Here are four unshakeable convictions in this one verse.
1) We know this to be true because the Bible says so
2) God is at work for the good of His people
3) God works out all things for good for those that love Him
4) Those that love Him, have been called for this exact purpose

This single verse is the underpinning for everything else in our Christian faith. It reminds us that God is in control. Our God is a God of transformation. He will take whatever we bring to Him and He will turn it into an ultimate good. This is not blind faith we have, but a faith in a supreme, omniscient, glorious, loving, generous and purposeful God who is taking care of our every need.

<u>One Minute Reflection</u>
In what profound way can this Scripture transform your life?

"If you don't see the greatness of God then all the things that money can buy become very exciting. If you can't see the sun you will be impressed with a streetlight. If you've never felt thunder and lightning you'll be impressed with fireworks. And if you turn your back on the greatness and majesty of God you'll fall in love with a world of shadows and short-lived pleasures."
(John Piper)

Go And Proclaim

<u>Mark 16:15</u>
"And He said to them, 'Go into all the world and proclaim the Gospel to the whole creation'."

Why should we share the Gospel? Because Jesus declared that He has "good news" that can transform human existence.

How do we share the Gospel?
Most of us don't feel educated enough about the truth of the Bible, or we are not comfortable expressing our "religious views". What we need to remember is that Christ cared about relationship not religion. Christ commands us to tell others about Him.

Go
First of all, we have to get moving. The word "go" is a directive. Jesus is telling us not to sit around and keep the news to ourselves. We need to get up off the couch, move out of the church pew, flee from daily distractions and get out into the world.

Proclaim the Gospel
Proclaim is a strong word, which means, "to declare publicly, typically insistently, proudly, or defiantly". The Gospel is called the 'good news' because it addresses the most serious problem plaguing the human condition, which is sin. God is Holy, and we are not. We are going to be judged either on the basis of our own righteousness or the righteousness of Christ. The good news of the Gospel is that Jesus lived a life of perfect obedience to God and then He offered Himself as a sacrifice to atone for the sins of mankind, which ultimately satisfied the righteousness of God.

To the whole creation
Finally, we have to proclaim the Gospel to all of creation because in every nook and cranny of the globe, man is the same. We are all sinful, corrupt, and alienated from God. Regardless of color, race, geography, education or birthright, we all are in need of redemption.

<u>One Minute Reflection</u>
Who will you share the "Gospel" with today?

"Do not be afraid. Do not be satisfied with mediocrity. Put out into the deep and let down your nets for a catch."
(John Paul II)

Praying Parent

Lamentations 2:19
"Arise, cry out in the night: in the beginning of the watches pour out thine heart like water before the face of the LORD: Lift up your◻hands unto Him for the sake of your children who faint for hunger at the head of every street."

The Bible is replete with wonderful suggestions on parenting. Learning to pray regularly for our children and with our children is one of the most effective methods to insure peace and protection.

Our Scripture today comes from Lamentations. Lamentations is one of those Old Testament books, which is not recognized by most people. It is considered a very somber look at how Jeremiah weeps over the ruins of Jerusalem; however, today's passage is really an affirmation of faith in the justice and goodness of God.

Our text reminds us to pray round the clock - right on through the night, until sunset; continually *"pouring out our hearts like water before the face of the Lord".* When we cry out to God for the sake of our children, we need to have an expectation of receiving a divine blessing with each plea.

What will praying for our children do?
Prayer will create a God centered child
Prayer will help children feel loved and cared for
Prayer will release kids from fear
Prayer will motivate them to do the right thing
Prayer will establish strong family bonds
Prayer will show young people how to discern God's wisdom
Prayer will teach our children to understand God's ways
Prayer will remind kids to take the high road in all things

One Minute Reflection
How will you pray for your child today?

"Each day of our lives we make deposits
in the memory banks of our children."
(Charles Swindoll)

Pray Without Ceasing

1 Thessalonians 5:17
"Pray Without Ceasing."

What did the Apostle Paul mean when he said, *"Pray without ceasing"*?

We find this exhortation in a letter Paul writes to the church in Thessalonica where new Christians were being persecuted for their faith. The Thessalonian letters are a set of paired books written as Book 1 and Book 2 found in the New Testament. Thessalonica exists today as the Greek city of Salonika.

To pray without ceasing means to adopt a new attitude and outlook on prayer so that it becomes ingrained as our "go to" strategy for any situation. Paul is encouraging us to make prayer so much a part of our natural behavior that we never think to not pray.

Prayer can incorporate praise, thanksgiving, confession, pleading for ourselves, interceding for others, looking for guidance, wisdom, forgiveness or accessing God's will for our life.

"Without ceasing" basically means recurring. It doesn't mean non-stop talking, instead it conveys a continual surrendering of everything back over to God.

The great thing about prayer is that we can pray whenever we want; morning, noon or night, where ever we want; a car, a gym, a beach, a hospital, a street corner, and we can pray about whatever important or trivial matter we desire to share with God.

Daily, regular communion with God generates intimate fellowship with our Creator and leads to divine blessing.

One Minute Reflection
What do you think of the suggestion to pray without ceasing?

"Faith is the heroic effort of your life,
you fling yourself in reckless confidence on God."
(Oswald Chambers)

Why Confess?

<u>Psalm 32:5-7</u>
"Then I acknowledged my sin to You and did not cover up my iniquity. I said, 'I will confess my transgressions to the Lord.' And you forgave the guilt of my sin."

The Biblical meanings of confess is to "say it as it is" or to "acknowledge the reality".

The Hebrew word used in the Old Testament for confess is "yadah" meaning to throw down, and the Greek word used in the New Testament for confess is homologeo meaning to say the same thing as or acknowledge.

Why does God want us to acknowledge our sin if He is already aware of it?

Confession is important to God.
Confession of sin demonstrates our acknowledgment that we have sinned. If we look at God's instructions in the Old Testament regarding the sacrifices for sins, we see that God wants us to acknowledge and confess our sins whenever we become aware that we have fallen short of His instruction.

The Bible also says, if we are faithful to confess our sin, He is faithful and just to forgive us. Christians confess their sins to God to practice humbleness before a Holy and righteous God. We are challenged to exercise and promote confession as a regular spiritual practice.

How do we do this?
One way we can ensure regular confession is to consider confession as a starting point for any prayer. In other words before we praise God, before we ask for anything, before we thank God for all He has done, we can start with confessing our sins and asking God for forgiveness.

<u>One Minute Reflection</u>
What do you need to confess today?

"Confession heals, confession justifies, confession grants pardon of sin, all hope consists in confession; in confession there is a chance for mercy."
(St. Isidore of Sevillea)

Holy And Pleasing

Romans 12:1-2

"Therefore, I urge you, brothers and sisters, in view of God's mercy, to offer your bodies as a living sacrifice, Holy and pleasing to God-this is your true and proper worship."

In today's society, the entire concept of holiness has become somewhat obsolete. Thankfully God does not change with the opinions of man. Holiness is important to God. It always has been and from what we read in Scripture, it always will be.

What God declares as Holy cannot be denigrated by man's agenda. God does not diminish His righteous standards even when man does.

The Holy Bible, The Holy Word, The Holy Spirit, Holy Ground, Holy People, and Holy Matrimony all still matter to a Holy God.

Holiness is a scriptural principle.
The word Holy, in various forms, is found more than 600 times in the Bible.

Webster's Dictionary defines holiness as anything "dedicated to religious use; belonging to or coming from God; spiritually perfect or pure; untainted by evil or sin; sinless; saintly...or sacred referring to that which is set apart as Holy or is dedicated to some exalted purpose".

Here in Romans Chapter 12 verse 1, the Apostle Paul beseeches followers of Christ to *"offer your bodies as a living sacrifice, Holy and pleasing to God".*

In other words because God is Holy, we are meant to be Holy also. It is crucial that we understand that our bodies belong to God just as much as our souls do. God wants visible, lived-out, bodily evidence that our lives are built for His holiness and that our bodies are the temples of a Holy God, which houses His Holy Spirit.

We are meant to use our bodies as a place of worship to honor God with our lives.

One Minute Reflection
In what way can you offer your body as a living sacrifice today?

"Holiness is nothing less than conformity to the character of God."
(Jerry Bridges)

Holy Bible

2 Timothy 3:15

"And how from infancy you have known the Holy Scriptures, which are able to make you wise for salvation through faith in Christ Jesus."

Nothing is more important than the Holy Bible.

The Bible is not some obsolete, dusty old book stuck in the back of a pew at our local church. The Bible is Holy and God intended us to treat it as an invaluable gift that He gave to us - His people.

The Bible is Holy because it is "set apart" for sacred purposes; in other words it is a book set apart from all others in history. It is the only book written by God Himself, the only book that has the power to set men free, to change our lives and give us insight to God's ways. It is also the only book that gives life, comfort, and hope because of its super natural origin, which endures until the end of time.

In our passage today, Paul's use of the word "Holy" in combination with the word "Scriptures" is significant. The word "Scripture" means "a sacred writing; the sacred writings of the Bible" The word "Holy" means "belonging to, derived from, or associated with a divine power". Paul was stressing that the Scripture is divinely inspired.

Scripture was written by men under the direction and influence of the Holy Spirit. Therefore, the Bible is actually God speaking about His will and His ways.   Since God, the Holy Spirit, is the author of Scripture, we must conclude that all the words of the Bible are Holy as well.

We can put full trust in the words of the Holy Bible because a Holy God writes it. He is true, faithful, just, and completely perfect in every way and so are the words that He proclaims. The purpose of the Holy Bible is to make us Holy too.
Or as we are reminded from our passage today,
"to make us wise for salvation through faith in Christ Jesus".

One Minute Reflection
How will reflecting on the Bible as Holy impact you today?

"All Word and no Spirit, we dry up; all Spirit and no Word, we blow up; both Word and Spirit, we grow up."
(David Watson)

Holy Matrimony

<u>Matthew 19:4-6</u>
"And He answered and said to them, 'Have you not read that He who made them at the beginning made them male and female, and said, 'For this reason a man shall leave his father and mother and be cleaved to his wife, and the two shall become one flesh'?' 'So then, they are no longer two but one flesh.'

In our passage today from Matthew 19, Jesus is quoting Genesis 2:24. Here we have God's perfect blueprint concerning perfect marriage. Marriage is God's idea, designed and instituted by the Creator, Himself.

When we speak of "Holy Matrimony" we are referring to a marriage that has been officiated in a ceremony performed by clergy, often in the context of a church. It is deemed "holy" by virtue of the fact that the union between a man and a woman is sanctified ("made holy") by vows to God as well as to each other. God is to be a witness and participant in the ritual as He divinely blesses the marriage union.

In today's passage, we discover that at the heart of God's design for Holy Matrimony is companionship and intimacy spelled out in very specific terms.
1) We must leave our families of origin
2) We must cleave to one another in a permanent commitment
3) We must become one flesh

Becoming "one flesh" is what God intended for marriage.
One flesh is more than physical union. It means the sharing of life, material possessions, money, thoughts and dreams, joys and hardships, hopes and fears, successes and failures, as well as producing and raising children. In Holy Matrimony, there are no longer two entities (two individuals), but now there is one entity (a married couple).
In short, we are actually meant to operate as one person in marriage.
One In Spirit: Growing together in love for Christ.
One In Physical Union: An exclusive, intimate commitment.
One In Emotional Intimacy: exclusive feelings for each other only.
One in Family: Going the same direction to benefit the whole family unit.

<u>One Minute Reflection</u>
Are there areas of your marriage that need "one flesh" commitment?

"There is, hidden or flaunted, a sword between the sexes till an entire marriage reconciles them." (C.S. Lewis)

Faith & Works

<u>James 2:4</u>
"What does it profit, my brethren, if someone says he has faith but does not have works? Can faith save him?"

The Book of James is found almost at the end of the New Testament and yet is one of the earliest writings by James who was the half-brother of Jesus. The book is short and easy to read and has one central message: genuine faith in Christ is lived out in a life of obedience to Christ's teachings.

Today we look at the question of whether faith needs to be manifesting itself in works.
We are asked to consider whether if someone has faith but works does not back it up, can faith save him?

In summary, both faith and works are important to our salvation.

Faith
We know that believers are "saved" (declared righteous before God) by God's Grace through faith alone in the atoning work of Jesus Christ at the cross.

Works
Works, on the other hand, are the evidence of genuine salvation. They are the "proof in the pudding". Good works demonstrate the truth of one's faith.

In other words, works are the obvious, visible results of being justified by faith. Jesus referred to this often as "bearing good fruit".

For many people, Christianity is merely a spectator sport, but that is not what Christ intended. We were made to serve. Ephesians 2:10 explains:
"For we are God's handiwork, created in Christ Jesus to do good works, which God prepared in advance for us to do."

<u>One Minute Reflection</u>
Do you see the connection of faith and works?

"Let us touch the dying, the poor, the lonely and the unwanted according to the graces we have received and let us not be ashamed or slow to do the humble work."
(Mother Teresa)

Send Me

Isaiah 6:8
"Then I heard the voice of the Lord saying, 'Whom shall I send? And who will go for us?' And I said, 'Here am I. Send me!'"

We can learn a lot from the life of Isaiah about hearing the voice of the Lord. Little is known of the personal life of the prophet, but Isaiah is considered to be one of the greatest Hebrew prophets. He lived and worked in Jerusalem from about 750 to 700 B.C.

Isaiah has been called the "Evangelical Prophet," because the writings attributed to him are the most frequently quoted Old Testament prophecies by Jesus and the New Testament writers.

Whether we hear God's call or not depends on two things: the condition of our hearts and the attitudes of our minds. This is a critical point for us to understand.

God did not direct His call to Isaiah; instead Isaiah overheard God saying,
"Whom shall I send? Who will go for us?"
Isaiah was in the presence of God, and he overheard the call. His response, performed in complete freedom, was, *"Here am I! Send me."* In the same way Jesus did not force the disciples to follow Him but invited them by saying, "follow me". They were willing!

God has a specific call for our lives also but we must be prepared to hear Him. We can do this by:

Get in the presence of God so we can hear His calling
Consider that God is calling us and be open to what God says
Listen intentionally during times of meditation and prayer
Journal what God impresses upon us and look for patterns over time
Step out in Faith because God has a miraculous plan for our life!

One Minute Reflection
Where does God need you today?

"It is a false assumption that there is a special calling, a vocation, to which superior Christians are invited to observe the counsels of perfection while ordinary Christians fulfill only the commands; but there simply is no special religious vocation since the call of God comes to each at the common tasks."
(Martin Luther)

Connection

<u>John 15:5</u>
"I am the vine; you are the branches. If you remain in me and I in you, you will bear much fruit; apart from me you can do nothing."

This Scripture passage comes from the Gospel of John. John was one of Jesus' closest companions. Within the group of original disciples, Jesus invited John, Peter and James into more serious fellowship with times of prayer, personal insight and instruction. Here John reminds us of the words Jesus spoke about the vital union we must maintain with Christ Himself. Jesus chose the metaphor of a vine because of its significance. The figure of a vine pictures an intimate union with branches that are totally dependent upon it. Jesus is demonstrating that if we stay connected to Him several things will occur:

1. We will always have a power source.

2. We will always bear good fruit.

3. We will never hunger or thirst for anything.

4. God is as close to us as a vine to its branch - we are never alone.

5. We can do all things through Christ who strengthens us.

The promise of having a deep abiding connection to Christ is that not only will we bear much fruit in our lives, we can also do it joyfully and with a full purposeful heart. We need to ask ourselves how many things we attach ourselves to for our own well-being. Is it food, alcohol, shopping, approval, work, busyness, fame, status, wealth, or possessions? God invites us to have no substitutes for the real thing. Christ desires to be the sole source of everything we need and desire!

<u>One Minute Reflection</u>
Is Christ sufficient for all your needs?

"The amount of time we spend with Jesus - meditating on His Word and His majesty, seeking His face - establishes our fruitfulness in the kingdom."
(Charles Stanley)

Conduct

Romans 7:14-15
"We know that the law is spiritual; but I am unspiritual, sold as a slave to sin. I do not understand what I do. For what I want to do I do not do, but what I hate I do."

How do we operate? - That is the question.

The words written by the Apostle Paul sum up perfectly how each of us often feels about our own conduct. Paul illuminates us from his experience, *"I do not understand what I do. For what I want to do, I do not, but what I hate I do"*.

Sound familiar?
No matter how much we may wish to serve God in our minds, we find ourselves sinning in our bodies. We might agree with the laws of God or commands of Christ as we say to ourselves, "no cheating, lying, stealing, gossiping or unforgiving heart here", but then we venture out into the real world and circumstances catch us off guard.

We want to do what is right, but often our conduct does not follow the plan.

God offers us a solution!
God has offered us the Holy Spirit to dwell in our hearts and help us do what we cannot do by our own strength. For those of us not familiar with the Holy Spirit - He is a full person of the Trinity and has several attributes to help us with our behavior.

The Holy Spirit will
Convict us of our sin
Remind us of right living
Empower us to walk away from any temptation
Enable Christ to be our guiding light in how we operate

One-Minute Reflection
What conduct could you surrender to Christ?

"If we are to have a measure of victory over the power of sin, it will come only as we lean on the strength and wisdom of Christ. As His grace strengthens our hearts and minds, we can overcome our own worst inclination to make foolish choices."
(Bill Crowder)

Being Weak Is Being Strong

2 Corinthians 12:10
"For the sake of Christ, then, I am content with weaknesses, insults, hardships, persecutions, and calamities. For when I am weak, then I am strong."

Today we are examining one of the most profound paradoxes of the Christian faith. A paradox is "a seemingly absurd or self-contradictory statement or proposition that when investigated or explained may prove to be well founded or true." From the human perspective, biblical paradoxes can be daunting to understand but from God's perspective, they reveal important truth.

Here are just some of the paradoxes of the Bible
We must lose our life to find it
The last will be first and the first will be last
Love your enemies and pray for those that hurt you
To be victorious, we must humble ourselves
Pain and suffering results in triumph

The paradox we are examining today is found in 2 Corinthians 12:10; *"For when I am weak, then I am strong".*
Here we find the Apostle Paul in his deep despair. Paul is experiencing sorrow as he feels betrayed, and maligned over what was most precious to him - his faith. However, even though Paul had lost his way, he grasped one of the most important concepts of Christian living - Christ's power is perfected in weakness.

Why is this important for us to know?
Because when you or I have tried every conceivable answer, spoken to every expert, relied on our intellect, our strength, our will power, and still have been broken to the point of having no confidence, and no trust in our own resources; this is when we finally surrender and allow God to show up and take over. In our weakness - God's grace will be undeniably on display. Grace is a dynamic force by which God gives us everything we need. He saves us, He enables us, He delivers us, He teaches us, He heals us, and ultimately He glorifies us.

One Minute Reflection
Can you apply the power of Christ in your weakness?

" Christ beside me, Christ before me, Christ behind me, Christ within me, Christ beneath me, Christ above me." (Saint Patrick)

Love Of Money

Ecclesiastes 5:10
*"He who loves money will not be satisfied with money,
nor he who loves wealth with his income; this also is vanity."*

Our passage today is taken from Ecclesiastes, found in the Old Testament. The book of Ecclesiastes is a book written by a man who never identifies himself but simply calls himself, "teacher". Some point to Solomon as the author. We know from reading the book that this man tries to find happiness in everything the world had to offer and finds it all meaningless.

The biblical wisdom of today's passage warns us that the more we love our money, pursue it, live for it and give up everything for it - the less it satisfies.
The opposite is also true. The less we love money, the less we pursue it, the less we live for it and the less we give up everything for it the more content we become with what we already have

Christ certainly teaches the same refrain in Matthew 6:19-21 when He says, *"Do not store up for yourselves treasures on earth, where moth and rust destroy, and where thieves break in and steal. But store up for yourselves treasures in heaven, where moth and rust do not destroy, and where thieves do not break in and steal. For where your treasure is, there your heart will be also."*

The lesson is that God wants the focus on Him
because He will provide all His riches in Christ Jesus.

We have to trust the Creator to bring us ultimate satisfaction.

One Minute Reflection
How much do you love your money?

"Money has never made man happy, nor will it, there is nothing in its nature to produce happiness. The more of it one has the more one wants."
(Benjamin Franklin)

Beautiful Planet Earth

<u>Genesis 2:5</u>
*"The Lord God took the man and put him in the Garden of Eden
to work it and take care of it."*

We know in the beginning, God put Adam into the Garden of Eden and commanded him to take care of it. As followers of Christ, we should be known as good and proper stewards of God's creation as well.

The Bible also teaches that God did not create nature primarily for man's use.
Psalm 24:1 reminds us that, *"The earth and everything in it are God's and for His good pleasure".* Throughout Scripture, God demonstrates that He personally cares for nature and finds absolute joy in His creation.

And what an amazing planet God created.
Vast oceans, plummeting waterfalls, brilliant scores of creatures, flowers, butterflies, fruits and vegetables come in every size and shape and color. White sand beaches, coral blue seas, and mountains that bristle with cascading hues of grasses, flora and fauna.
Everywhere our eyes can see, our ears can hear, our fingers can touch, and our mouths can taste and our nostrils can smell; there is wonder to behold.

God invites us as men and women created in His image to be stewards and caretakers of this great, big, beautiful planet Earth.

<u>One Minute Reflection</u>
How will you be a steward of Planet Earth today?

"The earth will not continue to offer its harvest, except with faithful stewardship. We cannot say we love the land and then take steps to destroy it for use by future generations."
(Pope John Paul II)

Be Encouraging

Romans 15:5-6
"May the God who gives endurance and encouragement give you the same attitude of mind toward each other that Christ Jesus had, so that with one mind and one voice you may glorify the God and Father of our Lord Jesus Christ."

We are reminded in our passage from Romans 15 to "pay it forward". God gave us Christ to provide encouragement, and now it is our turn *to "be of the same mind toward each other"*. When we encourage each other, we become one voice glorifying God.

"Courage" is the root of encouragement. We instill courage in others by speaking encouraging words. We can help people believe in themselves and strengthen their belief in God simply by putting the focus on what is possible.
We live in a time where we all need more encouragement.

How can we encourage someone else today?
All it takes is a "word" of encouragement.

We could
send a friend an email of support
call a family member just to see how they are doing
greet a homeless man, instead of walking by
include the person no one else wants to invite
catch our child doing something right
thank the cleaning person at our office or school
brainstorm with someone who is out of work
inject a positive trait when others are gossiping
remind someone that they are loved by God

One Minute Reflection
Who can you intentionally encourage today?

"One of the highest of human duties is the duty of encouragement... It is easy to laugh at men's ideals; it is easy to pour cold water on their enthusiasm; it is easy to discourage others. The world is full of discouragers. We have a Christian duty to encourage one another. Many a time a word of praise or thanks or appreciation or cheer has kept a man on his feet. Blessed is the man who speaks such a word."
(William Barclay)

Learn From Mary Magdalene

John 20:13-15
"They have taken my Lord away," she said, 'and I don't know where they have put him.' At this, she turned around and saw Jesus standing there, but she did not realize that it was Jesus. He asked her, 'Woman, why are you crying? Who is it you are looking for?'"

After Jesus died on the cross, He made a number of appearances to His followers; many of these are recorded in Scripture. However the first appearance was to Mary Magdalene in a garden near the empty tomb.

Mary is thought of as the second most important woman in the New Testament after Mary, the mother of Jesus. Mary Magdalene traveled with Jesus as one of His followers. She was present at Jesus' two most important moments: the crucifixion and the resurrection. And within the four Gospels, she is named at least twelve times, which is more than most of the apostles.

In our passage today from John, we can learn several important things from the exchange between Mary and Jesus.

One
It was Mary's deeply personal relationship with Jesus that enabled her to become the first person He spoke to after His resurrection. We can enjoy that same kind of intimate relationship with Jesus as well.

Two
When we seek Jesus, we will find Jesus. Mary's heart earnestly sought to find Jesus even when she viewed the empty tomb. Christ made Himself known by speaking to her. It is through His words that Christ will speak to us as well.

Three
We are called to live by faith, not by sight. When Mary could not find Jesus, she began to cry. But Jesus questions her weeping and reminds her He is near. Jesus promises to never leave or forsake us and we must take Him at His word.

One Minute Reflection
What can you learn from Mary Magdalene?

"Do not abandon yourselves to despair.
We are the Easter people and hallelujah is our song." (Pope John Paul II)

Eternal Message

Matthew 28:19-20
"All authority has been given to Me in Heaven and on earth. Go and make disciples of all the nations, baptizing them in the name of the Father and of the Son and of the Holy Spirit, teaching them to observe all things that I have commanded you; and lo, I am with you always, even to the end of the age."

After Jesus died on the cross and was resurrected, He spent forty days on earth. The gospels of Matthew, Mark, Luke and John provide an overview of Jesus' teachings, instructions and inspiration as the resurrected Christ.

Jesus made a number of appearances to His followers, and many of these are recorded in Scripture.

The Bible tells us that:
Jesus was crucified and buried. Three days after His death, His body went missing. There were reported appearances of Jesus over the course of forty days to both believers and unbelievers. People were transformed by the appearances, and they began to proclaim Christ's resurrection even to the point of being martyred for their belief.

Jesus tells us four significant things in today's passage

1)   Jesus proclaims His power over earth and heaven.

2) Jesus declares His purpose to make disciples of all nations.

3) Jesus explains the power of the Trinity - Father, Son and Holy Spirit.

4) Jesus promises He is with us, even to the end of the age.

One Minute Reflection
How will you respond to the words of the risen Christ?

"The great gift of Easter is hope - Christian hope which makes us have that confidence in God, in His ultimate triumph, and in His goodness and love, which nothing can shake."
(Basil Hume)

Bloom Where You Are Planted

Ephesians 3:20
"Now to Him who is able to do exceedingly abundantly above all that we ask or think, according to the power that works in us."

God has given each of us a skill and ability that the world needs. We are filled with possibilities. However, we often allow others to put us in a box, tell us what we can or cannot accomplish, and fall prey to discouragement, defeat, and dream stealing.

Today's passage tells us to believe in the awesome life-changing power of Jesus Christ. As Ephesians 3:20 above points out; *"now to HIM who is able to do exceedingly abundantly above what we ask or think."*

When God is working for us and in us - He can do more than we can ever imagine because what we accomplish is based on God's power not our own.

We can use:
Prayer - Ask God to Use You For Service
Purpose - Envision Your Destination & The Steps to Get There
Positive Energy - Encourage Yourself and Others Along the Way
Persistence - Do our best and leave the results up to God

Remember
No one can climb beyond the limits he places on him/herself.
But with God ALL things are possible.

<u>One Minute Reflection</u>
What can God accomplish in you?

"Your ability needs responsibility to expose its possibilities.
Do what you can, with what you have, where you are."
(Theodore Roosevelt)

Time Management

Ephesians 5:15-17
"Therefore be careful how you walk, not as unwise men but as wise, making the most of your time, because the days are evil. So then do not be foolish, but understand what the will of the Lord is."

The one thing most people agree on about time is that we never seem to have enough of it.

In today's passage, the Apostle Paul is writing to a group of Christians in Ephesus. He is trying to convince them that they are rich, not because of their wealth, but because of their faith and loyalty to Jesus Christ. Paul reminds all of us to use our time wisely and for the right purposes.

From God's point of view, time equals opportunity. And because of Jesus, we have an incredible spiritual wealth and spiritual power available to us daily. We are advised: *"be wise for the days are evil, do not be foolish but understand what the will of the Lord is."*

Many distractions can grab our attention, and if we are not careful we too can give into the "evil" of our present culture. We must give considerable thought to whether we spend our time, waste our time or invest our time wisely. Paul warns us that every moment here on earth will count toward eternity. Paul desires that we intentionally live a life worthy of God's calling, being sensitive to God's will not just our own.

One Minute Reflection
Are you making good use of your God-given time?

"Time is free, but it's priceless. You can't
own it, but you can use it. You can't keep
it, but you can spend it. Once you've lost it
you can never get it back."
(Harvey MacKay)

A Time For Every Purpose

Ecclesiastes 3:1
"To everything there is a season, a time for every purpose under heaven."

Above is the most famous passage in the Bible on the subject of time. Found in the Old Testament, Ecclesiastes is written to teach us that for everything there is a season; a set determined time, when everything shall come into being, how long it shall continue, and in what circumstances; all things that have been, are, or shall be, were foreordained by God.

God is the Author, Creator and Person who gives everything its purpose.

King Solomon, the writer of Ecclesiastes, was demonstrating that if we want to know the purpose for anything, we need to look to the source that created it. And that is why it is so crucial to read the Bible. The Bible lays out the thoughts, motivations and plans of God for everything in creation.

God has an appointed time for all things.

What does Ecclesiastes 3:1 teach us?

1) There is a specific season for all things

2) We must use our time wisely

3) How we spend our time - demonstrates our priorities

4) Everything has its purpose here on earth

5)) We can always trust God's timing for it is perfect in every way

One Minute Reflection
Do you believe there is an appointed time for all things?

"Oh, how precious is time, and how it pains me to see it slide away, while I do so little to any good purpose."
(David Brainerd)

Delight Yourself In Abundance

Isaiah 55:2
*"Why do you spend money for what is not bread,
And your wages for what does not satisfy?
Listen carefully to Me, and eat what is good,
And delight yourself in abundance."*

This word "abundant" in Greek is perisson, meaning, "exceedingly, very highly, beyond measure, a quantity so abundant one would never expect or anticipate."

In short, Isaiah 55:2 above reminds us that God promises us a life far better than we could ever imagine or manifest by our own abilities. It proclaims that if we listen carefully to God, we will delight in abundance.

Most of us tend to have a scarcity mindset. The challenge is to replace a "scarcity" mindset with an "all things are possible" way of thinking. After all we serve a God who created the entire universe out of nothing.

God's covenant to us is a covenant for abundant life. From the very beginning of Scripture, we are shown that God wanted us to be well cared for by Him. In Genesis, we are told that God made everything and declared it to be good. The Bible also tells us that wealth, prestige, position, and power in this world are not God's priorities for us. Clearly the abundant life does not consist of only an abundance of material things.

Abundant life is eternal life, a life that begins the moment we come to Christ and receive Him as our Savior. The biblical definition of "life" is provided by Jesus Himself when He said, *"Now this is eternal life: that they may know You, the only true God, and Jesus Christ, whom you have sent" (John 17:3).*

This definition mentions that the only thing necessary for an abundant life is knowledge and love of God Himself.

One Minute Reflection
Can you claim the abundance found in God alone?

"Whatever the blessing in your cup, it's sure to run over. With Him the calf is always the fatted calf, the robe is always the best robe, the joy is unspeakable, the peace passeth understanding. God's way is always characterized by... overflowing bounty."
(F.B. Meyer)

Are You Salty?

<u>Matthew 5:13</u>
"You are the salt of the earth; but if salt has lost its taste, how shall its saltiness be restored? It is no longer good for anything except to be thrown out and trodden under foot by men."

Jesus tells us:
"You are the salt of the earth"

Notice that this is a statement of fact.
Jesus is not telling us to strive hard to become salt.
He is declaring that we already are salt.

The only question for us to consider is "are we salty?"

The truth is Jesus has called us - His disciples - for a specific purpose. God has a plan on how to redeem the entire world and we are part of that plan. We are His hands, feet and heart in a needy, sinful, hurting world.

Jesus tells us the first thing we must do is operate like salt.
To understand salt, we need to examine how it functions. Salt is put on food for the purpose of flavoring or preserving. It benefits food by its presence.
In some way then, our presence in the world is for its benefit as well.

Here are the qualities of salt we can emulate:
Salt is desired - God desires disciples to follow and obey Him
Salt is distinctive - We are meant to stand out amongst the crowd
Salt preserves - We can stop the decaying effects of sin
Salt purifies – We could demonstrate purity in all things
Salt makes things better – We might encourage others in their faith
Salt causes people to become thirsty. In the same way, Christians should cause people to thirst for Jesus Christ and His gospel truth.

<u>One Minute Reflection</u>
In what way can you operate like salt today?

"A disciple is literally a follower, a pupil, a learner, an apprentice. He is one who has decided not only to follow his master but also to become like Him."
(Dann Spader)

Whoever Wants To Be My Disciple

Mark 8:34
"Then He called the crowd to Him along with His disciples and said: 'Whoever wants to be my disciple must deny themselves and take up their cross and follow me.'"

Today we are looking at what it really means to be a "disciple" of Jesus Christ.

In our passage today from Mark 8, Jesus tells us that those who want to be disciples of His, *"must deny themselves and take up their cross and follow Him"*.

Christian discipleship is the process by which men and women become equipped by the Holy Spirit to become more and more Christ-like. This process requires believers to respond to the Holy Spirit's prompting to examine their thoughts, words and actions and compare them with the Word of God.

This requires that we be dedicated to studying God's Word daily, praying over it, and then obeying each and every command. A disciple of Christ needs to live in the world and yet be set apart from it. Our focus should be on our Lord and pleasing Him in every area of our lives. We must put off self-centeredness and put on Christ-centeredness.

Jesus invites us to "deny ourselves" and "follow" Him.
Here are several ways to model His behavior
Jesus spent much time in prayer
Jesus was obedient to God the Father
Jesus forgave His enemies
Jesus served the poor with humility
Jesus resisted earthly temptations
Jesus knew Scripture well and referred to Scripture often
Jesus ministered to everyone He met and was always available
Jesus glorified God on earth with everything He did

One Minute Reflection
How will you be more of a disciple of Christ today?

"There are many willful, wayward, indifferent, self-interested Christians who cannot really be classified as followers of Christ. There are relatively few diligent disciples who forsake all to follow the Master." (Phillip Keller)

What Is My Vocation?

<u>Romans 12:6-8</u>
"We have different gifts, according to the grace given to each of us."

The Latin root of the word vocation is "vocare" meaning to "call".
God calls each of us specifically and has a purpose for our time here on earth.
A great place to start to understand God's call is by discovering our spiritual gifts.

The Bible speaks prominently about gifts. Generally speaking, spiritual gifts are God-given abilities meant to benefit and build up the body of Christ as a whole.

The spiritual gifts can be found in the following passages of Scripture:
Romans 12:6-8; 1 Corinthians 12:4-31; Ephesians 4:7-13; 1 Peter 4:10

The key is for us to know both what they are
and also how to use them.

The Bible mentions at least 20 gifts
Administration / Apostleship / Pioneering/ Craftsmanship
Creative Communication/Discernment
Encouraging / Exhorting/ Evangelism
Faith/ Giving/ Hospitality
Intercession/ Knowledge/ Leadership
Mercy / Shepherding
Prophecy / Perceiving/ Teaching/Wisdom

To discover our vocation, we can investigate three areas:
Our Spiritual Gifts will point out what we should do
Our passion will point out where we can do it
Our style will show us how to go about our service to others

<u>One Minute Reflection</u>
What is one thing I could do today to discover my spiritual gift?

"A spiritual gift is a supernaturally designed ability granted to every believer by which the Holy Spirit ministers to the body of Christ. A spiritual gift cannot be earned, pursued or worked up. It is merely "received" through the grace of God."
(John MacArthur)

Unfading Beauty

<u>1 Peter 3:3-4</u>
"Your beauty should not come from outward adornment, such as elaborate hairstyles and the wearing of gold jewelry or fine clothes. Rather it should be that of your inner self, the unfading beauty of a gentle and quiet spirit is one of great worth in God's sight"

It turns out people are obsessed with beauty.
We have created a $160 billion-a-year global industry, encompassing make-up, skin and hair care, fragrances, cosmetic surgery, health clubs and diet pills and it is growing at a rate upwards of 7% a year, more than twice the rate of the developed world's GDP.

To put that number in even more perspective, Americans spend more each year on beauty than they do on education.
We are very concerned with our exterior life.

And not only are we obsessed with beauty for beauty's sake, we have the additional pressure to make sure everyone else knows just how beautiful our lives are too. We have become a nation of people utterly consumed with self-aggrandizement. Social media platforms from Facebook to Instagram invite us to share photos of our outwardly perfect selves. We now spend countless hours posting pictures of our best selves, our amazing vacations and our VIP events. Then we look to secure "fans", "friends" and "likes" as a stamp of approval on our lives.

However, God has a different viewpoint on true beauty and we find it in our passage from 1 Peter. He tells us quite profoundly that true beauty should not come from outward adornment. Instead it should be that of the inner self. The Bible tells us that, "*the unfading beauty of a gentle and quiet spirit is one of great worth in God's sight.*"

<u>One Minute Reflection</u>
How do you describe true beauty?

"Beauty without virtue is like a flower without fragrance."
(Woodrow Kroll)

Who Do You Say?

<u>Mark 8:29</u>
"But who do you say I am?" Peter replied, "You are the Messiah."

In Mark 8:29 above, Jesus asks His disciples a very important question that we need to contemplate ourselves.

"But who do you say I am?"
That may seem like a very simple question, but unfortunately the world does not seem to agree on just one answer.

Peter replies - *"You are the Messiah."* (The "anointed one")

Let us consider again what we know about Jesus Christ.

The birth and death of Christ
We understand that the birth of Jesus was natural, but His conception was supernatural. We recognize that His death was natural, but His resurrection was supernatural.

Jesus claimed that He came to the earth to do three things
First, He claimed to be the fulfillment of the Old Testament Scriptures.
Second, He claimed to be the Son of God.
Third, He claimed to be the Savior and Judge of the world.

Jesus' power
There is historical testimony to Jesus' power and authority. He taught thousands of people, He healed the sick, He governed nature, He had power over death, He performed miracles and He forgave sins.

What Jesus asks
Finally, Jesus Christ asks us to repent of our sins and to follow Him.

<u>One Minute Reflection</u>
What will be your answer when asked who is Jesus Christ?

"Either this man was, and is, the Son of God, or else a madman or something worse. You can shut Him up for a fool, you can spit at Him and kill Him as a demon or you can fall at His feet and call Him Lord and God, but let us not come with any patronizing nonsense about His being a great human teacher. He has not left that open to us. He did not intend to."
(C.S. Lewis)

Glory, Glory Hallelujah

<u>Isaiah 6:3</u>
*"Holy, Holy, Holy is the Lord God Almighty;
the whole earth is full of His Glory."*

Glory is the goal of life!

Every living thing was created with the potential to release God's glory including you and me. We were created in God's image and because God is full of glory then our purpose is to reveal that glory daily in our own lives.

Glory is whom we really are, the full expression of the true person hidden inside of us that God wants to bring out. Our full glory is everything we were born to do.

We can each display God's glory in our own unique and powerful way.

A painter paints
A teacher teaches
A healer heals

We also know that the glory of Jesus Christ was most clearly on display at the cross. The Bible tells us that Jesus spoke about His own glory when He said,
"The hour has come for the Son of Man to be glorified."
(John 12:23)

Releasing our own personal glory means showing God to the world through our gifts, talents, unique perspective, and energy.

This is our true vocation in Christ.

<u>One Minute Reflection</u>
How will you display God's Glory today?

"We human beings are never happier than when we are
expressing the deepest gifts that are truly us."
(Os Guiness)

Dream Stealer - Fear

Psalm 56:3-4
"When I am afraid, I will trust in You. In God, whose word I praise, in God I trust; I will not be afraid. What can mortal man do to me? "

The Bible mentions two specific types of fear.

The first type is beneficial and is to be encouraged and that is fear of the Lord. This is described as "reverent awe" of an Almighty God.

The second type of fear is a detriment and is to be overcome. Some common fears are dread of scarcity, death, loneliness, commitment, heights, small spaces, flying, failure, rejection, being laughed at or criticized.

Multitudes of people never fulfill the call of God on their lives simply because they are afraid. Fear can paralyze us and keep us from stepping out in faith.

How can we handle our fear?

First, turn it over to Christ.
Don't deny your fear. Confess it to Christ, and then surrender it. Our passage today reminds us that God is ultimately in control and we can trust in Him.

Second, stand firmly on God's promises.
God says, *"Never will I leave you; never will I forsake you."* (Hebrews 13:5). Jesus declared, *"In this world you will have trouble."* But He immediately added, *"But take heart! I have overcome the world."* (John 16:33) God promises us hope that someday all injustices of this life will be destroyed.

Finally, pray diligently and in faith.
The Bible's answer to fear couldn't be clearer. Praise God's word and trust in Him. Stay in faith through prayer and supplication. If God is for us then Psalm 56 declares, *"No mortal man can be against us".*

One Minute Reflection
What fear do you have that you need to surrender to God?

"When you are tempted to give up,
your breakthrough is probably just around the corner."
(Joyce Meyer)

Anger Management

James 1:19-20

"My dear brothers and sisters, take note of this: Everyone should be quick to listen, slow to speak and slow to become angry, because human anger does not produce the righteousness that God desires. "

Handling anger is an important life skill. Christian counselors report that fifty percent of people who come in for counseling have problems dealing with anger. Uncontrolled anger is a devastating sin. It shatters friendships and destroys marriages; it causes abuse in families and discord in business; it breeds violence in community and war between nations.

We need to remember that getting angry is a temptation. With God's help we can stop anger before it takes over our life and learn strategies to choose differently. If we read our passage today from James, we are told to be *"slow to speak and slow to anger for the anger of man does not produce the righteousness of God".*

What can we do about anger?

1) Choose our battles
Much of what gets us worked up can be classified as nuisances that threaten to make us lose control. We can decide that the small stuff is not worth our time.

2) Confess our anger to God, and seek His forgiveness and help.

3) Be honest and speak about what is upsetting us before our anger builds up in us.

4) Act, don't react.

5) Attack the problem, not the person.

6) Seek help.

One Minute Reflection
How can you handle your anger differently today?

"No matter how just your words may be, you ruin everything when you speak with anger."
(John Chrysostom)

Dealing With Discouragement

Psalm 55:22
"Cast your cares on the LORD and He will sustain you; He will never let the righteous fall."

All of us deal with discouragement in one form or another because it covers a broad range of emotions. The verb "to discourage" means "to deprive of confidence, hope or spirit; dishearten, daunt."

Discouragement can be mild, strong or sometimes disabling. However God gives us the answer to overcoming discouragement in our text today found in Psalm 55:22. The Bible assures us that if we are willing to cast our cares upon the Lord, He will sustain us and never let us fall.

God declares both His ability and His willingness to be our strength and support. He can take anything that threatens to overwhelm us and use it for our benefit instead.

How can we overcome discouragement?

1) Take a break.
Identify what's causing our spiritual energy to run low and then step away from attempting to fix the problem. Rest and renewal are the first line of defense.

2) Cast our cares to God.
God always has a better plan than we do. Surrender all the worries to God.

3) Flee from our own negative thinking.
We must intentionally replace discouraging thoughts with prayer and Scripture instead.

4) Get around encouraging people.
Invite friends or co-workers to brainstorm and be solution oriented.

5) Trust that God has a plan for our life.

One Minute Reflection
What strategy will you use to overcome discouragement?

"If we're going to bring out the best in people, we, too, need to sow seeds of encouragement." (Joel Osteen)

The Power Of Our Own Words

Ephesians 4:29

"Let no corrupting talk come out of your mouths, but only such as is good for building up, as fits the occasion, that it may give grace to those who hear."

Of all the creatures on this planet, only man has the ability to communicate through the spoken word. The power to use words is a very unique and powerful gift from God.

Let's remember that God created the entire world from the spoken word. The entire first chapter of the first book of the Bible, Genesis, is about God bringing forth creation through His spoken word. *It states, "In the beginning God created the heavens and the earth. Now the earth was formless and empty, darkness was over the surface of the deep, and the Spirit of God was hovering over the waters. And God said, "Let there be light," and there was light".*

Words do not simply convey information. Words have real power.

As God's chosen people, we must be vigilant about what we say. We may talk a lot and yet pay no attention to what we are actually saying; let alone think seriously about the impact of our words. Our words go into our own ears as well as other people's, and then they descend into our hearts and souls where they shape character and destiny.

The question we need to consider is what kind of life do our words create. Do we have a life of possibility and positive options or do we speak words of discouragement and despair.

The Old Testament records King David praying,
"Let the words of my mouth, and the meditation of my heart, be acceptable in thy sight, O Lord, my strength, and my redeemer." (Psalm 19:14)

We can use this prayer before we start the day and before we open our mouths.

One Minute Reflection
How can you use your words differently today?

"When we understand the power of words and realize that we can choose what we think and speak, our lives can be transformed. "
(Joyce Meyer)

Happy Mother's Day

<u>Luke 1:38</u>
"And Mary said, Behold the handmaid of the Lord; be it unto me according to thy word. And the angel departed from her."

Today we are looking at the life of Mary - Mother of Jesus.

Mary was the most honored mother in the Bible.
God knew that Mary was a woman of rare strength and obedience and so He chose her for a very important historical occasion. She was the only human being to be with Jesus throughout His entire life - from His birth until His death. She gave birth to Him as her baby and watched Him die as a Savior to the world.

When the angel appeared to Mary in the passage from Luke above and told her the baby would be God's Son, Mary replied,
"Let it be unto me according to Thy Word."

Mary did not offer any of the following excuses:
Let me think about it.
I don't have time.
This is way too scary for me.
The cost is simply too high.
I have better plans in mind for myself.
Isn't there someone else who can do this?
I'll get back to you.

And although Mary was a young, poor female, and not the most obvious choice to be used mightily by God, she accepted God's will for her life which contained great joy and immense suffering. And because of her faith, she is a shining example of obedience and trust in the Father's will.

<u>One Minute Reflection</u>
How can Mary inspire you in a daily walk of faith?

"Mary, give me your heart: so beautiful, so pure, so immaculate; your heart so full of love and humility that I may be able to receive Jesus in the Bread of Life and love Him as you love Him."
(Mother Teresa)

My Body Is A Temple?

<u>1 Corinthians 6:19-20</u>
"Do you not know that your bodies are temples of the Holy Spirit, who is in you, whom you have received from God? You are not your own; you were bought at a price. Therefore honor God with your bodies."

Whenever we are asked a question in the Bible, it is God's way of emphasizing that we really need to consider the subject more deeply.

Today's passage highlights that point.
We are asked,
"Do you not know that your bodies are temples of the Holy Spirit?"

Notice that Paul, the writer of Corinthians uses the word "temples". He could have used other words to describe our bodies such as "places", "houses," or "castles." But by choosing the word "temples" to describe the Spirit's dwelling place, he conveys the idea that our bodies are a sacred space where the Spirit not only lives, but also where it is worshiped and revered.

We are privileged to house the Holy Spirit but are we behaving as a worthy choice?

Would a temple of God use vulgar language, gossip or slander?
Would a temple of God act in provocative, promiscuous ways?
Would a temple of God degrade, abuse or harm itself?
Would a temple of God cheat, steal, or lie to others?
Would a temple of God starve itself, or over indulge with food, drugs or alcohol?

We are urged to remember that God the Father created our bodies, God the Son redeemed them, and God the Holy Spirit indwells them. This makes our bodies not our own but claimed by God for His use and purposes.

<u>One Minute Reflection</u>
What can you do today to preserve your body as a temple?

"Our bodies are inclined to ease, pleasure, gluttony, and sloth. Unless we practice self-control, our bodies will tend to serve evil more than God. We must carefully discipline ourselves in how we "walk" in this world, else we will conform more to its ways rather than to the ways of Christ."
(Donald Whitney)

Personal Mission Statement

Luke 4:18-19
*"The Spirit of the Lord is upon me, because He has anointed me
to proclaim good news to the poor. He has sent me to proclaim liberty to
the captives and recovering of sight to the blind, to set at liberty those who
are oppressed, to proclaim the year of the Lord's favor."*

In a real way, our text above from Luke 4 summarizes
the "mission statement" of Jesus.

Even as early as age 12, Jesus knew He was to be about His Father's
business. He spent His life being true to His mission of glorifying God
through proclaiming good news to the poor, healing the sick, freeing the
oppressed and proclaiming the greatness of God's favor.

We usually think of a mission statement as summarizing the purpose of
a company, organization or charity and its reason for existing. A good
mission statement guides actions, spells out overall goals, and informs
decision-making.

**However we can develop a personal or family mission statement
too.**

Although most of us have unspoken goals - financial, spiritual, physical,
and emotional, these ideas seldom translate into reality. One way to
prioritize what our personal and family goals are is to write them
down. It can help establish a family's identity and reinforce what is
important to each person. A clear mission statement can help us stay on
track or sound the alarm when we go off course. It supplies a
foundation to mark if we are fulfilling the mission we originally set out
to do.

One Minute Reflection
Will you commit to a personal mission statement today?

"Everyone has his own specific vocation or mission in life; everyone
must carry out a concrete assignment that demands fulfillment. Therein
he cannot be replaced, nor can his life be repeated, thus, everyone's task
is unique as his specific opportunity to implement it."
(Viktor E. Frankl)

Change Your Morning Routine

<u>Psalm 118:24</u>
"This is the day the Lord has made;
We will rejoice and be glad in it."

If you want a radical new way to start your day,
Psalm 118:24 are the key to true transformation.

Before your feet hit the floor in the morning, memorize this key passage
of Scripture and declare it to be true each and every day. It points us in
the right direction and sets a tone of gratitude for the day. It reminds us
that God created this beautiful planet, full of wonder, delight, surprise
and unexpected gifts and all we need to do is notice, be engaged and give
thanks to the Lord.

The psalmist is telling us two specific things in this verse:

1) *"This is the Day the Lord hath made"*. This is the only day we have.
Yesterday is gone and tomorrow has not yet been manifested. God has
given us only today. It is a fresh start and a new beginning.

2) "We will rejoice and be glad in it". God created us with free choice.
We can make the day miserable with our thoughts, words and deeds or
we can choose differently. We can decide to rejoice and be glad in it.

Henry Drummond, a noted spiritual teacher, advised spending at least
two minutes daily thinking only of the Lord, Jesus Christ. Visualize Him
clearly in your mind, and strongly affirm "*This is the day which the Lord
hath made; we will rejoice and be glad in it.*"

<u>One Minute Reflection</u>
How do you start your day?

"When you cannot rejoice in feelings, circumstances or conditions,
rejoice in the Lord."
(A. B. Simpson)

Exercise Of Conformity

<u>Romans 8:29</u>
"For those God foreknew He also predestined to be conformed to the image of His Son, that He might be the firstborn among many brothers and sisters."

Today we are looking at a transformational exercise that might enable us to be more "Christ-like" in our daily life. We are told in Romans 8:29 above that *"God has predestined us to be conformed to the image of His Son".*

God's desire is for us to become more like Christ. However we cannot become what we do not know or understand. Of course, knowledge alone will not produce a Christ-like character. The knowledge we gain from God's Word must impact our hearts and convict us of the need to obey and model what we have learned.

One of the best ways to emulate Christ is to concentrate on one attribute and then spend the day manifesting it into our daily life.
Some of the attributes of Christ are:
gentleness
quietness
wisdom
being charitable
providing comfort
being a peacemaker
finding the best in people
faithfulness
offering forgiveness
being compassionate
showing kindness
standing up for what is right
extending love

God gave us the Holy Spirit to enable us to do things we may not be able to do with our own strength or desire. We learn in the Scripture above that conforming to the likeness of Christ is part of God's plan and destiny for our lives and has been since the beginning of the creation of the world.

<u>One Minute Reflection</u>
What attribute of Christ can you emulate today?

"Christianity without discipleship is always Christianity without Christ."
(Dietrich Bonheoffer)

Blocked By Pride

Psalm 10:4
*"In the pride of his face the wicked does not seek Him;
all his thoughts are, 'There is no God.'"*

We all want to experience the blessings from God that are promised in the Bible. However, it is crucial to also realize that there are some areas of our lives that may be blocking the free flow of His favor.

Nowhere is this more evident than pride.

Pride is described as "undue confidence in and attention to one's own skills, accomplishments, state, possessions, or position". Often pride is easier to recognize in others than in ourselves.

The Bible speaks of pride often while highlighting two important warnings for us:

1) Pride is a sin
2) God will humble the proud if they do not humble themselves

Psalm 10:4 above states that the proud are so consumed with themselves that to them *"there is no God".*

Why is pride so sinful?
Pride misaligns our priorities so that we become our own first consideration rather than God Himself. Pride is giving ourselves the credit for something that God has accomplished and it is taking the glory that belongs to God alone and keeping it for ourselves. Pride is essentially self-worship and therefore a sin because it becomes a hindrance to seeking Him. God desires our fellowship. We were created to be in relationship with God first and foremost but we must yield to His ways and develop our righteousness. We cannot do that if we are not yielding to His spirit.

If we want the blessings of God to flow freely into our lives, we must make sure pride is not blocking the way.

One Minute Reflection
Will you ask God to reveal any hidden areas of pride today?

"God sends no one away empty except those who are full of themselves."
(D.L. Moody)

Why Do We Doubt?

Matthew 14:29-31
"Then Peter got down out of the boat, walked on the water and came toward Jesus. But when he saw the wind, he was afraid and, beginning to sink, cried out, 'Lord, save me!' Immediately Jesus reached out His hand and caught him. 'You of little faith,' he said, 'why did you doubt?'"

Today we take on doubt.
In Matthew 14 above we find the story regarding Peter walking on water toward Jesus. It crystalizes how doubt gets in our way:

Here is a summary of the events:
After feeding the 5000, Jesus sends His disciples ahead of Him in a boat to cross the Sea of Galilee. Several hours later in the night, the disciples encounter a storm. Jesus comes to them, walking on the water and tells them, *"Take courage! It is I. Don't be afraid."* Then Peter replies, *"Lord, if it's you, tell me to come to you on the water."* Jesus invites Peter to come but as Peter begins walking, he focuses on the wind and waves, and as he begins to sink, he cries out "Lord, save me".
Jesus replies: *"You of little faith, why did you doubt?"*

We can learn two important lessons from this encounter with Peter.

1) Peter doesn't begin to sink until he takes his eyes off of Jesus and begins to look at the wind and the waves and the storm around him.

2) Peter starts out with good intentions. His faith has both high points and low points. Faith, for all of us, is a journey. However it is crucial to remember in whom we have faith. We serve a mighty, loving, omniscient, purposeful God.

The remedy for doubt is faith.
If we can stay in the Word and keep our attention focused on Jesus, all will be well.

One Minute Reflection
Why do you doubt Almighty God?

"Every temptation, directly or indirectly, is the temptation to doubt and distrust God."
(John MacArthur)

Blessings Of Obedience

Exodus 19:5
"Now therefore, if you will obey my voice indeed, and keep my covenant, then you shall be a peculiar treasure to me above all people: for all the earth is mine."

Obedience is defined as "dutifully complying with the commands, orders, or instructions of one in authority."

Obedience to God does several things:

Proves our love for Him
Demonstrates our faithfulness to Him
Glorifies Him in the world
Opens avenues of blessing for us

The Bible has much to say about obedience. In fact, obedience is the essence of the Christian faith. Jesus Himself was *"obedient unto death, even death on a cross"*. (Philippians 2:8)

As we learn in our Scripture passage today, God desires that we not only come to Him and believe in Him, but also to follow Him through obedience to His voice and covenant. We are told the result of our obedience will be that we are considered a *"particular treasure"* above all people.

One Minute Reflection
Are you being obedient to the Word of God?

"See in the meantime that your faith brings forth obedience, and God in due time will cause it to bring forth peace."
(John Owen)

Do You Have A Confession To Make?

<u>James 5:6</u>
"Therefore confess your sins to each other and pray for each other so that you may be healed. The prayer of a righteous person is powerful and effective."

To confess means to "declare, acknowledge, profess, and admit". We confess something when we openly declare that a thing is true. Confession is the opposite of denial and of silence. All of us sin, however what God desires is that we confess that sin.

Why?

God requires confession of sin as the means of maintaining a close, personal relationship with Himself.

God already knows when we have committed the sin so we can think of confession as being "in agreement" with God.

Confession does several things:

1) Acknowledging sin in our lives is a first step to being reconciled back to God.

2) Only when we acknowledge our offenses toward God can our relationship with God be restored fully.

3) God desires and requires that we confess sin and acknowledge that Jesus Christ's action on the cross was sufficient for God to forgive our sins and cleanse us from all unrighteousness.

We need confession of sin before God, not to earn God's love; but to rest in it and know it more fully.

<u>One Minute Reflection</u>
When was the last time you really confessed your sin before God?

"Sin is not just breaking God's laws; it is breaking His heart."
(Adrian Rogers)

In The Beginning

<u>Genesis 1:1</u>
"In the beginning God created the heavens and the earth."

Today we start at the very beginning.
Genesis 1:1 tells us that in the beginning - God existed.
He was before all things, He created all things and all things belong to Him.

Genesis means "origin" or "beginning" and it lays the groundwork for God's purposes and God's story of creation.

If we want to understand the mind of God - we must read Genesis.

Genesis explains four monumental statements about the universe.

1) Genesis reveals the nature of God
He is Creator, Sustainer, Judge and Redeemer of everything

2) Genesis explains the value and dignity of the human race
We are made in God's image and therefore the first born of all creation

3) Genesis warns us about the consequences of sin in our lives

4) Genesis foreshadows the great promises of salvation

What we learn in Genesis is the start of a very important truth, which continues to be revealed throughout the entire Bible. God created and calls out a people to Himself. In the Old Testament it was the people of Israel and in the New Testament it is anyone willing to become a disciple of Jesus Christ.

<u>One Minute Reflection</u>
What is God teaching you in the Book of Genesis?

"While I know myself as a creation of God, I am also obligated to realize and remember that everyone else and everything else are also God's creation."
(Maya Angelou)

Delight In The Law

Psalm 1:1
*"Blessed is the one
who does not walk in step with the wicked
or stand in the way that sinners take
or sit in the company of mockers,
but whose delight is in the law of the Lord,
and who meditates on his law day and night."*

The Book of Psalms is perhaps the most widely read and used book in the Bible. The Book of Psalms is in fact a collection of 150 songs, prayers and poetry that run in themes from creation to jubilation, worship, judgment, prophecy, praise and lament. Each psalm is a stand-alone work emphasizing a particular topic.

What does Psalm 1:1 tell us?

The psalmist uses the familiar Old Testament form of pronouncing that a certain type of person is "blessed." In Psalm 1, "the blessed" is described as the one who does not engage in certain activities. He/she is someone who does not hang out with evildoers, engage in reckless sin or join the mocking crowd.

Instead, the blessed person is someone who *"delights in the law of the Lord and meditates on it day and night".*

The word "meditate" means to ponder something and thereby take it into one's being. The promise in Psalm 1 is that God loves us so much that He has left an instruction book called Scripture that will counsel us in the right way to go. It provides a manual to live by so that we will not be destroyed by sin but can enjoy a purpose-driven, successful life.

If we want to truly be blessed, we must learn to delight in the law of the Lord.

One Minute Reflection
What action will you take today based on Psalm 1:1?

"Do not have your concert first and tune your instruments afterward. Begin the day with God."
(Hudson Taylor)

Famous Last Words

Revelation 22:20-21
"He who testifies to these things says, "Yes, I am coming soon." Amen.
Come, Lord Jesus. The grace of the Lord Jesus be with God's
people. Amen"

Have you ever considered what the last words of the Bible are and if
they have significance to your life?

We are given the bottom line.
We must trust Christ's words and expect Christ's return.

It has been over 2000 years since Jesus spoke these words to John but
they are as true today as they were then.

This passage tells us several things

1) From God's perspective, one thousand years are the same as a day.
God is timeless and therefore when He tells us He is coming soon, that is
a time that is unknown to us.

2) God's delay in coming again soon gives us insight into His
mercy.   Each day that Christ's return is delayed is another day of His
unmerited favor being poured out upon a people who have turned away
from Him. He is giving us time to change our hearts and minds.

3) The last sentence of the Bible is really a summary of the entire Bible
wrapped up in one simply yet powerful, transformational word -
GRACE.   In our tired, sinful, messed up world we are still eternally
offered grace by and through Jesus Christ our Lord.

The book of Revelation offers hope in the coming of Christ and gives
certain knowledge of the overthrow of evil and the ultimate restoration
of all things. Christ is ultimately victorious and because we hope in Him,
we are victorious too.

<u>One Minute Reflection</u>
What do the last words of the Bible mean to you?

"We never grow closer to God when we just live life,
it takes deliberate pursuit and attentiveness"
(Francis Chan)

Choose Love

Galatians 5:22 -23
"But the fruit of the Spirit is love, joy, peace, forbearance, kindness, goodness, faithfulness, gentleness and self-control."

We know that the "Fruit of the Spirit" is a biblical term that sums up the nine visible attributes of a true Christian life. Collectively, these are the fruits that all Christians should be producing in their new lives with Jesus Christ.

The one attribute necessary to bear all the other "fruits" is love and that is why it is the first and most important fruit listed. The Apostle Paul makes it very clear that any gifts without love are useless. It is the first fruit of the Spirit because it is the only one that is absolutely required.

This love is a distinctly Christian love, which finds its source from God alone. The Holy Spirit is hard at work to reproduce this kind of love in each one of us. We are to show this kind of selfless love to one another and to the world.

How can we develop and demonstrate this kind of love?
We need to start with understanding the definitive qualities of this kind of love.

Love is sacred
We need to treat love as something to be valued and honored

Love is selfless
We must put others needs before our own

Love is sacrificial
Look to what Christ did on the cross and act accordingly

Love is sincere
We must be authentic as we extend love to others

One Minute Reflection
Where exactly can you manifest love today?

"When we make a true commitment to walk in love, it usually causes a huge shift in our lifestyle. Many of our ways - our thoughts, our conversation, our habits - have to change."
(Joyce Meyer)

Choose Joy

Psalm 16:11
"You make known to me the path of life; You will fill me with joy in Your presence, with eternal pleasures at Your right hand."

The goal of every Christian should be joy, which is from the Lord, and you can still experience joy during trials, suffering, and testing.

Today we are concentrating on joy, which is the second fruit of the Spirit.

Life is hard for all of us and too many Christians are not experiencing and therefore not exhibiting much joy because they believe their joy is connected to outward circumstances. However, biblical joy is defined as "cheerfulness or calm delight;" and it has nothing to do with our emotions. Joy is something that is manifested in the spiritual realm; it is a supernatural joy produced with the help of the Holy Spirit.

The word joy appears 60 times in the New Testament.
Biblical joy is a fruit, a byproduct, an additional blessing, not the end in itself. It flows into and grows within the person whose life is focused on God.

How can we manifest more joy in our own lives?
We must find joy in Christ, joy in our salvation and joy in daily living. The key is to keep our hearts focused on the Lord for our fulfillment. We can be joyful because we have found our purpose in God's plan. We are meant to reveal God's glory and express God's joy.

Remember Psalm 118:24 states,
"This is the day which the Lord has made; Let us rejoice and be glad in it."

One Minute Reflection
Will you choose joy today?

"Joy does not simply happen to us. We have to choose joy and keep choosing it every day."
(Henri Nouwen)

Peace

"The Lord turns His face toward you and give you peace."

When we become followers of Jesus Christ, all the fruit of the Spirit are planted inside us in seed form. Through the Spirit we can experience joy and peace in every circumstance, no matter how difficult or painful.

Today we are looking at peace, the third fruit of the Spirit.

Peace refers to a tranquility of mind, body, and soul. It is a spiritual well being that only God can give a person. Jesus said, *"The peace I give is not as the world may give".*

God's peace will never pass away. This doesn't mean that we will never have another problem, but instead that God will give us peace in the midst of the trials and temptation of life.

God's peace transcends earthly matters.

We are meant to call on the Holy Spirit to manifest peace with God, peace with our fellow man and also peace within ourselves.

One Minute Reflection
How often do you experience the peace of God?

"Because peace is a fruit of the Spirit, we are dependent upon the Spirit's work in our lives to produce the desire and the means to pursue peace. But we are also responsible to use the means He has given us and to take all practical steps to attain both peace within and peace with others."
(Jerry Bridges)

Forbearance

Ephesians 4:2
"Be completely humble and gentle; be patient, bearing with one another in love."

Our passage today does a good job of describing the word "forbearance" which is the fourth fruit of the Spirit. The Greek word for "forbearance" used in Galatians 5:22 is makrothumia, which means "longsuffering." In other words, a patient person can take a lot of provocation before reacting to circumstances.

This means we need to work on manifesting the quality of putting up with others and waiting through the difficult times, even when we are severely tired, exhausted, or weak. Forbearance also can be shown when we are in a position of power. A person might have the ability to take revenge or be condescending, but when we have a forbearing spirit, we will use self-restraint and careful thinking.

When we are demonstrating forbearance, we leave room for God to work in our hearts and in our relationships. We lay down our agenda and our need to be right and we trust God instead. We understand God's timing is different than our own and we respect it by waiting patiently for any outcome.

How can we develop forbearance?

Abide In Christ
Christ enables us to develop into the person God has called us to be.

Invite the Holy Spirit to do His work
Notice that the fruit of the Spirit is just that, of the Spirit. It is not our fruit, but the fruit of the Spirit of God. We can invite God to help us.

Wait on God
God's answer for any situation will be better than our own. We need to wait patiently and expectantly on God holding fast to His words and promises for our life.

One Minute Reflection
Is there a person or situation that needs forbearance today?

"Have patience with all things, But, first of all with yourself."
(Saint Francis de Sales)

Kindness

Galatians 5:22 -23
"Consider therefore the kindness and sternness of God: sternness to those who fell, but kindness to you, provided that you continue in His kindness. Otherwise, you also will be cut off."

Today we are examining the fifth fruit of the Spirit, kindness. One of the primary purposes of the Holy Spirit coming into a Christian's life is to transform that life. It is the Holy Spirit's job to conform us to the image of Christ, making us more like Him.

The Greek word for kindness means "benignity, tender concern, uprightness." It is kindness of heart and kindness of act.

As a Christian, we have experienced the kindness of God's salvation in Christ. God is now inviting us to clothe ourselves with the same kindness to others.

When we exhibit the kindness of God, we are tender, benevolent, and useful to others. Every action and every word should have the flavor of grace in it. In a world full of anger, selfishness, and contention, God desires that we cultivate the fruit of kindness in our lives.

The key to biblical kindness is that we must do good to others regardless of their character, conduct, or responses to us. We are to extend loving-kindness to all that come across our path regardless of how we feel about them or how they treat us.

We are called to take the high road for Christ.

One Minute Reflection
Would you define yourself as a "kind" person?

"Be kind, for everyone you meet is fighting a harder battle."
(Plato)

Goodness

2 Thessalonians 1:11
"With this in mind, we constantly pray for you, that our God may make you worthy of His calling, and that by His power He may bring to fruition your every desire for goodness and your every deed prompted by faith."

Goodness is the sixth fruit of the Spirit.

Goodness is virtue and holiness in action. It results in a life characterized by deeds motivated by a desire to be a blessing.

The Greek word translated "goodness," agathosune, is defined as "uprightness of heart and life." Agathosune is goodness for the benefit of others, not goodness simply for the sake of being virtuous.

In other words, we are to take action and become agents of God's goodness in the world. When we see a need we must meet it. When we discover a hurt we must heal it.
When we come across an injustice, we must make it right.

The virtue of goodness reminds to become the "hands and feet" of Jesus Christ, as if He Himself, were ministering to the needs of His people.

One Minute Reflection
In what tangible way will you demonstrate goodness today?

"The highest form of worship is the worship of unselfish Christian service. The greatest form of praise is the sound of consecrated feet seeking out the lost and helpless with goodness."
(Billy Graham)

Faithfulness

1 Samuel 26:23
"The Lord rewards everyone for their righteousness and faithfulness. The Lord delivered you into my hands today, but I would not lay a hand on the Lord's anointed."

Faithfulness is one of the most significant words in the Bible. It is used in a variety of ways to mean faith and it refers to being a person that others can rely upon. Faithfulness is steadfastness, constancy, or allegiance; it is carefulness in keeping what we are entrusted with. Scripture speaks often of God's faithfulness. Over and over we learn that when God says He will do something, He fulfills those promises. However today 1 Samuel is addressing our faithfulness back to God. It requires belief in what the Bible says about God-His existence, His works, and His character.

Faithfulness is the seventh fruit of the Spirit

You cannot have faith in God without being faithful to Him. Faithfulness is believing that God is who He says He is and continuing in that belief despite the circumstances of life. Faithfulness is the essence of living by faith not by sight.

1 Samuel gives us a hint of just how important faithfulness is to God. We are told that God rewards us for our righteousness and our faithfulness. We know that without faith it is impossible to please God. However when we demonstrate faithfulness, God will reward us in unimaginable ways.

We know how important faithfulness was to Christ who explained it in the Parable of the Bags of Gold. Matthew 25:21 *"His master replied, 'Well done, good and faithful servant! You have been faithful with a few things; I will put you in charge of many things. Come and share your master's happiness!'"*

One Minute Reflection
How would you rate your own faithfulness?

"I am not called to be successful, I am called to be faithful."
(Mother Teresa)

Gentleness

<u>Galatians 6:1</u>
"Brothers, if anyone is caught in any transgression, you who are spiritual should restore him in a spirit of gentleness. Keep watch on yourself, lest you too be tempted."

Today we are looking at gentleness, which is the eighth fruit of the Spirit.

Gentleness, also translated "meekness," does not mean weakness. Rather, it involves humility and thankfulness toward God, and polite, restrained behavior toward others. Gentleness refers mostly to actions, whereas meekness refers to one's whole state of mind that translates into actions.

Meekness produces gentleness.
We are to be meek - yielding, teachable, responsive - first of all in our relationship with God. Then we are to take what we learn from God and demonstrate that gentleness to others by being humble, gentle, and respectful.

How do we manifest gentleness?

Model Christ
The best way to understand gentleness is to look at our God. Christ had no problem being known as gentle.

Handle Others With Care
We put the words "handle with care" on packages to protect the contents from being damaged. We can use the same "handle with care" instructions when dealing with our fellow man.

<u>One Minute Reflection</u>
Where can you demonstrate some gentleness today?

"Both gentleness and meekness are born of power, not weakness. A Christian is to be gentle and meek because those are Godlike virtues. We should never be afraid, therefore, that the gentleness of the Spirit means weakness of character. It takes strength, God's strength, to be truly gentle."
(Jerry Bridges)

Self-Control

"For the Spirit God gave us does not make us timid, but gives us power, love and self-control."

Self-control ("temperance" in the KJV) is, of course, the ability to control oneself. It involves moderation, constraint, and the ability to say "no" to our more base desires that do not reflect the standards of a Holy God.

Self-Control is the ninth and last fruit of the Spirit.

There are many areas where we can manifest self-control.

Our Body - what we eat, drink, abuse, use, wear
Our Mind - what we think about, watch, read, or allow as self-talk
Our Emotions - extremes of anger, jealousy, despair
Our Time - how we spend it and our availability to others
Our Finances - money choices that do not reflect God's ways
Our Speech - the words we speak to injure, gossip, or slander

In a modern culture where standards of behavior have collapsed and accountability is in short supply, self-control is more relevant than ever before.

One Minute Reflection
What area of your life do you need self-control?

"I am a spiritual being. After this body is dead, my spirit will soar. I refuse to let what will rot rule the eternal. I choose self-control. I will be drunk only by joy. I will be impassioned only by my faith. I will be influenced only by God. I will be taught only by Christ."
(Max Lucado)

A Time To Remember

Psalm 106:13-16
*"Then they believed His promises
and sang His praise. But they soon forgot what He had done
and did not wait for His plan to unfold.
In the desert they gave in to their craving;
in the wilderness they put God to the test."*

We celebrate Memorial Day because it was a time to remember those who've died serving in the U.S. military. Civil War veteran General John A. Logan called in 1868 for Americans to decorate the graves of those who fell during the "War Between the States;" The holiday has grown since then and now commemorates the fallen from each of America's wars.

As Christians we want to remember and learn from the past also. The philosopher George Santayana said, "Those who do not remember their past are condemned to repeat their mistakes."

If you read the passage from Psalm 106 above it explains how the Lord was loyal to the Israelites but time and time again, the Israelites "forgot" the Lord. Because of their disregard, they wandered in the wilderness for forty years never making it to the Promised Land.

We don't want to make the same mistakes.

This is why it is so important to read the Old Testament. The stories there are rich in life lessons and warnings to help us navigate our relationship with God.

What can we learn as we memorialize the past?

Our greatest lesson is to never forget who God is and what He has done for us. We have to learn to be patient as we wait on the Lord and trust in His merciful plan to unfold in due time.

One Minute Reflection
How will you remember daily what God has done for you?

"A hero is someone who has given his or her life to something bigger than oneself." When we make God our King and advance His Kingdom in our nation, we serve both our Lord and our country."
(Joseph Campbell)

Soar On Eagles Wings

Isaiah 40:31
"But those who hope in the LORD will renew their strength. They will soar on wings like eagles; they will run and not grow weary, they will walk and not be faint."

The Book of Isaiah is a collection of oracles and prophecies, with the overall theme being a message of salvation.

Today's passage reflects one of the most important promises of God

Isaiah tells us:
"Those who hope in the LORD shall renew their strength. They will soar on wings like eagles."

The truth is that life is hard for many of us.
We live in a frantic, fast paced society where just keeping our families intact and paying the monthly bills can be a challenge. Nightly news is bombarding us with the misfortunes of the entire world and our 24/7 information cycle has put us into distracted overdrive. We often feel out of control, exhausted or simply depleted of any reserves. If we rely on our own strength, despair is inevitable.

So Isaiah reminds us that if we hope in the Lord we will *"run and not grow weary and we will walk and not faint"*. God wants us to surrender every part of our lives over to Him and rely solely on His power and strength.

It is a daily act of surrender and yet the promise is so sweet.
With God, we can soar above the trials and temptations of this life with majesty as gripping and beautiful as the wings of an eagle.

One Minute Reflection
Are you someone that hopes in the Lord daily?

"I've read the last page of the Bible.
It's all going to turn out all right."
(Billy Graham)

Truth & Freedom

"Jesus said, 'If you hold to my teaching, you are really my disciples. Then you will know the truth, and the truth will set you free.'"

Today's verse is about the famous words, *"the truth will set you free".*

This is a saying that the secular world uses often in many contexts but with no insight or regard to the fact that Christ said them first. When Jesus said, *"the truth will set you free",* He was not speaking of any truth but He was very specifically talking about Himself.

Jesus is the truth that sets us free.

He is the source of truth and the only standard for what is right. Jesus does not give us freedom to do whatever we want but freedom to follow God. As we seek to serve God, the perfect truth of Christ's teachings frees us to be all that God intended us to be.

However there is one caveat to discovering and enjoying freedom. If we look carefully at the Scripture above from John 8, Jesus says; *"if you hold onto my teaching, you are really my disciples".* This is a warning that we must remain in His truth, following His lead and obeying His commands. This is where ultimate freedom is found. The reason this is true is because we were created in His image and so His commands fit perfectly for our life and will ultimately lead us to good.

Jesus' freedom has three distinct core elements.
It is a gift - freely given by God
It is eternal, not temporary or only for this time and place
It is expressed in obedience to God not independence to do what we want

One Minute Reflection
What truth do you believe will set you free?

"True liberty is not the ability to do anything we please, but the liberty to do what we ought; and it is genuine liberty because doing what we ought now pleases us."
(Martin Luther)

Spiritual Gifts - How To Use Them?

1 Corinthians 12:31
"But strive for greater gifts. And I will show you a still more excellent way."

Discovering your spiritual gifts is the best way for you to understand part of God's plan for your life! Spiritual gifts affect our life and our work. They also empower us to respond to God's call on our life.

The key is to know both what our Spiritual Gifts are
and to know how to use them.
The passage above from 1 Corinthians tells us to strive for spiritual gifts and then God will continue to show us a more excellent way.

Spiritual Gifts come from God and their purpose is so we can serve each other. Gifts are first discovered and then developed as we use them Spiritual gifts should ultimately display the love of God to each other.

Some of us want to work in a soup kitchen ministering to the poor; others want to use their homes to host a Bible Study. Some like to arrange flowers for the Sunday service, while others may want to minister to a co-worker on the job.

To continue our search of a Spiritual Gift – We can ask:
If I could solve one problem in the world - what would it be?
What environment do I most enjoy working in?
What am I truly passionate about?
What gift is unique to me and where can I see myself using it?

One Minute Reflection
In what specific way could you use a spiritual gift?

"A spiritual gift is a supernaturally designed ability granted to every believer by which the Holy Spirit ministers to the body of Christ. A spiritual gift cannot be earned, pursued or worked up. It is merely 'received' through the grace of God."
(John MacArthur)

Follow Me

Mark 1:17-18
"Then Jesus said to them, "Follow Me, and I will make you become fishers of men." They immediately left their nets and followed Him."

If you read the account above from Mark 1 on how Jesus called His disciples you will notice two significant things.

One - Jesus simply said, "Follow Me."
Two - His disciples immediately left everything behind and followed Him.

Many of us remember the game called "Follow The Leader". One child goes to the front of the line and everybody else has to do exactly what the leader does. The leader moves around and all the children mimic the leader's actions exactly. Any player who fails to follow the leader needs to start again.
Following Christ is about as basic as this childhood game.

Here are ways we can follow Christ
Jesus spent much time in prayer
Jesus was obedient to God the Father
Christ forgave His enemies
Christ served the poor with humility
Christ resisted earthly temptations
Christ knew Scripture well and referred to Scripture often
Christ ministered to everyone He met and was always available

If we keep our eyes securely on Christ, the journey is elementary.
He leads and we follow.

One Minute Reflection
How well do you "follow" Christ?

"Going to church doesn't make you a Christian any more than going to a garage makes you an automobile."
(Billy Sunday)

Come To Me

Matthew 11:28-29
"Come to me, all you who are weary and burdened, and I will give you rest. Take my yoke upon you and learn from me, for I am gentle and humble in heart, and you will find rest for your souls."

In our passage from Matthew 11, Jesus avows, *"Come to me, all who are wearied and burdened, and I will give you rest". This* is one of the most poignant and beautiful passages of the Bible. Rest is important to God and rest is a necessity. Without proper rest the human body will break down and the human spirit will be depleted.

Deep, satisfying rest seems to elude us in our modern busy life. We can't get to sleep at night and we rarely feel peace during the day. And although the world is a mysterious and wonderful place, it is also filled with sadness, anxiety, pain and loss.

The passage today from Matthew 11 is a stark reminder that Jesus invites all who are *"weary and burdened"* to come to Him.

Jesus calls us to come to Him with all our problems, with all our sorrows, with all our burdens, with all our anxieties, with all our addictions, and with all of our sins.
Jesus does not invite us based on merit or because we do good works. Jesus' invitation is totally unconditional.

The Hebrew word "rest" is the root word for "Sabbath." It means to cease from busyness, toil, or strain. The rest God promises is essentially spiritual with physical benefits as well. Imagine how much lighter the weight of the world would be if we "yoked" ourselves to Christ and allowed Him to carry our heavy load.

So what burden are we shouldering alone; is it a rough marriage, financial debt, betrayal, sickness, worry or loss? Now is the time to answer Christ's invitation to come to Him. He is gentle and humble of heart. We can trust Him with the "rest" of our life.

One Minute Reflection
Will you find your rest in Jesus?

"Rest. Rest. Rest in God's love. The only work you are required now to do is to give your most intense attention to His still, small voice within."
(Madame Jeanne Guyon)

Tithe Your Time

2 Chronicles 31:5
"As soon as the command was spread abroad, the people of Israel gave in abundance the first fruits of grain, wine, oil, honey, and of all the produce of the field. And they brought in abundantly the tithe of everything."

The concept of tithing can be traced back to the Old Testament. The tithe was a requirement of the Law in which the Israelites were to give ten percent of the crops they grew.

First Fruits
In the truest sense, today tithing involves giving the first ten percent of our income - as opposed to giving whatever income we might have left over. In this manner, according to Scripture, we are assured that we are giving our first and very best back to God.
We can also tithe our time in the same way we tithe our money.
We do this by certain actions:

1) Be available
If we are too busy with our own schedules, we won't devote the best part of ourselves to God or take time to recognize His voice and miracles in our life.

2) Pray every day that God uses your life for His purposes
After we pray, we could spend a moment in complete silence, listening for God's response to His will for our lives.

3) Volunteer
We can give our time away to someone else in need. Read to an elderly neighbor, serve a hot meal at a soup kitchen, or open our home for a Bible study.

4) Devote scheduled time to knowing God
There is nothing more transformational than reading Scripture. This is where we find out what God has to say about Himself, His ways and His Kingdom. We should guard this precious time as if our very lives depended on it.

One Minute Reflection
What time can you tithe in pursuit of God today?

"We make a living by what we get; we make a life by what we give."
(Winston Churchill)

Pitching Our Tents

Genesis 13:10-13
"So Lot chose for himself the whole plain of the Jordan and set out toward the east. The two men parted company: Abram lived in the land of Canaan, while Lot lived among the cities of the plain and pitched his tents near Sodom. Now the people of Sodom were wicked and were sinning greatly against the Lord."

Today's scripture is a wonderful reminder that we all need to be careful where we *"pitch our tents".* "Pitching our tents" could be a metaphor for where we live, who we hang out with and what influences our daily decisions. We all need to carefully consider where we will invest our time, energy and money.

We learn in Genesis about the story of Abram, and his nephew Lot, who had been traveling together, but decided to separate. Lot chose to settle near the town of Sodom and Gomorrah, because of the rich plains there.

This is a simple story with profound lessons in decision-making.

1) The grass is not always greener
This story is a perfect example of choosing something based on its promise, only to find out that the value is short lived.

2) Don't be led to temptation
Sodom and Gomorrah are names virtually synonymous with evil, sin, and judgment and yet Lot voluntarily chose to remain in Sodom despite this wickedness. Lot convinced himself he would be able to stave off the temptation of sin. However his choices ended up costing him dearly. It is better to avoid the temptation altogether.

3) Always consider the spiritual dimension
Lot had much to think about when given his choice of where he wanted to pitch his tents. However he focused solely on the economic factors of what the land might yield. He forgot entirely about consulting God before making his decision.

One Minute Reflection
Where does God want you to pitch your tents?

"You weren't put on earth to be remembered. You were put here to prepare for eternity."
(Rick Warren)

Humility To Holiness

Philippians 2:3-5

"Do nothing out of selfish ambition or vain conceit. Rather, in humility value others above yourselves, not looking to your own interests but each of you to the interests of the others. In your relationships with one another, have the same mindset as Christ Jesus."

Our Scripture passage today from Philippians states that to practice humility, we need to have the same mindset as Jesus Christ. Jesus did not come to be served by others but He used His life in service to all.

Mother Teresa was a person who did have the same mindset as Christ. She can be a role model for us as well. Mother Teresa lived from August 26th, 1910 to September 5th, 1997. She was a Roman Catholic Religious Sister and missionary of Albanian origin who lived most of her life in India.

Mother Teresa founded the Missionaries of Charity, a Roman Catholic religious congregation, which consisted of over 4,500 sisters and is now active in 133 countries. They run hospices and homes for people with HIV/AIDS, leprosy and tuberculosis along with other charitable organizations. She was awarded The Nobel Peace Prize in 1979.

Mother Teresa firmly believed that to gain intimacy with God, one needed to practice humility. To gain holiness, we renounce self and prepare to receive God. She profoundly proclaimed, "For not even God can put anything into a heart that is already full."

How can we develop the humility of Christ?
Our passage tells us:
Do nothing out of selfish ambition
Do nothing out of vain conceit
Keep the focus off of your own interest
Keep the focus on the interests of others
Act like Christ in your relationships with others
Give God the credit

One Minute Reflection
How can Mother Teresa be your inspiration for humility today?

"The most holy men are always the most humble men; none so humble on earth as those that live highest in heaven."
(James H. Aughey)

Praise What We Enjoy

<u>1 Peter 1:3</u>
"Praise be to the God and Father of our Lord Jesus Christ! In His great mercy He has given us new birth into a living hope through the resurrection of Jesus Christ from the dead."

Our passage today reminds us of the importance of praising God. C.S. Lewis also wrote about this when he said, "I think we delight to praise what we enjoy because the praise not merely expresses but completes the enjoyment. It is appointed consummation".

Clive Staples Lewis (29 November 1898 - 22 November 1963), commonly called C. S. Lewis and known to his friends and family as "Jack", was a novelist, poet, academic, literary critic, essayist, lay theologian, and Christian apologist. Born in Belfast, Ireland, he became an atheist at 15, though he later described his young self as being paradoxically "very angry with God for not existing".

In addition to his career as an English professor and an author of more than 30 books, Lewis is regarded by many as one of the most influential Christian apologists of his time.

Our job as Christians is not just to have faith in Christ and obey Christ's teachings but also to enjoy and praise Christ's presence in our lives.

We learn in our Scripture passage today that God deserves our praise because He has given us a new birth into a living hope, which is only possible because of the resurrection of Jesus Christ.

Praise, according to the Scriptures, is an act of our will that flows out our reverence for God's glory. Praise turns our attention to the nature and character of God Himself. As we focus our minds on God and proclaim His goodness, we reflect His glory back to the world around us.

As Lewis reminds us, we delight to praise what we enjoy and praise is what completes that enjoyment.

<u>One Minute Reflection</u>
Do you enjoy Christ and is it evident in your praise of Him?

"Complain and remain. Praise and be raised."
(Joyce Meyer)

First Go And Reconcile

Matthew 5:23-24
"Therefore, if you are offering your gift at the altar and there remember that your brother or sister has something against you, leave your gift there in front of the altar. First go and be reconciled to them; then come and offer your gift."

God is always encouraging us to work on reconciling
the differences with our fellow man.

In our passage today from Matthew 5, Jesus contends that reconciliation is more important than our worship of God. This is a stark warning that harmonious relationships with people must take first place before any true fellowship with God can be received.

In other words anger and hatred toward our neighbors, family and friends has a direct impact on our relationship to God. They are not separate matters.

If we read the passage carefully, Jesus claims; *"If your brother or sister has something against you, leave your gift there in front of the alter. First go and be reconciled".* This is a directive to fix those relationships where we bear the responsibility of any damage before we offer our praise to God.

We need to ask ourselves whom we have offended.
If we have wronged someone, we must make restitution; if we owe someone a debt, we must make repayment; if we have assassinated someone's character, we should seek pardon and then rebuild. God knows all and sees all and therefore we cannot hide our sin from Him.

Jesus implores us to create the best possible relationship with God, by seeking the best possible relationships with our fellow man.

One Minute Reflection
Is there someone God is directing you to reconcile with today?

"As far as I know, this is the only time God tells you to slip out of Church early. Apparently, He'd rather have you give your olive branch than your tithe."
(Max Lucado)

Beloved

<u>Luke 3:22</u>
"You Are My Beloved Son. On You My Favor Rests."

Henri Nouwen, the internationally renowned priest and author, respected professor and beloved pastor wrote over 40 books on the spiritual life. Nouwen mused that he was firmly convinced that the decisive moment of Jesus' public life was His baptism, when he heard the divine affirmation quoted in Luke 3:22 above, *"You are my Beloved on whom my favor rests."*

Since our mission as Christians is to conform to the likeness of Christ we too need to come to terms with being "the beloved".

What does beloved mean?
Its definition is rendered "dearest, precious, adored, much loved, cherished, treasured, prized, highly regarded, admired, esteemed, worshiped, and venerated." We need to claim this identity of being "beloved" for ourselves as both children of God and followers of Christ.

The world tells us:
We are what we do, we are what others say about us, we are what we own and, we are our accomplishments.

God tells us:
In the New Testament "beloved" is used exclusively to explain the manifestation of divine Christian love.

How can we claim our "belovedness"?
We are told in Ephesians 5:1: *"Follow God's example, therefore, as dearly beloved children and walk in the way of love, just as Christ loved us and gave Himself up for us as a fragrant offering and sacrifice to God."*

From the moment we claim the truth that we are God's "beloved", we are faced with becoming what we already are.

<u>One Minute Reflection</u>
How will you respond to knowing you are beloved?

"Above all the grace and the gifts that Christ gives
to His beloved is that of overcoming self."
(Francis of Assisi)

Dealing With Hatred

1 John 4:20
"Whoever claims to love God yet hates a brother or sister is a liar. For whoever does not love their brother and sister, whom they have seen, cannot love God, whom they have not seen."

Norman Vincent Peale was one of the most influential clergymen in the United States during the 21st century. Born in Bowersville, Ohio, on May 31,1898. Peale grew up helping support his family by delivering newspapers, working in a grocery store, and selling pots and pans door to door. He went on to write the *Power of Positive Thinking*, which has sold more than 20 million copies worldwide.

Reverend Peale firmly believed that the key to a happy life was to "keep your heart free from hate and your mind free from worry". He based that philosophy on the New Testament teachings of Jesus Christ.

Our passage today from 1 John explains that if we hate anyone but claim to love God then we are liars. Biblically speaking it is okay to hate the offense but never the offender.

How can we keep our hearts free from hate and minds free from worry?

Surrender every burden to God and trust Him to make all things right. It is truly about letting go and letting God do His work.

Proverbs 3:5-6 says it this way:
"Trust in the LORD with all your heart, and lean not on your own understanding; in all your ways acknowledge Him, and He shall direct your paths."

One Minute Reflection
What burden of hate or worry will you surrender today?

"The reason why many are still troubled, still seeking, still making little forward progress is because they haven't yet come to the end of themselves. We're still trying to give orders, and interfering with God's work within us."
(A.W. Tozer)

Instruments Of Peace

John 14:27
"Peace I leave with you; my peace I give you. I do not give to you as the world gives. Do not let your hearts be troubled and do not be afraid."

Today we are examining what we can learn about God's peace. Jesus spoke of peace often and influenced Saint Francis of Assisi greatly in his writings.

Saint Francis of Assisi was born in Italy in the year 1811. His birth name was Giovanni di Pietro di Bernardone, but nicknamed Francesco ("the Frenchman"). St. Francis of Assisi was renown for drinking and partying in his youth. However, after he spent nearly a year in prison, he began receiving visions from God. Francis reportedly heard the voice of Christ, who told him to repair the Christian Church and live a life of poverty. Though he was never ordained to the Catholic priesthood, Francis is one of the most venerated religious figures in history.

He is most widely known for his well-known prayer:

"Lord, make me an instrument of your peace.
Where there is hatred, let me sow love. Where there is injury, pardon.
Where there is doubt, faith. Where there is despair, hope. Where there is
darkness, light. Where there is sadness, joy. O Divine Master, grant that I
may not so much seek to be consoled, as to console; to be understood, as to
understand; to be loved, as to love. For it is in giving that we receive. It is
in pardoning that we are pardoned, and it is in dying that we are born to
Eternal Life.
Amen."

In our Scripture passage today from John, we know that Jesus spoke to His disciples about the fact that He is the one that gives us peace. We are meant to receive God's peace and then pass this peace onto others.

One Minute Reflection
How will you be a peacemaker today?

"Peace demands the most heroic labor and the most difficult sacrifice. It demands greater heroism than war. It demands greater fidelity to the truth and a much more perfect purity of conscience."
(Thomas Merton)

He Will Never Leave Us

<u>Deuteronomy 31:8</u>
"The Lord Himself goes before you and will be with you; He will never leave you nor forsake you. Do not be afraid; do not be discouraged."

Today we are examining the need for security and belonging.

June is a month of graduations.
It is a time of commencements and final goodbyes.
It is also a time for us to inspire our youth with heartfelt, encouraging words before they go off into the world without us.

One of our biggest concerns is that they will be lonely, discouraged or afraid and we won't be there to comfort them.

Loneliness is a growing problem in our society. Some of the loneliest people in America can be college students as they assimilate to new surroundings far from home. Next on the list are divorced people, welfare recipients, single mothers, rural students, housewives, and the elderly.

By God's design we have an innate need to be in relationship and to belong.
Remember Genesis 2:18:
"The LORD God said, "It is not good for man to be alone."

The passage from Deuteronomy 31:8 reminds us that we are never alone. We are reminded that God will go before us, and will be with us. In fact, He will never leave or forsake us. Therefore we never have to be afraid or discouraged.

<u>**One Minute Reflection**</u>
Whom will you share this special Bible passage with today?

"Loneliness was the first thing that God's eye named not good."
(John Milton)

Our Self Worth

<u>Psalm 139:13-14</u>
"For You created my inmost being;
You knit me together in my mother's womb.
I praise You because I am fearfully and wonderfully made;
Your works are wonderful,
I know that full well."

Today we are looking at self-worth.

Self-worth is an important topic because we can all fall prey to discouragement, self-doubt, measuring ourselves against unrealistic standards and false expectations.

The Bible actually has many passages that tell us what God has to say about our worth and our value from His point of view. Genesis 1:26-27 says we *"are made in His image, the very image of God"*. And our passage from Psalm 139:13-14 today reminds us that we are, *"fearfully and wonderfully made".*

God knew what He was doing when He created us and, *"knit us together in our mother's womb".* If we have lost our sense of value it is because we are measuring against the world's system and not against what Our Creator deems to be true.

Often we align our significance too closely to our achievements, acquiring material possessions, climbing career ladders and other people's opinions. There's nothing inherently wrong with these, but what ultimately matters is what God declares in Scripture.

We need to constantly remind ourselves that God loves us so much that He became a man and walked among us, and then was crucified to save us from our inherent sin. He did this because of our great value. We need to get in agreement with that assessment and start behaving like the worthwhile men and women we were created to be.

<u>One Minute Reflection</u>
Can you value yourself from God's point of view?

"Self-worth and net worth are not the same."
(Rick Warren)

Omni Present

<u>Psalm 139: 7-10</u>
*"Where can I go from Your Spirit? Where can I flee from Your presence?
If I go up to the heavens, You are there; if I make my bed in the depths,
You are there. If I rise on the wings of the dawn, if I settle on the far side of
the sea, even there Your hand will guide me."*

One of the truths we need to understand and that the Bible makes very clear is that our God is "omni-present". The prefix "omni" comes from the Latin meaning "in all ways". So, to say that God is omnipresent is to say that God is present everywhere.

Omnipresence is a theological term that refers to the unlimited nature of God and His ability to be everywhere at all times. Unlike the idols of ancient cultures or the mythical gods of Greek and Roman culture, God is not limited to one time or place.

In our passage today from Psalm 139, we learn that there is no physical location in this universe where we can hide from the presence of God. King David asks above *"Where can I go from Your Spirit? Or where can I flee from Your presence? If I ascend into heaven, You are there; if I make my bed in the depths, You are there"*.

God's reach extends to every nook and cranny of the universe. God knows all things, sees all things and is everywhere all of the time.

If we are not feeling God's presence - it is because we are not making ourselves completely available to Him, not the other way around. God wants fellowship with us and He desires to reveal Himself to us.

To feel God's presence and understand His will for our life, we must make it our number one priority to gain access to God. We can do this through silence, meditation, prayer, reading God's Word and most importantly finding intimacy with His son, Jesus Christ.

<u>One Minute Reflection</u>
Does knowing that God is "omni-present" impact your life today?

"We are at this moment as close to God as we really choose to be. True, there are times when we would like to know a deeper intimacy, but when it comes to the point, we are not prepared to pay the price involved. "
(J. Oswald Saunders)

Holiness & Glory

<u>Isaiah 6:3</u>
"And they were calling to one another:
"Holy, holy, holy is the Lord Almighty;
the whole earth is full of His glory."

The phrase "holy, holy, holy" appears twice in the Bible, once in the Old Testament (Isaiah 6:3) and once in the New (Revelation 4:8). Both times, the phrase is spoken by heavenly creatures, and both times it occurs in a vision: first by the prophet Isaiah and then by the apostle John.

"Holy, holy, holy," expresses both the supreme Holiness of God and also the triune nature of God - Father, Son and Holy Spirit.

It is significant to note that in today's passage Holiness and Glory are intertwined. Glory is the full manifestation of God expressing Himself. God is Holy and He expresses His power and majesty through His very nature.

If you look closely at the universe, you will see the manifestation of God's glory everywhere, from a flower in full bloom to a color-stained sunset; from a starlit evening sky to a lightning storm erupting at sea. God's glory is always on display.

We also are meant to display God's glory. Since human beings were created in the image of God, we need to take the manifestation of God's glory in our own lives very seriously.

We need to ask ourselves these questions surrounding glory:

What is our own personal glory?
In what way are we manifesting God's glory?
Does holiness have anything to do with our own glory?

<u>One Minute Reflection</u>
How will you manifest God's glory today?

"There is no greater purpose in life than to expose one's personal glory. It is a fact of creation that every living thing possesses its own glory and exists for the purpose of manifesting its glory."
(Dr. Myles Munro)

How To Pray For God's Will

<u>Colossians 1:9-10</u>
"For this reason also, since the day we heard of it, we have not ceased to pray for you and to ask that you may be filled with the knowledge of His will in all spiritual wisdom and understanding, so that you will walk in a manner worthy of the Lord, to please Him in all respects, bearing fruit in every good work and increasing in the knowledge of God."

God has both a universal will and a personal will for each and every one of us. In the passage from Colossians above, we are reminded that it is crucial to pray for things that are in accordance with the Will of God.

In what ways can we pray for the will of God?

Paul tells us there are three specific areas to concentrate on.

First, request that we *"be filled with the knowledge of His will in all spiritual wisdom and understanding"*. *In* other words, we need to ask God to give us the ability to see life from His point of view.

Second, ask that we *"walk in a manner worthy of the Lord"*. We want God to fill us with a longing desire to please Him in thought, word and deed.

Third, pray that our lives are *"bearing fruit in every good work"*. There is a difference between being busy and being fruitful. Effectiveness in God's kingdom depends on what He calls each person to do as we increase in the knowledge of God.

<u>**One Minute Reflection**</u>
Are you currently "walking in a manner worthy of the Lord"?

"Love is a fruit in season at all times, and within reach of every hand."
(Mother Teresa)

Mercy Not Sacrifice

Luke 9:12-13
"On hearing this, Jesus said, 'It is not the healthy who need a doctor, but the sick. But go and learn what this means: I desire mercy, not sacrifice. For I have not come to call the righteous, but sinners.'"

Jesus' remarks in Luke 9:12-13 above arises during a controversy with the Pharisees over Jesus spending time with tax collectors. Jesus quoted the prophet Hosea (Hos. 6:6) that says, *"For I desire mercy, not sacrifice, and acknowledgment of God rather than burnt offerings".* Jesus was trying to convince the Pharisees that they had missed the whole point of whom He was and what He came to do. They valued the technicalities of law more than the people the law was there to serve.

The Pharisees' motive was not love for people, but love for themselves. They loved the law because they used the law to feel valuable.

We often do the same thing.
We want to be right rather than to be merciful.

Jesus is reminding us today that mercy trumps sacrifice every time.

If the Pharisees were in a place of having the right relationship with God, then they would have recognized their own pride and shown compassion to sinners.

In today's terms, we can visit the soup kitchen, sing in the choir, teach Sunday school, and even follow every command in the Bible but if we can't show mercy for the rest of humanity, we have missed Christ's most valuable lesson.

Christ avows that He did not come to call the righteous, but us sinners.

One Minute Reflection
Which do you think is more valuable - mercy or sacrifice?

"I think we too are the people who, on the one hand, want to listen to Jesus, but on the other hand, at times, like to find a stick to beat others with, to condemn others. And Jesus has this message for us: mercy. I think - and I say it with humility - that this is the Lord's most powerful message: mercy."
(Pope Francis)

The Least Of These

Matthew 25:37-40

"Then the righteous will answer Him, 'Lord, when did we see you hungry and feed you, or thirsty and give you something to drink? When did we see you a stranger and invite you in, or needing clothes and clothe you? When did we see you sick or in prison and go to visit you?' The King will reply, 'Truly I tell you, whatever you did for one of the least of these brothers and sisters of mine, you did for me.'"

There is probably no clearer illustration in the Bible on how we are supposed to treat each other than in the exchange that takes place in Matthew 25:37-40.

The "righteous" could be anyone of us who thinks we are doing a pretty good job of being a Christian. The "righteous" ask Jesus when they ever fed Him, dressed Him, cared for Him, visited Him or invited Him in. Jesus responds very profoundly, *"truly I tell you, whatever you did for one of the least of these brothers or sisters of mine, you did it for me".*

Jesus is challenging our faith in how we deal with those in need.

In every instance that we care for the hungry person, the homeless man, the unemployed neighbor, the naked child, the dying relative, or the woman in prison - we are in fact caring for those whom Jesus identified with Himself. The identity is so significant to Christ that He tells us it is as if we were caring for Him directly when we care for the *"least of these".*

The message is clear
1) We are accountable to each other
2) Judgment awaits each of us in the most personal way
3) The heart of Christianity is about relationship with Christ, which shows itself in sacrificial acts of love toward our fellow man

One Minute Reflection
Could you serve Christ disguised in "the least of these"?

"Being unwanted, unloved, uncared for, forgotten by everybody, I think that is a much greater hunger, a much greater poverty than the person who has nothing to eat."
(Mother Teresa)

Fatherhood

John 14:9-10
"Anyone who has seen me has seen the Father. How can you say, 'Show us the Father'? Don't you believe that I am in the Father, and that the Father is in me? The words I say to you I do not speak on my own authority. Rather, it is the Father, living in me, who is doing His work."

Today we celebrate Fathers.
We find many names in the Bible for God but none more endearing than "Father". God the Father is the first Person of the Trinity, which also includes His Son, Jesus Christ, and the Holy Spirit.

The Bible teaches us:
God the Father is omnipotent (all powerful),
God the Father is omniscient (all knowing),
God the Father is omnipresent (everywhere).

Jesus urged us to think of God as our loving father and went a step further by calling Him, "Abba". "Abba Father" is one of the most significant names in understanding how God relates to people. The word Abba is an Aramaic word that would most closely be translated as "daddy." It was a common term that young children would use to address their fathers. It signifies the close, intimate relationship of a father to his child. The name helps demonstrate how intimate our relationship with God is or can be.

God the Father is the perfect example for all earthly fathers. To know the Father, we don't have to look any further than knowing the Son. Jesus Christ Himself explains all this in the passage above in John 14 when He says: *"Anyone who has seen me has seen the Father."* Jesus shows us what God the Father is like. He shows us the Father's love, His compassion, mercy, righteousness, humility, holiness, authority, truth, purpose and most importantly, His everlasting glory.

One Minute Reflection
How do you perceive God as a Father?

"A good father is one of the most unsung, unpraised, unnoticed, and yet one of the most valuable assets in our society."
(Billy Graham)

High Anxiety

<u>Philippians 4:6-7</u>
"Do not be anxious about anything, but in everything by prayer and supplication with thanksgiving let your requests be made known to God. And the peace of God, which surpasses all understanding, will guard your hearts and your minds in Christ Jesus."

Today we are looking at anxiety.
We are told in today's passage; *"do not be anxious about anything."*
However it does seem that there is a lot to worry about.

We worry about where we are going to live, what clothes should we wear, what others think about us, who our kids hanging out with, and what will happen if our spouse loses a job. We agonize over aging parents, health scares, a downward turn in the stock market, hurricanes, torrential flooding, outbreaks of Ebola virus, shooting sprees and the threat of a nuclear bomb attack.

It is surprising we can even get out of bed!
Thank God the Bible gives us a straightforward answer to our anxiety dilemma and it's outlined in Philippians 4.

The answer to anxiety is prayer and thanksgiving.
If we practice both of those things we will experience
a peace that surpasses all understanding.

Why does God's peace surpass all understanding?
Because in the midst of uncertainty, or danger, or sadness, or grief, we simply have to surrender our worries to God in prayer and thanksgiving and He will grant us peace.

Concrete Things To Do To Overcome Anxiety
Surround ourselves with hopeful people
Repeat, *"I can do all things through Christ who strengthens me"*
Turn off the evening news and read a newspaper instead
Bring everything to God with prayer and thanksgiving
When we master our faith, we master our fear!

<u>One Minute Reflection</u>
How will you master your anxiety today?

"Anxiety does not empty tomorrow of its sorrows, it only empties today of its strength." (Charles Spurgeon)

A Little Goes A Long Way

Matthew 14:17-19
"We have here only five loaves of bread and two fish," they answered.⬚ 'Bring them here to me,' He said.' And He directed the people to sit down on the grass. Taking the five loaves and the two fish and looking up to Heaven, He gave thanks and broke the loaves. Then He gave them to the disciples, and the disciples gave them to the people."

Aside from the resurrection, the story of Jesus' feeding of the 5,000 is the only miracle recorded in all four Gospels. There are many significant lessons for us to learn in this one short story.

First
Jesus wanted the disciples to see how impossible their situation was when they needed to feed the masses with only five loaves and two fish.

Second
The disciples had to trust Jesus for everything they distributed. They could only give as they received and therefore were put in a position of total dependence upon God for the supply.

Third
Jesus took the five loaves and two fish and then He prayed a blessing over the food. It was a simple prayer but one offered in faith and thanksgiving, which resulted in a miracle. According to Scripture, everyone in the crowd had as much as they needed to eat. Plus, there were leftovers, twelve baskets full. Christ did not just meet the need; He lavished everyone with extras.

What is the ultimate take away from our Scripture passage?
God will use the ordinary, everyday, meager things we bring to Him to create extraordinary gifts and blessings. We should never believe our resources are too little to serve God. The next time we think, "I can't do this", we need to remember that it is never about us. God promises to exponentially multiply our measly offering into a provisional feast for whatever our need might be.

One Minute Reflection
What can you ask God to bless today?

"God meets daily needs, not weekly or annually.
He will give you what you need when it is needed."
(Max Lucado)

I AM

<u>Exodus 3:14</u>
"And God said unto Moses, 'I Am That I Am:' and He said, 'Thus shalt thou say unto the children of Israel, I Am hath sent me unto you.'"

Names are very important to God. In Scripture a person's name often signifies his character or ability especially when God gives the name. "I AM" is the first name that God gave Himself as seen in the above Scripture from Exodus 3:14.

There are seven "I Am" statements in the Book of Genesis.

There are also seven "I Am" statements in the Gospel of John.
Here Jesus uses the "I am" to describe Himself and His divinity.

"I am the bread of life" (John 6:35,48,51).

"I am the light of the world" (John 8:12).

"I am the door of the sheep"(John 10:7,9).

"I am the good shepherd" (John 10:11,14).

"I am the resurrection, and the life" (John 11:25).

"I am the way, the truth, and the life" (John 14:6).

"I am the true vine" (John 15:1,5).

Why should we care?
Because Jesus' I AM statements reflect and express His saving relationship toward the world. We can call on God for any need we have and He will answer.

<u>One Minute Reflection</u>
What do these "I AM" statements tell you about God's Character?

"This King lives independently of all other life forms. He is the origin of all other life forms. His life is non-derivative. He does not live because of who anyone or anything else is or who or what anyone or anything else does. He simply *is*, irrespective and independent of all other *is's*. His life is beyond the ravages of death, decay, or disintegration."
(Sam Storms)

In Your Presence

Psalm 16: 11
"You will show me the path of life;
In Your presence is fullness of joy;
At Your right hand are pleasures forevermore."

Today's verse from Psalm 16:11 provokes us to ask two questions:

Do I have fullness of Joy?
Am I in God's presence?

The truth is that God is most glorified when we are most satisfied in Him.

Too many of us believe that life is meant to be endured instead of enjoyed. Depression, unhappiness, anxiety, frustration, anger, unfulfilled hopes and dreams, dissatisfaction, and emptiness describe the experience too many of us are having daily.

Possessing joy is a choice.
We can choose whether to value God's presence and promises.
We can choose to yield to His Spirit.
We can choose to allow His word to permeate our thoughts, words and deeds.

When we open our hearts and minds to experience God's grace, we are filled with supernatural joy.

Psalm 16 affirms: *"In your presence there is fullness of joy; at your right hand are pleasures forevermore".*

One Minute Reflection
Have you ever experienced fullness of joy?

"To fall in love with God is the greatest of all romances; to seek Him, the greatest adventure; to find Him, the greatest human achievement."
(Augustine)

Receive The Blessings

Chronicles 4:10
"Jabez cried out to the God of Israel, 'Oh, that You would bless me and enlarge my territory! Let Your hand be with me, and keep me from harm so that I will be free from pain.' And God granted his request."

Jabez is the story of an ordinary man with an extra-ordinary transformation as God granted his request.

The lesson of Jabez is that all of us could be leading a more dynamic life but we are afraid to ask for God's best. Personal change begins when we cry out to God to bless us with what He already longs to give us. The word "bless" occurs 400 times in the Old Testament alone and it means to "favor", "bestow special gifts or status" or "honor".

The story of Jabez encourages us to ask for God's blessing not because we deserve it, or because we can earn it, but simply because God can grant it based on His supernatural ability and love. God desires to bless His children and the blessing is concretely based on His character and greatness.

Asking is the beginning of receiving.
Jabez teaches us to release ourselves over to God's guidance and to His will. We often harbor preconceived notions about ourselves, our limits, our comfort zones, and even our beliefs about what God is really capable of anyway. Instead, we can break out in a new direction and expect the best God has to offer.

We Can Start Today
1) Ask God to bless us - leave the details to Him
2) Get out of our comfort zone and do something great for God
3) Get around folks that inspire us to be more and do more for God
4) Find one piece of Scripture based on a promise of God and read it daily until it is fully manifested into our life

One Minute Reflection
Have you asked God for anything impressive lately?

"A man may lose the good things of this life against his will; but if he loses the eternal blessings, he does so with his own consent."
(Augustine)

The Parable Of The Prodigal Son

<u>Luke 15: 11-12</u>
"Jesus continued: 'There was a man who had two sons. The younger one said to his father, Father, give me my share of the estate. So he divided his property between them. Not long after that, the younger son got together all he had, set off for a distant country and there squandered his wealth in wild living.'"

Today we are reviewing The Parable of the Prodigal Son.

Here is the overview
There was a father who had two sons. The younger one asks for his share of his inheritance, receives it and leaves immediately to a far-away country where he squanders it all on frivolous living. He returns home with shame and a changed heart and to his surprise is greeted with open arms by his father and a celebration fit for a prince.   However, this reception angers his older brother who has never left home, always done the right thing and has a strong moral record.

Here Jesus gives us a story of two brothers who each represent a different way to be alienated from God.   The younger brother walks away from his father in search of something that will satisfy him; fun living and sin are at the top of his list. However the older brother also walks away from his father because of pride in his own moral record and his unwillingness to welcome his younger brother home into the fold.

The moral of this story is that pride in our own good deeds is just as destructive as reveling in bad behavior because both separate us from fellowship with God. What is profoundly striking is that the older is in fact in worse off than the younger, because he is blind to his true condition.

<u>One Minute Reflection</u>
Which brother do you relate to more?

"Lukewarm people don't really want to be saved from their sin; they want only to be saved from the penalty of their sin."
(Francis Chan)

The Ten Commandments

Deuteronomy 4:13
"He declared to you His covenant, the Ten Commandments, which He commanded you to follow and then wrote them on two stone tablets."

The Ten Commandments, also known as the Decalogue, are a set of biblical principles relating to ethics and worship, which play a fundamental role in Judaism and most forms of Christianity. The Ten Commandments appear twice in the Old Testament, in the books of Exodus and Deuteronomy. Originally, God inscribed them on two stone tablets, which He gave to Moses on Mount Sinai. He declares He is our God and our deliverer and asks us to demonstrate our love for Him by following these set of laws.

The first four Commandments define our relationship with our Heavenly Father. Establishing, developing and maintaining that personal relationship is the most important commitment we can ever make. The next six commandments define our relationship to one another.

We can find two levels of meaning in the Ten Commandments. There is both a positive declaration or command, and a negative prohibition. We should view the Ten Commandments as a guide to how to live life successfully and a warning that they are much more than a set of rules to follow. The Ten Commandments are in fact God's way to help us navigate an uncertain world.

1. You shall not worship any other gods but GOD alone.
2. You shall not make a graven image.
3. You shall not take the name of GOD in vain.
4. You shall not break the Sabbath.
5. You shall not dishonor your parents.
6. You shall not murder.
7. You shall not commit adultery.
8. You shall not steal.
9. You shall not bear false witness.
10. You shall not covet.

One Minute Reflection
Can you close your eyes and name the Ten Commandments?

"If God would have wanted us to live in a permissive society He would have given us Ten Suggestions and not Ten Commandments."
(Zig Ziglar)

First Commandment - Have No Other Gods

Exodus 20:1-3
"And God spoke all these words: 'I am the Lord your God, who brought you out of Egypt, out of the land of slavery. You shall have no other gods before me.'"

The introduction to the Ten Commandments establishes the identity of God by both His personal name and His historical act of delivering Israel out of Egypt. The definition that God assigns Himself is significant. God is establishing Himself as both Lord and Savior.

The First commandment summons man to believe in God, to hope in Him, and to love Him above all else. It is God's demand for exclusive worship.

We worship a lot of different things in 21st century life. God is not often one of them. It might be wealth, fame, celebrity, ambition, popularity, excellence, prestige or a political affiliation. None of these are wrong in and of themselves, however they become a sin when they are idolized and push God out of His rightful first place position.

Exalting the creation rather the creator is the cornerstone of today's materialistic, worldview in which we live, work and raise our families. Moreover, religion has conditioned us to think of worship as something that we take part in once a week. This is inadequate for fulfilling God's purpose of creating us in His image. God desires our complete allegiance.

We should love, honor and respect God so much that He alone is the supreme authority and model in our lives. We should allow nothing to prevent us from serving and obeying Him 24 hours a day, seven days a week.

One Minute Reflection
What is standing in the way of you honoring God above all?

"A true love of God must begin with a delight in His holiness, and not with a delight in any other attribute; for no other attribute is truly lovely without this."
(Jonathan Edwards)

Second Commandment - A Jealous God

"You shall not make for yourself an image in the form of anything in Heaven above or on the earth beneath or in the waters below. You shall not bow down to them or worship them; for I, the LORD your God, am a jealous God, punishing the children for the sin of the parents to the third and fourth generation of those who hate me, but showing love to a thousand generations of those who love me and keep my commandments."

It is tempting to understand the second commandment to be like the first - a prohibition against idolatry. However, Moses makes it clear that God's commandment was intended to forbid us from making graven images of Yahweh Himself.

It is a critical distinction!

Why is God so concerned with man representing Him by means of a symbol?

Humans rely on symbolism. People create idols and images out of metal, wood, stone, and plastic. They also fashion idols mentally, and in the process they create false ideas about who God is and what role He plays in our lives.

It is an insult to Almighty God when we make things up about Him because ultimately we completely distort the truth of Him. This is why God gave us Scripture in the form of the Holy Bible. Everything God wants us to know about Himself is written there. God is omnipotent, God is omnipresent and God is omniscient. Mere symbolism does not begin to represent His inherent, divine and majestic nature.

The Second Commandment goes to the heart of our relationship with our Creator. How do we perceive God? How do we explain Him to ourselves and to others? We have a responsibility to represent Him accurately. Moreover, God proclaims, *"I am a jealous God"*. He wants our full attention and devotion. He will stand for nothing less than our full and utter devotion.

One Minute Reflection
What one thing can you do to honor The Second Commandment?

"An idol of the mind is as offensive to God as an idol of the hand."
(A.W. Tozer)

Third Commandment - A Name In Vain

Exodus 20:7
"You shall not misuse the name of the LORD your God, for the LORD will not hold anyone guiltless who misuses His name."

Today we are examining the Third Commandment, which ultimately has to do with reverence for God.

The name of God represents the very nature and character of God. To use God's name in vain is more than a bad choice of words, it goes to how we treat God in front of others and respect God Himself.

The use of God's name in a casual, degrading or disrespectful manner dishonors the relationship we have with Him. The Hebrew name for vain means, "falsehood", "iniquity" or "emptiness"; all summarizing disrespect. Try and imagine someone in your own family who vows to love and honor you and then speaks flippantly or degradingly about you to others. The sense of betrayal would be enormous.

We are told in Scripture that God's name is to be "hallowed" because His very essence and glory are wrapped up in His name.

Moreover, we can misuse God's name with more than just words. There is a larger sense in which people today take the Lord's name in vain. To call God the "Lord" of our life and then not follow His commandments is also a misuse of God's name in thought, word and deed.

We need to carefully consider the "name" of God.

One Minute Reflection
Do you "misuse" the name of the Lord?

"Nothing is a greater, or more fearful sacrilege than to prostitute the great name of God to the petulancy of an idle tongue."
(Jeremy Taylor)

Fourth Commandment - Remember the Sabbath

"Remember the Sabbath day by keeping it Holy."

Why would God start the Fourth Commandment with the word
"remember"?

Is it because He knew we would forget it, or even worse, completely disregard this commandment all together? It seems God knew all along our penchant for disregarding the sanctity of the Sabbath.

God asks that we set one day apart each week for Holy purposes so we can draw nearer to Him. The Fourth Commandment to remember the Sabbath helps define a proper relationship with God. God planned it and purposed it as one day to love, worship and relate to Him.

The Sabbath is a divine institution where the seventh day of the week was set apart by God as a time of resting in God and experiencing spiritual rejuvenation. We are required by this commandment to treat the Sabbath as something Holy. Holy means sanctified and set apart in honoring God.

The Sabbath has traditionally been on Saturday. Some early Jewish Christians observed the Sabbath on Saturday and then gathered with Christian believers to worship on Sunday.

Today our Sabbath has been hijacked by other demands and distractions. Stores are open, children's sports schedules abound and our endless to do list is encroaching on our time with God.

It seems we do need to "remember" that God set the Sabbath apart and established it as Holy. The Sabbath whether celebrated on a Saturday or a Sunday should still be a day of joyful remembrance, rest, and worship in which we celebrate God's inexhaustible provisions available through faith in Jesus Christ.

One Minute Reflection
How will you reclaim the Sabbath?

"Most of the things we need to be most fully alive never come in busyness. They grow in rest."
(Mark Buchanan)

It Is About Honor

Exodus 20:12-16
"Honor your father and your mother, so that you may live long in the land the LORD your God is giving you. You shall not murder. You shall not commit adultery. You shall not steal. You shall not give false testimony against your neighbor."

The Fifth, Sixth, Seventh, Eighth and Ninth Commandments introduce us to a series of Laws that define proper relationships with other people. Commandments are all prohibitions about not taking away from our fellow man what is most precious to him/her.
Family (Honor Your Father and Mother)
Life (thou shall not kill)
Honor (thou shall not commit adultery)
Property (thou shall not steal)
Reputation (thou shall not bear false witness)

We start with honoring our parents because families are the building blocks of life here on earth. God designed the family unit and when families are fractured, it has a negative influence not just on us individually but also society at large.

God had to require us not to murder each other because He understood the hearts of men engaged in sin can lead to serious consequences. God then asks us to express and demonstrate our love for our partner in marriage by not committing adultery.

God also instructs us to show our love and respect for others by not stealing what belongs to them. The 8th Commandment safeguards everyone's right to legitimately acquire and own property.

Finally, the Ninth Commandment is the one we break and then justify most often. We do this by gossiping as if it were real concern, degrading others within the label of a "joke", being silent instead of standing up for our friends, and not correcting untrue statements about our neighbors.

<u>One Minute Reflection</u>
What Commandment do you need to work on?

"God's commands are not arbitrary. They are grounded in His moral character, what He is like within Himself, and orientated towards His purposes for His creation."
(Melvin Tinker)

Tenth Commandment - Secret Sin

Exodus 20:17

"You shall not covet your neighbor's house. You shall not covet your neighbor's wife, or his male or female servant, his ox or donkey, or anything that belongs to your neighbor."

Today we are looking at the last of the Ten Commandments, which is aimed directly at the heart and mind of every human being.

You Shall Not Covet!

Covetousness takes place beneath the surface of our lives and therefore we can easily hide this sin in our hearts and minds, away from the view of others.
However we cannot hide it from God.
Hebrews 4:13 warns us, *"Nothing in all creation is hidden from God's sight. Everything is uncovered and laid bare before the eyes of him to whom we must give account".*

At its root, to covet means, "to crave or desire, especially in an excessive or improper way". Coveting is usually the result of envy, and is especially insulting to God because it conveys that we are not really grateful for what He has bestowed upon us.

The real purpose of all the Ten Commandments is to expose sin and encourage us to realize we cannot save ourselves.

Ultimately and in all ways, we need the saving grace of Christ.

One Minute Reflection
What does your coveting expose in you?

"Take heed and beware of covetousness. The Lord saw the need of doubly warning against that besetting sin."
(William Tiptaft)

Spiritual Discernment

1 Corinthians 2:4-5
"My message and my preaching were not with wise and persuasive words, but with a demonstration of the Spirit's power, so that your faith might not rest on human wisdom, but on God's power."

Discernment is a term used to describe the activity of determining the value and quality of a certain subject or event. Typically, it is used to describe the activity of going past the mere perception of something, to making detailed judgments about that thing.

Spiritual discernment is not something we are born with but instead it is a supernatural ability that we receive from God Himself in the power of the Holy Spirit. Understanding God's word is simply an academic endeavor without the help of the Spirit. When we become Christians we are not instantly in possession of the knowledge of God, instead we grow to maturity through a process.

Discernment requires time and patience and effort.
To grow in discernment we need to grow in Christian Faith.

Simply reading God's word is not enough.
We need to invite the Holy Spirit to manifest wisdom and discernment into our lives. We need to step out in faith and to obey God even when it is counter intuitive to how we might normally approach any given situation.

First God wants to do an important work "in us" and then eventually do an important work "through us". As Paul reminds us in the passage above in 1 Corinthians, the message regarding faith does not come from *"wise and persuasive words"'* but it does *"rest on God's power"*.

One Minute Reflection
How can you grow in spiritual discernment today?

"God does not judge the condition or quality of His church by how good the meetings are on Sunday morning, but by how good the people are on Monday morning. The main calling of our life is more than just knowing the truth; it is having that truth become our life. "
(Rick Joyner)

You Are An Heir

Romans 8:17
"Now if we are children, then we are heirs-heirs of God and co-heirs with Christ, if indeed we share in His sufferings in order that we may also share in His glory."

It is critical that we comprehend that God has already proclaimed who we are in Him, and then realize that our task is to manifest that reality into our lives daily.

Paul declares in our passage:
"We are heirs-heirs of God and co-heirs with Christ".

An heir apparent is a person who is first in line of succession and cannot be displaced from inheriting what is rightfully his or hers.

A good analogy is that of Prince William. Today he is simply a prince but he has been declared the future King of England. Everything he is and everything he does, prepares him for that future role. In the same way, we have been declared heirs of God's kingdom and although the crown has not yet been given to us, we know that we must also prepare for that future, lofty coronation.

If we look closely at our passage today in Romans, we will notice that there is one qualification in being co-heirs with Christ. The emphasis is on suffering as part of the path to glory. We will experience suffering in the form of testing, refining, or persecution when standing up for Christ's principles and defending God's kingdom.

Our inheritance is well described in 1 Peter 1:3-5
" In His great mercy He has given us new birth into a living hope through the resurrection of Jesus Christ from the dead, and into an inheritance that can never perish, spoil or fade. This inheritance is kept in heaven for you, who through faith are shielded by God's power until the coming of the salvation that is ready to be revealed in the last time."

One Minute Reflection
Do you see yourself as an heir?

"The main thing that God asks for is our attention."
(Jim Cymbala)

The Revelation

<u>Revelation 1:3</u>
"Blessed is the one who reads aloud the words of this prophecy, and blessed are those who hear it and take to heart what is written in it, because the time is at hand."

It is clear that if we know our destination we are much more likely to get there. So today we are going to take a glance at The Book of Revelation. This is the last book of the Bible. Many people shy away from reading Revelation because they fear it is confusing and scary.

The Book of Revelation is actually a letter written by the Apostle John. John, at the time of this writing, was an old man who had been exiled to Patmos, a prison island in the middle of the Aegean Sea. However, we must remember that John was also the beloved disciple of Jesus. He loved Jesus so much that John was known as "the disciple of love". Whenever three disciples went aside with Jesus, as they did at the transfiguration, John was one of them.

The word "revelation" means unveiling and we can understand that the Scripture written in Revelation "unveils" the deepest truth about Jesus Christ.

The book is sometimes hard to understand because John is trying to describe prophecy that he had never experienced before and so he was choosing words to describe the unknown mysteries of things to come.

Revelation is the only book in the Bible that contains a promise to everyone that reads it that they will be abundantly blessed. ☐
Specifically, Revelation 1:3 states *"the one who reads aloud the words of this prophecy, will be blessed...take heart what is written here because the time is at hand"*.

The Book of Revelation illustrates human history culminating in the fulfillment of Jesus Christ as He sets up His eternal kingdom of glory and justice.

<u>One Minute Reflection</u>
Will you commit to learning more about the Book of Revelation?

"Jesus is the God whom we can approach without pride and before whom we can humble ourselves without despair."
(Blaise Pascal)

Principle Or Preference

<u>Roman 1:17</u>
"For in the gospel the righteousness of God is revealed--a righteousness that is by faith from first to last, just as it is written: 'The righteous will live by faith.'"

We perceive our world through the five senses; sight, hearing, smell, taste, and touch. Yet God tells us that there is a higher reality, even though our perceptions appear as truth. Throughout Scripture God commands us to live by faith, not according to what we see.

So, what does *"the righteous shall live by faith"* really mean? It is the confident conviction that God is all He claims to be in His Word and that His promises are true. We cannot simply look around at the world to determine truth but instead we must believe God.

This has profound importance in how we operate. Will we respond by principle or by preference?

A preference is a moral choice based on likes and dislikes or whatever seems best in the moment. When we let our preferences guide us, then every day is up for grabs. Every situation will be dependent upon our emotions, other people's opinions, our temptations and desires and our bad judgment. We will go one way today and another way tomorrow.

A principle is a fixed or predetermined mode of conduct, or a moral rule based on the Word of God. When we live by God's principles then our conduct, character and choices are set in stone. We will know in very certain terms what is required of us and how we should present ourselves to the world. This is also a critical yet valuable lesson for our children as well. We must practice surrendering every part of our life to God, knowing that His principles lead to righteousness when we are walking by faith.

<u>One Minute Reflection</u>
What principles of faith will you commit to today?

"Religion finds the love of happiness and the principles of duty separated in us; and its mission—its masterpiece is, to reunite them."
(Alexandre Vinet)

Faith Not Sight

<u>2 Corinthians 5:7</u>
"For we live by faith, not by sight."

In 2 Corinthians 5:7 above, the apostle Paul exhorts the believers in Corinth to make a distinction between the way they used to live and the new way of life now that they are walking with Jesus.

He proclaims, *"For we live by faith, not by sight"*

In the Bible, faith is not explained in ethereal or spiritual terms but it is rather defined in very practical ways. Faith is not only to simply believe, but also to be lived out. Faith in the Bible is described *as "being sure of what we hope for and certain of what we do not see".* (Hebrews 11:1)

What does this mean?
To walk by faith, is to live in the confident expectation of things that are to come and in the belief of unseen realities that God is capable of manifesting by His power.

Most people today are influenced by things that are seen. They live by the cliché, "seeing is believing". However Christians are asked to live by the very opposite notion. 2 Corinthians underscores the fact that we trust God to fulfill his promises for the future (the unseen) based on what He has already fulfilled in the past. Thus, our faith is not blind, but based squarely on God's proven faithfulness.

If we turn on the evening news or look around at the mess we may have created in our own lives – the "sight" of things might cause great anxiety. However God is inviting us to live by faith, not sight.

No matter what we are facing - illness, discouragement, a job loss, a serious betrayal, an unexpected circumstance, marriage trouble, or any kind of trial or tribulation, we can focus on God's promises for the future not on what the circumstances might be telling us today.
We can rejoice daily in the reality of faith in God.

<u>One Minute Reflection</u>
What do you think it means to live by faith not by sight?

"Faith is to believe what we do not see, and the reward of this faith is to see what we believe."
(Augustine)

Refuge And Strength

Psalm 46:1
"God is our refuge and strength, an ever present help in trouble."

God is always revealing Himself.
We see that demonstrated in the various and marvelous ways God is described in the Bible.

Today, Psalm 46:1 tells us that God *is "our refuge and strength an ever present help in trouble"*. Whether it is a national tragedy affecting hundreds of people or devastating news we hear at home alone, God declares He is available during the trials of daily life and He can be a security for us in three distinct ways.

God is our refuge
The Bible describes God as our refuge; a place to which we may flee to for safety. We need not fear situations or people who threaten our well-being. God is always there for protection.

God is our strength
The word strength and its derivatives are mentioned over 360 times in the Bible. God assures us that we do not need to fight our battles with our own natural power but instead we can rely on His supernatural strength.

God is an ever-present help in trouble
"Ever-present" is not just a theological term describing God's ability to be everywhere at the same time, it is also a description of the adequate help God supplies for this moment and beyond.

All we need to do is call on God and He will help us.
He is available right this moment and also whenever we need Him.

One Minute Reflection
Do you turn to God first in times of trouble?

"Our "safe place" is not where we live, it is in whom we live."
(Tom White)

The Gift Of The Rest

Genesis 2:2
"By the seventh day God had finished the work He had been doing; so on the seventh day He rested from all His work."

"Rest" is defined as "peace, ease or refreshment." The Bible speaks quite highly of rest. It is a repeated theme throughout Scripture, beginning with the creation week where even God rested from His work; to The Ten Commandments where resting on the Sabbath is a requirement; to Christ assuring all of us that HE would provide rest for our weary souls.

Rest is physical
Our bodies need time to recuperate and re-energize. We need time to pause from our busy schedules and rest.

Rest is spiritual
God commanded us to take the seventh day and honor the Sabbath. It is a time "set apart" to reflect on the greatness and goodness of God.

Rest is emotional
Jesus reminds us to put our trust and faith in Him. We can let go of every burden and know that He is capable of handling our lives.

Rest is a gift from God
Rest is good. It is necessary. It is healing. Rest is from God. The importance of rest is not just a side note of Scripture-not some trivial idea that God added as an afterthought. Rest is intentional, meaningful and allows us precious time to delight in God and all that He has created.

One Minute Reflection
Are you intentional about resting in God, for God and with God?

"You have created us for yourself, and our heart
cannot be stilled until it finds rest in You."
(Augustine)

Unconditional Love

<u>Romans 8:35</u>
"Who shall separate us from the love of Christ? Shall trouble or hardship or persecution or famine or nakedness or danger or sword?"

Today's lesson contends that the truth that God's love is unconditional and is central to the gospel message itself. This may be the best news we will ever hear because most things have a condition attached to them.

One of the most amazing things about God's love is that it is extended to us when we do not deserve it and continues to be offered even when we do not respond to it. That certainly is different from human love because we operate in a "performance based" society. We have a tendency to show more love to the people who are good to us and less love to the ones who are not.

Moreover we have probably been on the receiving end of this as well. We may have felt approval and acceptance when we met someone's needs, and disapproval and rejection when we failed to live up to their standards.

God offers us something better called grace.
A great way to remember the word grace is by using an acronym.
GRACE - God's Riches At Christ's Expense.

Grace essentially means that there is not one thing any of us can do to earn God's love because it is a free gift. God does not love us because we are worthy instead we are worthy because He loves us first. This is a critical distinction.

Today's passage reminds us that nothing we come across in this world can separate us from the love of Christ.

<u>One Minute Reflection</u>
Do you accept God's love based on faith in Jesus Christ?

"Grace, then, is grace, --that is to say, it is sovereign,
it is free, it is sure, it is unconditional, and it is everlasting."
(Alexander Whyte)

Why Do The Righteous Suffer

<u>Job 1:1</u>
"In the land of Uz there lived a man whose name was Job. This man was blameless and upright; he feared God and shunned evil."

Job is one of the most well known books of the Bible because it plays out like a serious Shakespearean drama. The Book of Job does not specifically name its author and because the author is not really known, the date of this story is somewhere between 1440 B.C. and 950 B.C.

What makes the book of Job relevant to us is that Job questions God on issues that we all want the answer to.

Today's question:
Why do the righteous suffer?

This is the question raised after Job loses his family, his wealth, and his health. In other words, if we live our lives well, love God and do our very best, why would God still allow us to suffer?

We know that Job was a family man of integrity and great wealth. We also discover that Job had done nothing to deserve the suffering that takes over his life. Job's response to his suffering was not to sink into despair and blame God but instead he declares: *"Naked I came from my mother's womb, and naked I will depart. The Lord gave and the Lord has taken away; may the name of the Lord be praised."*

The Book of Job helps us to understand the following:
God has power over what Satan can and cannot do
Humans will never understand all the suffering in the world
We live in a world plagued by sin and its devastating effects
Suffering may be allowed in our lives to purify, test, and teach
Ultimately, God provides the answer to all situations in our life

<u>One Minute Reflection</u>
How do you explain suffering in this world?

"Suffering is part of the human condition, and it comes to us all. The key is how we react to it, either turning away from God in anger and bitterness or growing closer to Him in trust and confidence."
(Billy Graham)

Understanding God's Ways

<u>Job 2:11-13</u>
"Now when Job's three friends heard of all this adversity that had come upon him, they came each one from his own place, Eliphaz the Temanite, Bildad the Shuhite and Zophar the Naamathite; and they made an appointment together to come to sympathize with him and comfort him."

Many of us know the story of Job and his unimaginable suffering. In today's passage above, we meet Job's friends who try to help Job with sympathy and comfort when they hear of his adversity. However as the conversation continues they quickly turn to accusing him of sin to explain his suffering. Job's three friends end up only making him feel worse because they don't understand Job or God enough to give sound advice to this situation.

The interaction of Job and his friends shows us the folly of trying to understand God's ways from our limited point of view.

They argued with Job from the human perspective based on their own experience, tradition and merit. They were wrong in their theology and wrong in their conclusions. They believed that man must do things to earn God's favor and therefore Job's suffering is a sign of God's displeasure.

The truth is we will never fully understand God's ways.

As Isaiah 55:8-9 reminds us:
"For my thoughts are not your thoughts, neither are your ways my ways," declares the Lord. *"As the heavens are higher than the earth, so are my ways higher than your ways and my thoughts than your thoughts."*

However what we do know for sure is that if we offer our suffering to God, He will ultimately use it for good. Therefore, we must trust God with every circumstance in our life.

<u>One Minute Reflection</u>
What can you learn from the story of Job's friends?

"God will not permit any troubles to come upon us, unless He has a specific plan by which great blessing can come out of the difficulty." (Peter Marshall)

The Truth About Satan

Job 2:2

"And the LORD said to Satan, 'From where do you come?' So Satan answered the LORD and said, 'From going to and fro on the earth, and from walking back and forth on it.'"

What makes the book of Job relevant to all of us is that it presents questions that we all want the answer to. One such question is:

Does Satan really exist?

The Bible explicitly informs us of the existence of Satan. He is described as the enemy of man (Genesis 3:15), the father of lies (John 8:44), and the accuser (Revelation 12:10). The name "Satan" means adversary. The Bible states that Satan is cunning, intelligent, powerful, and resourceful. In the Book of Job we see that Satan has power in two realms.

Heavenly Realm

Satan's power has repute in the spiritual realm where he has access to the presence of God. The book of Job provides insight into the relationship between God and Satan. In Job 2:2 above we learn that Satan stands before God and reports that he has been *"going to and fro on the earth"*. God asks Satan if he has considered Job, and Satan immediately accuses Job of only loving God for the blessings God gives. God grants Satan permission to destroy Job's possessions and family.

Earthly Realm

The Bible says, *"the whole world is under the control of the evil one"* (1 John 5:19), and we *must "be self-controlled and alert. Your enemy the devil prowls around like a roaring lion looking for someone to devour"* (1 Peter 5:8). Satan's greatest advantage is that many people do not believe he exists. Over the centuries he has been portrayed as a caricature with horns, a spiked tail and a pitchfork so that millions consider him a myth. However, Jesus took Satan very seriously.

Job's story is a warning that we need to always place our trust in God because Satan is a real and dangerous force we will be battling.

One Minute Reflection
Do you believe in the reality of Satan?

"There is no neutral ground in the universe; every square inch, every split second, is claimed by God and counter-claimed by Satan."
(C.S. Lewis)

Full Restoration

Job 4:12-13
"The Lord blessed the latter part of Job's life more than the former part. He had fourteen thousand sheep, six thousand camels, a thousand yoke of oxen and a thousand donkeys. And he also had seven sons and three daughters."

Most people don't consider that the Book of Job has a happy ending.

What Job teaches us is that how we handle the bad stuff in life is just as important as how we handle the good stuff. It is poignant to recognize that we will only know our own faithfulness if we are tempted with situations that provide a choice of unfaithfulness.

The story of Job is really about what choices Job made in the midst of his own trials and what principles he was willing to adhere to during the worst time of his life.

The message of Job has deep implications for all of us because trials and suffering provide spiritual enrichment and a bridge to building an even stronger relationship between God and us.

It affirms that God is still God and always worthy of our love, reverence and worship. Job vindicated himself by remaining faithful to God at the worst time of his life. As we see in our passage today taken from the last chapter of Job, faithfulness results in a beneficial outcome, *"The Lord blessed the latter part of Job's life more than the former part".*

We serve a God of redemption and restoration.
And nowhere is that more evident than in the life and death of Jesus Christ. We must remember that as Christians we partake in Jesus' suffering but at the same time we also partake in His resurrection and restoration to a full and risen life.

One Minute Reflection
What lesson will you take from the end of Job's story?

"Come work for the Lord. The work is hard, the hours are long, and the pay is low, but the retirement benefits are out of this world."
(Billy Sunday)

God And Our Treasure

<u>Luke 12:34</u>
"Where your treasure is, there will your heart be also."

The movement of our money signifies the movement of our heart. Where our money goes tells the world where our heart is going also.

If we value food - our money might be spent on expensive dinners
If we value education - our money will go to a private school
If we value entertainment – we enjoy Broadway, ball games and movies

Here in Luke 12:34 -Jesus is reminding us to be careful about what we value because the money will testify to what we really love. What Jesus desires is for us to value Him first and foremost and to be invested in things of eternal value.

There are three areas God points to in Scripture that are of supreme importance to Him and where we could invest more of our money.

The poor
We are to reach out to those in desperate circumstances

The lost
We need to support missionaries so that the Gospel is shared

The church
We are to support its leaders, teachers and ministries

When Jesus said, *"Where your treasure is, there will your heart be also."* He is not just stating a fact of the human heart; instead He is giving a prescription for it. Jesus implores us to invest our money in the right things, and then allow our hearts to follow.

<u>One Minute Reflection</u>
Does your money management reflect your Christian values?

"Jesus Christ said more about money than about any other single thing because, when it comes to a man's real nature, money is of first importance. Money is an exact index to a man's true character. All through Scripture there is an intimate correlation between the development of a man's character and how he handles his money."
(Rev. Richard Halverson)

Confess Christ

Matthew 10:32-33
"Whoever acknowledges me before others, I will also acknowledge before my Father in heaven. But whoever disowns me before others, I will disown before my Father in heaven."

The entire 10th chapter of Matthew is Jesus' preparation and sending out of the twelve disciples He had called to follow Him. It is in the context of this instruction and training of these men that Jesus gives us some of his best teaching about discipleship.

In our passage above, Jesus explains to us that the mark of a true disciple is to confess that He is Jesus Christ the Lord.

What does that mean? To confess means "to affirm, to acknowledge, and to agree". The idea is a verbal statement of identification and a proclamation of our relationship with Christ. When we confess, we are telling the world that we believe in Jesus as our Lord and Savior. It is the outward verbalization of our inner faith.

Confession includes:
1) Belief in the heart that a certain thing is true.
2) A decision that we are willing to make an open commitment to the truth.
3) A public statement declaring this conviction before others.

Jesus reminds us not just to confess Him but also to confess Him before men. We are not to keep Jesus a private matter. Instead we are to profess our allegiance to Jesus in front of our neighbors, friends, co-workers, families, and all the people we come into daily contact with in our lives.

If we confess Jesus before men, then He will confess us before God. Of course another response is possible too. We can also deny Jesus before men. If we do this, Jesus warns us that He will then also deny us before God. As you can see, Jesus takes away all middle ground. He invites us to make a decision either way.

One Minute Reflection
Are you more likely to confess or deny Jesus among your peers?

"Yield yourself to Christ's claims. Give Him the throne of your heart. Turn over to Him the regulation of your life. Trust in His atoning death. Love Him with all your soul. Obey Him with all your might and He will conduct you to heaven." (A.W. Pink)

Bless Those Who Curse You

Luke 6:27-29
"But to you who are listening I say: Love your enemies, do good to those who hate you, bless those who curse you, pray for those who mistreat you. If someone takes your coat, do not withhold your shirt from them."

We all have people in our lives that have caused us pain, betrayal, and unimaginable harm. There are people who have been rude, excluded us, been downright mean or even crossed serious emotional and physical boundaries.

The best strategy for dealing with any of these betrayals was given to us by Jesus Christ Himself and is our passage today from Luke 6 above.

We are told, *"love your enemies and do good to those who hate you."*

How we do we do this?
1) Ask the Holy Spirit to help us do what we cannot do by our own strength or desire
2) Lift our enemies up in prayer and ask God to bless them
3) Visualize wonderful things happening in the life of our foes
4) Reach out in love even when we don't "feel" like it
5) Ask ourselves if we love God more than we hate our enemy. If the answer is "yes", following His command to forgive is much easier.

One Minute Reflection
Is there an enemy you could respond to in love?

"Do all the good you can. By all the means you can. In all the ways you can. In all the places you can. At all the times you can. To all the people you can. As long as ever you can."
(John Wesley)

Get Excited

"Never be lacking in zeal, but keep your spiritual fervor, serving the Lord."

In today's passage from Romans 12:11, the apostle Paul is emboldening his readers to get excited about the work of the Lord. He gives us three easy and helpful suggestions for our own life as well.

1) Never Lack Zeal
In other words be enthusiastic about God. Enthusiasm is one of the greatest words in the English language. It is derived from two Greek words, en and theos, literally meaning, "full of God." The Bible uses several different words for this idea of being filled with enthusiasm: ardor, zeal, whole-heartedness, or to be eager.

2) Keep Our Spiritual Fervor
The word used for fervor literally means, "to boil." This refers to the heat of our emotions. What we feel inwardly about the business of God ought to be so hot that it literally boils outward to every area of our lives. Whether we are teaching a Bible study, sharing our faith, working at a homeless shelter, arranging flowers for a Sunday service or praying for world peace - God expects us to "keep our fervor" for His line of work.

3) Serving the Lord
Ultimately we are not serving people, we're not serving ourselves, and we're not serving the church. We are serving God. He is our audience of One that we want to impress.

Jesus is not interested in "lukewarm" Christians. He told us in Revelation 3:15-16, *"I know your works: you are neither cold nor hot. So, because you are lukewarm, and neither hot nor cold, I will spit you out of my mouth."* Our passage today emphasizes that we need to get busy and excited serving the Lord.

One Minute Reflection
How fervent are you for the work of God?

"Enthusiasm is one of life's greatest qualities, but it must be practiced to become a dominant factor in one's life. There is real magic in enthusiasm. It spells the difference between mediocrity and accomplishment."
(Normal Vincent Peale)

Righteous Judge

2 Timothy 4:8

"Now there is in store for me the crown of righteousness, which the Lord, the righteous Judge, will award to me on that day-and not only to me, but also to all who have longed for His appearing."

Today we are examining God as a Righteous Judge. Since everything in this world belongs to God, we are accountable to Him for all things. As our Maker, He owns us and He has the right to judge us according to His standards.

The proof that God is the perfect, righteous judge is that He is deeply concerned with questions of right and wrong, good and bad, moral and immoral. God's righteousness is the natural expression of His Holiness. God is infinitely pure and opposed to all sin and He judges sin as something that cannot be tolerated. God has therefore set standards for our behavior as well and He will judge us according to those same standards.

God is the perfect righteous judge for many reasons.

God is Righteous
His actions and decisions are always right 100% of the time

God Knows Everything
He never misses an important piece of evidence. He has all the facts

God is Everywhere
He is the witness to everything we do.

God is All Powerful
No one can coerce God to judge unfairly. Jesus Christ satisfied God's perfect righteousness by His death on the cross, and now we can claim that righteousness on Judgment Day

One Minute Reflection
What are your thoughts on God being the final judge?

"God is not unjust. No one will be condemned for not believing a message they have never heard. Those who have never heard the Gospel will be judged by their failure to own up to the light of God's grace "
(John Piper)

God Is The Same

<u>Hebrews 13:8</u>
"Jesus Christ is the same yesterday and today and forever."

Today we are looking at the promise that God is always the same.

The Bible tells us that God is faithful, loving, patient, forgiving, and kind and cares deeply about justice and mercy. However, we also learn from our passage today that God is unchangeable and therefore thoroughly dependable.

God is who He says He is and His nature and character never change.

What does this mean for us personally?

Change happens all around us. Days change into nights, the seasons alternate regularly, weather is completely unpredictable and the circumstances of our lives shift in a moment's notice without regard to our personal desire. Ultimately, the world is a very fragile place and we don't seem to have any real control over our lives. One day we may be up and the next day we are down. Even those closest to us can change, leave, or die.

We live in a world that is always transforming.

However we can always count on God because He never changes.

This is the ultimate security package.
We can rely on His promises and believe what He tells us in the Bible because, *"Jesus Christ is the same yesterday and today and forever"*.

God is sovereign over all things.
The good news is we can put our faith securely in Christ. He will forgive our past sins, take care of our present worries and secure a future with Him into eternity.

<u>One Minute Reflection</u>
Does knowing God is always the same, give you security today?

"God is not who you think He is; He is who He says He is."
(Clarice Fluitt)

Proverbs - Trust In The Lord

Proverbs 3: 5-6
"Trust in the Lord with all your heart, And lean not on your own understanding; In all your ways acknowledge Him, And He shall direct your paths."

A proverb is derived from the Latin, "proverbium" and is a simple and concrete saying which expresses a truth. Written mostly by King Solomon, proverbs are wise sayings and ethical, common sense teachings on how to live a Godly life. We can find an entire book of the Bible dedicated to proverbs.

Proverbs are brief
Proverbs are instructive
Proverbs are often metaphorical
Proverbs are probabilities not promises

Proverbs 3:5-6 tells us:
"Trust in the Lord with all of your heart and do not lean on your own understanding."

Here we have the basic tenet of Christianity. It all starts with trusting God. Jesus actually reflected the same idea when He uttered, *"But seek first the kingdom of God and His righteousness, and all these things shall be added to you."*

Both King Solomon and Jesus were speaking about a profound truth. We were created in the image of God and created to be in fellowship with God. If we want to understand how the world works, we must not lean on our own understanding but trust in God who knows everything.

If we trust in God, then He will make our paths straight.
We will have no regrets for yesterday, stress for today or worries for tomorrow because God has all things under His control.
We simply need to acknowledge God and allow Him to direct our paths.

One Minute Reflection
Is there something you need to trust God with today?

"Trust is not a passive state of mind. It is a vigorous act of the soul by which we choose to lay hold on the promises of God and cling to them despite the adversity that at times seeks to overwhelms us."
(Jerry Bridges)

Proverbs - Train Up A Child

<u>Proverbs 22:6</u>
*"Train up a child on the way they should go,
and even when they are old they will not turn from it."*

Most of us are diligent about training our children in manners, safety concerns, and getting ahead in school and sports. However we need to ask ourselves how much time we train them in the ways of the Lord.

Today's proverb is a great reminder that the seeds of biblical wisdom we plant in our children's lives today may stay hidden for years to come but if we continue to water them, they will take root later on.

The words "train up" come from a Hebrew word that literally means, "to narrow". This proverb tells us to narrow the way in which our children go and then when they are old, they will not turn away from it.

How can we train up our child?
Go to church as a family
Model Godly behavior
Enroll them in a Sunday school class
Pray before a family dinner
Write a favorite Bible verse and put it on their desk
Create a family mission statement you can all get excited about
Be enthusiastic about all God has done in your life
Share your testimony with your kids

<u>One Minute Reflection</u>
Is there one thing you could do today to train up your child?

"A wise person truly said, it ought to be as impossible to forget that there is a Christian in the house as it is to forget that there is a ten-year-old boy in it."
(Roger J. Squire)

Proverbs - Pride And Humility

Proverbs 16:18-19
"Pride goes before destruction, and a haughty spirit before a fall. Better to be of a humble spirit with the lowly, than to divide the spoils with the proud."

Today's proverb is a great teaching on the two opposite character traits of pride and humility.

Selfish pride can be defined as "excessive confidence or glorification in one's self, possessions or nation." This concept is found in The Bible, along with words such as arrogance, haughtiness and conceit, all of which are opposite of Godly humility. Self-centered pride can cause us problems in two areas. On a spiritual level, it inevitably leads to disregard, disrespect and disobedience to God. On a worldly level, selfish pride very often results in self-destructive behavior.

As we read in the proverb above, *"pride before destruction and a haughty spirit before a fall."*

Two things are foretold in Proverbs 16 above; Selfish pride is a sin and God will humble those who don't humble themselves. Humility on the other hand is a much more elusive virtue. Christ is our best example of humility. Jesus was the incarnate God who became the self-emptying servant.

To keep our pride in check and develop humility:
Give God the credit for everything
Say you are sorry first and often
Offer forgiveness whether or not the other person deserves it
Give away something of value to someone in need
Intentionally speak well of others
Serve someone less fortunate
Choose to be humble

One Minute Reflection
Do you think you exhibit more pride or humility in your daily life?

"Humility is the mother of all virtues; purity, charity and obedience. It is in being humble that our love becomes real, devoted and ardent. If you are humble nothing will touch you, neither praise nor disgrace, because you know what you are."
(Mother Theresa)

Proverbs - God's Purpose

<u>Proverbs 19:21</u>
"Many are the plans in a man's heart, but it is the Lord's purpose that prevails."

In our passage today from Proverbs 19:21, we find the original declaration about man's plans and God's purposes spelled out.

We can save ourselves a lot of heartache by
taking note of this profound biblical wisdom.

Since we were created with free choice, we have the ability to design, manipulate and push our plans to fruition but ultimately it is God's purposes that prevail.

The Bible reveals that God has a purpose in everything, and specifically He has a plan for your life and mine. It is wise to align ourselves with God's purposes.

How do we do this?

Enjoy God
Model Christ
Set Apart time to spend with God
Meditate on His word
Serve others with your talents and gifts
Glorify God in everything you do
Ask God to show you His way of doing things

<u>One Minute Reflection</u>
Do you believe that it is God's plans that will prevail?

"It's not about you. The purpose of your life is far greater than your own personal fulfillment, your peace of mind, or even your happiness. It's far greater than your family, your career, or even your wildest dreams and ambitions. If you want to know why you were placed on this planet, you must begin with God. You were born by His purpose and for his purpose."
(Rick Warren)

Proverbs - Guard Your Heart

<u>Proverbs 4:23</u>
"Above all else, guard your heart, for everything you do flows from it."

It turns out we all have a heart condition!

Scripture clearly teaches us that the real issues of life are spiritual and are really matters of the heart, the inner man. Maybe it's for this reason the word "heart" is found close to 1,000 times in the Bible.

We must guard our hearts for 3 reasons:

Our heart is extremely precious both physically and spiritually

Our heart contains the source of everything we care about

Our heart is under attack

Best explained by Bishop T.D. Jakes in his book,
Man of God, Guard Your Heart
"Finally, my brother, guard your heart. The enemy wants to embitter and corrupt you. Guard your heart against contamination by lust and loneliness, bigotry and arrogance, and everything in between."

We all have broken hearts; corrupted and contaminated by sin.
This is the sole reason that Jesus Christ came to save us. Only God, our creator, can do the repair that we all so desperately need.

Jesus Christ is the ultimate heart surgeon.
He will not only save our life, He will make it work better than before.

<u>One Minute Reflection</u>
In what way can you guard your heart today?

"A divided heart loses both worlds."
(A.B. Simpson)

Secret Of The Holy Spirit

John 14:15

"If you love me, keep my commands. And I will ask the Father, and He will give you another advocate to help you and be with you forever-the Spirit of truth."

We all want more power.
As a matter of fact we spend a lot of our waking day trying to figure out how to get more power in every area of our life. We want power over our finances, power at work, power to improve our marriages, power to control our tempers, power over our diet, power to pray, power to please, power to overcome trials, power to persevere.

The Bible introduces us to the greatest power on the face of the earth and the secret to how we can manifest into our lives daily.

Welcome to the Power of the Holy Spirit

The Apostle Paul clearly taught that we receive the Holy Spirit the moment we receive Jesus Christ as our Savior. And Jesus assures us that those who keep His commands will have the third Person of the Trinity, the Holy Spirit, living in him.

The Holy Spirit gives the believer the life of God, eternal life, which is really His very nature. It is within this life that we receive power.

We cannot have a relationship with an "it" but we can have a relationship with a person; the Person of the Holy Spirit.

Jesus also tells us Himself in our passage today from John 14 that He will give us another advocate who is the Spirit of truth and will be with us forever.

We can invite the Holy Spirit to be with us daily.

One Minute Reflection
Will you invite the Holy Spirit to reveal Himself to you this week?

"Divine power is displayed not in dramatic manifestations that intrigue men but in lives of quiet confidence and steady persistence that glorify God."
(Alistair Begg)

What The Holy Spirit Can Do For You

John 14:26
"But the Advocate, the Holy Spirit, whom the Father will send in my name, will teach you all things and will remind you of everything I have said to you."

Understanding the Holy Spirit is vitally important because our entire destiny and purpose for life on earth is to know God, to love God and to manifest God's glory. Everything is wrapped up in this sole design because we were made in God's image.

Since it is the job of the Holy Spirit to reveal all truth, we need to pay attention to Him. In John 14:26 above, Jesus explains that the Holy Spirit will teach and remind us of everything Christ has said.

What does the Holy Spirit do specifically?

He works on our behalf - making our requests known to God
He speaks to us because He has a voice
He leads - He is out in front
He guides - He stands next to us
He brings revelation of God's Word
He is "active, living"
He holds us accountable and He grieves for us when we sin
He convicts us of our sin to make us Holy
He advises us, as He is our "counselor"
He teaches us and reminds us of what Jesus said
He comforts us and promised to always be with us
He glorifies Jesus by revealing the truth of who Jesus is
He enables us to become like Christ

Once we understand the Power of The Holy Spirit,
We can use His power to manifest great things into our own life.

One Minute Reflection
What one manifestation of the Holy Spirit will you use today?

"God specializes in the impossible, so that when the victory is won and the task is complete, we cannot take any credit. Others know we didn't do it, and we know we didn't do it. We must always remember that we can only live the Christian life and serve God through the power of His Holy Spirit."
(Nancy Leigh DeMoss)

But Now We Know God

Galatians 4:9
"But now that you know God-or rather are known by God-how is it that you are turning back to those weak and miserable forces."

Our passage comes from Galatians, which may be the earliest letter Paul ever wrote, and it can be found in the New Testament.

Paul had come to the province of Galatia on his first preaching journey. Christians gathered for prayer and worship and encouragement about the basic beliefs of their newfound faith.

Paul was reminding them that although they were once slaves to sin they are now sons and daughters of God set free by Christ. He implores them not to return to those weak and miserable forces now that God knows them.

A new world order is possible in Christ.
The lesson is true for us as well.

How can our lives be different now that we know God?
We can take the high road
We can forgive regardless of circumstance
We can turn the other cheek
We can let go of offense
We can be available
We can stay the course
We can do all things patiently and joyfully
We do it all in the name and power of Christ Himself

One Minute Reflection
How can you be different now because you know God?

"Do all the good you can. By all the means you can. In all the ways you can. In all the places you can. At all the times you can. To all the people you can. As long as ever you can."
(John Wesley)

God Supplies

Luke 12:23-24

"For life is more than food, and your body more than clothing. Look at the ravens. They don't plant or harvest or store food in barns, for God feeds them. And you are far more valuable to Him than any birds."

One of the most cherished promises of the Bible is that God will meet all of our needs. However, It may also be one of the promises that we doubt is true for us personally.

In our passage today, Jesus invites us to look at the ravens.

We might find ourselves asking:
Why hasn't God answered my prayer and met my specific need?

The value of any promise is based on two things.
One is the ability of the promise maker to fulfill his promise and the other is the integrity of the promise maker to follow through on his word.
God qualifies on both accounts!

So if God is not the problem in an unmet need, then we must look to ourselves.
God wants us to be solely dependent on Him. We must trust God completely, obey His commands, wait on His promises and leave all the consequences to Him.

If we have an unmet need, we can use the time wisely to seek the answer to what else God might be doing in our lives. He may be meeting a deeper need than the one we originally put in a request for.

God might desire to teach us a valuable biblical lesson.
God may want us to deal with an unresolved area of conflict.
God could be shaping us for a greater mission.

God has a purpose for everything under Heaven.

<u>One Minute Reflection</u>
Why did Jesus use the example of a raven to make His point?

"We want to see results, and preferably instantly,
But God works in secret and with a divine patience."
(Henri J. M. Nouwen)

Summer Sabbatical

<u>Leviticus 25:1-2</u>
"The Lord said to Moses at Mount Sinai, 'Speak to the Israelites and say to them: When you enter the land I am going to give you, the land itself must observe a Sabbath to the Lord.'"

The idea of a sabbatical is deeply and indisputably rooted in Scripture. The term is derived from the Old Testament idea of "Sabbath." The Hebrew word means, "rest." God created the world in six days and rested on the seventh (Genesis 2:1-3).

In our passage today from Leviticus we learn that among the Israelites, God instituted the Sabbath year. It was a time to refrain from farming the land while allowing the earth rest. Moreover, it was a time to honor God by trusting in His resource and provision.

We can use this ancient practice of Sabbatical in our own lives this summer season. Our modern life keeps the focus on the "achieving" of life. We earn, we purchase, we strive, we compete, we challenge, we fix, and we are constantly on the hunt for faster, bigger, and better.

However, Scripture suggests that there is a rhythm to life. And as much as there is a time to build up, there is a time to slow down. Even Jesus had a deep understanding and appreciation for time off. He would often depart from the demands of His ministry to retreat into prayer and reconnection to His father.

How do we practice Sabbatical in our own lives?
It is about going inward instead of outward, deeper instead of wider. We can stop and simply enjoy all that God has done. We can take time to contemplate Scripture, lean into Christ through prayer and reflection, enjoy our families and friends and yield to the promptings of the Holy Spirit.

<u>One Minute Reflection</u>
How will you impose a Sabbatical this season?

"God wants us to follow a recurring pattern of intense work and then rest, intense work and then rest, and so forth. Whatever view one takes of the Sabbath, surely the six days of work and the one day of rest embedded in the creation remain relevant in some sense. Any routine of life that is unsustainable long-term cannot be of God. He calls us to work. But he also calls us to rest, in order to work most fruitfully."
(Ray Ortlund)

Everything A Loss

Philippians 3:8
"What is more, I consider everything a loss because of the surpassing worth of knowing Christ Jesus my Lord, for whose sake I have lost all things. I consider them garbage, that I may gain Christ."

We all desire to be complete. There is no greater example of being complete in Christ than the Apostle Paul.

Paul the Apostle (AD 5 - AD 67) has his first appearance in the Bible as a zealous young Pharisee named Saul of Tarsus who witnesses the stoning of the first Christian martyr. Paul leads a persecution against Christians, which eventually takes him to Damascus. It is while traveling to the city that he hears the voice of Jesus. This miracle eventually leads to Paul's repentance and baptism.

Paul is perhaps the most influential early Christian missionary. The writings ascribed to him by the church form a considerable portion of the New Testament. In the passage above Paul is explaining that He considered everything he'd ever attained as a loss for the sake of gaining Christ. His worthy reputation, his education, his birthright, his Jewish heritage and all of his achievements, he considered rubbish and of no value in light of what he had gained in Jesus Christ.

At the same time, Paul also considered all of his sufferings and trials mere garbage compared to the majestic divinity of knowing the supremacy of Christ. During his ministry, Paul spends at least five years in prison, is whipped, beaten, survives a stoning and endures being shipwrecked in the Mediterranean.

Yet, Paul is faithful to Christ to the very end of his life because this is where he finds everything he needs and desires. He is complete in Christ. We can gain Christ too.

One Minute Reflection
Do you consider everything a loss for the gain of knowing Christ?

"Until we know Jesus, God is merely a concept, and we can't have faith in Him. But once we hear Jesus say, "He who has seen Me has seen the Father", we immediately have something that is real, and our faith is limitless. "
(Oswald Chambers)

Simple Hindrances

<u>Psalm 66:16-19</u>
"Come and hear, all you who fear God; let me tell you what He has done for mi. cried out to Him with my mouth; His praise was on my tongue.
If I had cherished sin in my heart, the Lord would not have listened;
but God has surely listened and has heard my prayer."

Unanswered prayer is something that frustrates all of us. However, we can be aware of simple hindrances that can block a fruitful prayer life.

Doubt
We are not really sure God is big enough or cares enough to solve our dilemmas. Scripture tells us that God is all-powerful. He can handle any concern we bring to Him and so let's go ahead and be bold in our prayer requests.

Not wanting to bother God with the small stuff
God wants us to be specific in our requests to Him. When we share the details of our life, we create a foundation of God. God wants relationship not religion.

We have a preconceived idea of the solution
We may be looking for a new job when God would prefer we reconcile with our boss.
Remember that God will always provide a better outcome than anything we could have possibly imagined.

Asking for things not in accordance with the will of God
We might be asking for a new car when the man up the street doesn't have enough to eat. Often our desires are not the same as God's. We need to line up our request with what we think God would want for our life.

We expect answers too quickly.
God works in His own time zone and since He is eternal, things may take longer than we like. God has three answers; yes, no and wait.

<u>One Minute Reflection</u>
What might be a hindrance to your prayer life?

"There is not in the world a kind of life more sweet and delightful than that of a continual conversation with God."
(Brother Lawrence)

Don't Miss God's Best

Proverbs 4:20-21
*"My son, pay attention to what I say; turn your ear to my words.
Do not let them out of your sight, keep them within your heart."*

(Taken from an archive of The Washington Post)
"If you were among the 1,097 commuters hurrying through D.C's Metro station at L'Enfant Plaza on January 12th, 2007, you might have witnessed a once in a life time extraordinary experience. There amid the shoeshine, newspaper and lottery booths, was the world's greatest musician whose performances usually earn $1,000 a minute. He was playing Bach's most difficult and exquisite violin piece on a 3.5 million dollar, 300 year old Stradivarius."
"And he was playing for free"
"For those that knew him, they would have recognized Joshua Bell, a child prodigy violinist. However, Most folks didn't even glance in his direction and were completely unaware of the majesty that seemed irrelevant to their agenda."

This story above is extremely analogous to our own lives and how we often miss the best that God has to offer. We miss God's best because we are rushing through life, busy with trivial matters and constantly distracted. Our minds, hearts and souls are not attentive to God. God reminds us in Proverbs 4:20
"My son, pay attention to what I say; turn your ears to my words"

When folks were asked how they could have missed the majesty of Joshua Bell's performance, one gentleman answered, "Your ear has to be trained for the most part to understand and appreciate the beauty of what you are listening to".

Our ears also have to be trained to listen to the divinity and wisdom of God's voice.

One Minute Reflection
How will you attune your ears to God's voice?

"Few people arise in the morning as hungry for
God as they are for cornflakes or toast and eggs."
(Dallas Willard)

Repent

Matthew 3:2
"Repent ye: for the kingdom of Heaven is at hand."

Think about how many times the Bible uses words that start with the "re" prefix. There is redemption, revelation, repent, resist, reclaim, rebuild, rejoice, revive, recreate, restore, return, remain...and it turns out there are another 6023.

Is God trying to give us a message??

The answer is yes.
"Re" means again, (and again, and again).
God is persistently and lovingly calling His people back to Himself.
He is a God who is always "re"-inviting us back into relationship with Him.

Tim Laniak, author and teacher at Gordon Cromwell explains it this way:
"The theology of the "re-" prefix has implications for our own relationships. Have we given up on people, marriages, churches, schools, our government...the world? God's resilience presents us with a sometimes disturbing agenda that is eternally optimistic. He issues a prophetic "re-" word to let people know that He will find a way to bring them back to His original design. I must ask if we are as committed to restoration and return to God's ideals as He is?"

The word we are examining today is repentance.
It means, "turning back", "taking in a whole new point of view", "looking at it God's way". In other words, God simply asks us to turn from our own stubborn opinions about how the world works and listen to Him.

If your reread the passage from Matthew 3:2 above, Jesus explains it this way, *"Repent, for the kingdom of God is at hand".* Jesus is telling us that we won't see or understand God's Kingdom unless we turn from our own ways of doing things.

One Minute Reflection
Have you truly repented before God?

"Every year during their High Holy Days, the Jewish community reminds us all of our need for repentance and forgiveness."
(Billy Graham)

It Is Good To Resist

<u>James 4:7</u>
"Therefore submit to God. Resist the devil and he will flee from you."

Today we are looking at the word "resist" in the Bible.
The one thing God is often clear about in the Bible is that we must
"resist" the devil and flee from *"temptation"* because the world is filled
with both.

What temptations are we meant to resist?
Anything that does not honor God:

Foul Language
Gossip
Pride
Arrogance
Stealing
Cheating
Meanness
Brutality
Abuse
Pride
Stinginess
Drugs, alcohol, over consumption, gambling, debt

How are we meant to resist?
James reports that we must first *"submit to God"*.
Temptation is analogous to a bird landing on our head that starts to
build a nest. We don't have to allow those thoughts to take root but we
simply resist and swipe them away before they dig in for the long haul.
We are told to flee and use any means necessary to get away from the
strong hold of temptation.

<u>One Minute Reflection</u>
What do you need to resist today?

"Satan gives Adam an apple, and takes away Paradise. Therefore in all
temptations let us consider not what he offers, but what we shall lose."
(Richard Sibbes)

Rejoice

<u>Philippians 4:4</u>
"Rejoice in the Lord always. I will say it again: Rejoice!"

What a great word!!
Rejoice!

We spend very little time "rejoicing" about anything in life. We may be grateful, appreciative, deeply moved, momentarily thrilled but certainly we are rarely "rejoicing always", even in the Lord.

The word rejoice means, "to feel great joy or delight".

If you re-read Philippians 4:4 above - you will notice several things!

Joy is an obligation
The apostle Paul tells us, "Rejoice in the Lord!" and just in case we didn't get it the first time, he repeats it.

Joy is a mindset
Joy is different from happiness. Happiness is tied to circumstances that are often out of our control but joy is an attitude that we can control. It is an approach to life rather than a reaction to it.

Joy is based in the Lord
Joy comes into our lives because of our relationship with Christ.

Why should we rejoice?
Because:
We are loved by God
We are forgiven by God
We are granted eternity in Heaven with God
We are under God's providential care now and forever
God is good, life is good, and joy demonstrates our gratitude

<u>One Minute Reflection</u>
What can you intentionally rejoice in today?

"Joy is not the absence of suffering. It is the presence of God."
(Robert Schuller)

Remain

John 15:4
"Remain in me, as I also remain in you. No branch can bear fruit by itself; it must remain in the vine. Neither can you bear fruit unless you remain in me."

Remain means, "to stay in the same place or with the same person or group." The 15th chapter of John is one of the most important chapters in the entire Bible because we are introduced to one of the most meaningful analogies regarding the Christian faith. Jesus said He is the True Vine and we are the branches.

What does our passage tell us today?

Of themselves, branches are weak and useless. The branch cannot produce its own life. It must draw its life from the vine. Therefore, there are two types of branches; one is good for bearing fruit, and the other is only fit for burning.

The one that bears fruit does it because it draws its life and energy from the vine. Christ is advising us to remain with Him, just like the connected branch, so we can bear much fruit.

This is a foundational principle for living the Christian life:
-We must remain in Christ and then we will bear much fruit-

Dave Whitehead, Senior Pastor, Grace Church, writes about the experience of remaining with Christ: He says, *"This is both sobering and liberating! To experience a growing, vibrant spiritual life with Jesus is not just an intellectual exercise. Nor is it an exhausting series of good deeds. It is in remaining in the vine that our fulfillment comes."*

<u>One Minute Reflection</u>
How will you remain with Christ today?

"Outside of Christ, I am only a sinner, but in Christ, I am saved. Outside of Christ, I am empty; in Christ, I am full. Outside of Christ, I am weak; in Christ, I am strong. Outside of Christ, I cannot; in Christ, I am more than able. Outside of Christ, I have been defeated; in Christ, I am already victorious. How meaningful are the words, "in Christ."
(Watchman Nee)

Revelation

1 Corinthians 1:7
"So that you come short in no gift, eagerly waiting for the revelation of our Lord Jesus Christ."

God is a God of Revelation. He wants to reveal Himself to His creation.

Revelation means "a usually secret or surprising fact that is made known."
Can there be any better revelation than God making Himself known to us? Below are several of the ways God has revealed Himself to us in Christ.

Christ is the Eternal God
The divine nature of Christ is amply illustrated in the Bible
The Lord exclaims: *"I am the Alpha and the Omega, the first and the last, the beginning and the end."*

Christ Jesus is Messiah of Old Testament Prophecy
Jesus' lineage from David is established both legally (Matthew 1:1) and biologically (Luke 3:23) by means of the New Testament genealogical records.

Christ is The Sacrificial Lamb
He shed His blood for our sins.

Christ is the Ruler of the Universe
God has declared He is the Lord of Lords and King of Kings.

Christ Jesus is EVERYTHING we need
He provides comfort when we experience sorrow
He provides friendship when we are lonely
He provides hope in place of despair
He provides forgiveness in place of hatred
He provides answers for our dead ends
He provides peace amidst trials
He provides love now and forever

One Minute Reflection
How has God revealed Himself to you?

"Our knowledge of God is totally dependent on revelation."
(Robert Reymond)

Genesis

Genesis 3:8-9

"Then the man and his wife heard the sound of the Lord God as he was walking in the garden in the cool of the day, and they hid from the Lord God among the trees of the garden. But the Lord God called to the man, 'Where are you?'"

The first five books of the Bible are the foundation on which the whole Bible rests. Every major theme of the Bible has its beginning in Genesis, life, human life, marriage, family, language, government, purpose, destiny, disobedience, sin, separation from God, and ultimately God's plan to restore us to a right relationship with Himself.

Genesis, Exodus, Leviticus, Numbers and Deuteronomy are the books that make up the Pentateuch (two Greek words meaning five and scrolls).

The important thing to note about Genesis is that everything begins there except God because God already existed when the book opens. It is God who is the Creator and the Bible does not argue His existence - it simply declares it to be true. God is the source of everything.

We learn in Genesis the story of the human race and the history of the Hebrew race are weaved together and are the themes that still affect us today.

1) We are created by God.
2) We have all been marked by sin.
3) God takes the initiative to restore relationship with us.

Our passage today in Genesis 3 sums up these points. Directly after Adam and Eve sin, God inquires, *"Where are you?"* God is always on a relentless pursuit of us. Even when we are trying to hide in shame from Him, God seeks us out. God wants our restoration and fellowship because we were created in His image and our purpose is to glorify Him with our lives.

The entire Bible is a story of God wanting us back in right relationship with Himself.

One Minute Reflection
Do you believe that God is reaching out to you right now?

"Though our feelings come and go, God's love for us does not."
(C.S. Lewis)

Exodus - A God Who Rescues

Exodus 24:7
"Then he took the Book of the Covenant and read in the hearing of the people. And they said, 'All that the Lord has said we will do, and be obedient.'"

Today we are looking at Exodus – the second book of the Bible
The title Exodus comes from the Greek translation of the Hebrew Old Testament and means "to go out" or "departure".

Exodus - In A Nutshell
The end of the book of Genesis ends with Jacob and his family moving to the land of Egypt. But 400 years after Egypt had welcomed Israel, the Pharaoh decided to make them slaves. One Hebrew mother hides her baby in a waterproof basket near the Nile where Pharaoh's daughter eventually finds him, adopts the boy as her own and names him Moses. The rest is history.

Three themes dominate Exodus
God delivers His People (Parting of the Red Sea)
God deals with His People (The Ten Commandments)
God dwells with His People (The building of the Tabernacle)

What we learn from Exodus is that God is a Rescuer
God entered into agreement with Israel at Mount Sinai.
He rescued them from bondage, gave them laws to live by, and then He dwelt among them. As you can see from the passage of Scripture above from Exodus 24, the people had every intention of keeping their promise to obey God. They said, *"All that the Lord has said we will do, and be obedient."*
However, obeying God is often hard to do. So He devises a rescue plan, which is spelled out in the rest of the Bible. Jesus Christ is offered to save us from our own bondage to sin and lead us into the eternal Promised Land.

One Minute Reflection
Do you believe God can rescue you?

"The Lord Jesus regarded the Old Testament as a trustworthy, authoritative, unerring guide in our quest for enduring happiness. Therefore we who submit to the authority of Christ will also want to submit to the authority of the Book He esteemed so highly."
(John Piper)

Leviticus - Understanding Sacrifice

"This is the law of the sin offering: In the place where the burnt offering is killed, the sin offering shall be killed before the Lord. It is most Holy."

The Book of Leviticus helps us understand God's stance on sin and His plan to deal with it. Here we are introduced to the special regulations and sacred days that set the nation of Israel apart to exemplify "Holy living" as God's chosen people.

Israel worshiped God through offerings. There were burnt offerings, grain offerings, peace offerings, sin offerings and guilt offerings. We know that Israel had their sins forgiven through animal sacrifice. The blood of the animal "covered" Israel's sin and guilt for breaking God's law. This system removed God's anger against their sin and restored relationship between God and His people.

Why does God require sacrifice?
Because God is Holy - He cannot tolerate sin
The penalty of sin is death and blood must be shed

So what does this mean for us today?
All of the past sacrifices we learn about in Leviticus point to the one final sacrifice of Jesus Christ on the cross. Jesus Christ is the Lamb of God.

This means three significant things.
1) When we put our faith in Jesus Christ, we are forgiven eternally.
2) We can have a personal relationship with God through His son Jesus Christ.
3) God loves the world so much that He sacrificed His only begotten Son for each and every one of us.

The God that we find in Leviticus is the same God we worship today. God has offered us a way to have intimate fellowship with Him and to understand the depth of His sacrificial love.

One Minute Reflection
Do you fully understand the need for sacrifice?

"Sin and the child of God are incompatible. They may occasionally meet; they cannot live together in harmony."
(John Stott)

Numbers

<u>Numbers 20:12</u>
"Then the Lord spoke to Moses and Aaron, 'Because you did not believe Me, to hallow Me in the eyes of the children of Israel, therefore you shall not bring this assembly into the land which I have given them.'"

Today we are looking at the Book of Numbers – the fourth book of the Bible

There is an old joke that people avoid the book of Numbers because they think it has something to do with math. The book actually gets its name from original census reports and the counting of people. The truth is that Numbers traces the trip of the Israelites from Mt Sinai, where they had received God's law, to the land of Canaan. This was the very same land that God had promised to Abraham 500 years earlier.

However the story takes a dramatic turn when The Israelites refuse to enter the Promised Land because they believe it is dangerous. Not listening or trusting God costs them dearly and they have to wander for 40 more years. It is a time marked by complaining, rebellion, judgment and ultimately death.

We learn some valuable lessons from Numbers.

1) Fear and lack of trust in God results in a missed blessing. We should not let the same thing happen to us.

2) If we are in a "wilderness" time in our own life – we should seek God. He promises to bless those who seek Him and obey Him.

3) God brought Israel out of Egypt, across the Red Sea and He provided for them in the wilderness with manna from heaven. Unfortunately in the end they turned away from God and went their own way. We need to remember all the past times God has provided for us to bolster our faith in times of fear and doubt.
God will always see us through if we put Him first in our life!

<u>**One Minute Reflection**</u>
What lesson will you take from today's teaching?

"Take courage. We walk in the wilderness today and in the Promised Land tomorrow."
(D. L. Moody)

Farewell To Moses - Deuteronomy

Deuteronomy 24:4
"Then the Lord said to him, 'This is the land of which I swore to give Abraham, Isaac, and Jacob, saying, I will give it to your descendants. I have caused you to see it with your eyes, but you shall not cross over there.'"

Today we are looking at Deuteronomy- the fifth Book of the Bible. Here Moses is speaking to a younger generation of believers and he records what he wants them to know. Moses gives three distinct sermons.

Looking to the past
Moses reminds Israel that God is faithful and rescued them from the bonds of Egypt. Moses wants to impress upon this younger generation that although their parents would not enter the Promised Land, they should choose differently.

What God expects in the present
Moses reviews the laws of God and reminds the people of their responsibility to follow God joyfully and obediently.

How God handles the future
Moses reminds his followers that disobedience will bring disaster while obedience will bring blessings.

What can we learn and apply today?
Moses foreshadowed a greater leader still to come. He points the way to Christ who will set humanity free and offer all people power over sin and death. Ultimately Jesus is the way to the true Promised Land.

Remember the Old Testament is just as important as the New Testament in understanding God and His purposes. The Bible should be read in context to the whole manuscript. Every word of God has its place and significance in shaping whom we are and what we are meant to know as God's people.

One Minute Reflection
Which of the three sermons resonates with you today?

"Discouraged not by difficulties without, or the anguish of ages within, the heart listens to a secret voice that whispers: "Be not dismayed; in the future lies the Promised Land."
(Helen Keller)

Faith In God

1 Peter 1:21
"Who by Him do believe in God, that raised Him up from the dead, and gave Him glory; that your faith and hope might be in God."

We could all use more hope in our day-to-day lives. Hope is both a strong belief and the anticipation that something good is going to happen.

Since it is often difficult to remain optimistic in the face of an uncertain world, things completely out of our control and unmet expectations for our own lives; our passage today reminds us that we must rely on our faith.

We are told faith is a confidence and assurance about what we do not see.

Trusting in God will never disappoint us because all of His promises are in Christ.
And what God promises, always come to fruition.
We can never go wrong putting our hope in God.

Knowing this does three things.

(1) Faith shifts how we see ourselves.
When we live by faith and not by sight, we realize that everything here on earth is a temporary sojourn and our real inheritance is stored in Heaven.

(2) Faith changes what we value.
Hope, if biblical, makes us heavenly minded rather than earthly minded. We are more concerned with God's will, timing and ways than our own way of doing things.

(3) Faith affects what we do with our lives.
We have a greater understanding that everything is God's anyway and we have been blessed as stewards to take good care of things while we reside here on earth. Our talents, time and treasure are invested in God's kingdom and not just our own.

One Minute Reflection
On what have you fixed your hope?

"Do not look to your hope, but to Christ, the source of your hope."
(C.H. Spurgeon)

Golden Rule

<u>Matthew 7:12</u>
"Do to others whatever you would like them to do to you.
This is the essence of all that is taught in the law and the prophets."

The "Golden Rule" is the name given by Bible translators to a principle Jesus taught in His Sermon on the Mount. That is to say, the actual words "golden rule" are not found in Scripture, just as the words "Sermon on the Mount" are also not found.

Jesus has condensed the entire Old Testament into this one "golden rule" principle when He proclaims in our passage today, "This is the essence of all that is taught in the law and the prophets."

The command to love is what highlights the Christian ethic. In fact, the Bible is so radical in its command to actively love that we are told to even love our enemies.

Bernard Rimland who was an American research psychologist conducted a study on the principle of the Golden Rule. Each person involved in the study was asked to list ten people he knew best and to label them as happy or not happy. Then they were to go through the list again and label each one as selfish or unselfish.

In categorizing the results, Rimland found that all of the people labeled happy were also labeled unselfish. He wrote that those "whose activities are devoted to bringing themselves happiness are far less likely to be happy than those whose efforts are devoted to making others happy".

<u>One Minute Reflection</u>
Will you follow the Golden Rule today?

"If you contemplate the Golden Rule, it turns out to be an injunction to live by grace rather than by what you think other people deserve."
(Deepak Chopra)

God And Money

Matthew 6:24

"No one can serve two masters. Either you will hate the one and love the other, or you will be devoted to the one and despise the other. You cannot serve both God and money."

Money is usually about a lot more than dollars and cents.
For many of us money can be about:
Control, Self-Worth, Greed, Generosity
Coveting, Power, Trust, or Fear

Matthew 6:24 points out that money is in fact a "master".
And today's passage warns us that nobody can serve two masters and therefore, we are either going to serve God or we are going to serve money. The subject of money appears over 800 times in the Bible because God wants us to consider our relationship to money very seriously.

Why?
It seems money is in direct competition with God for our devotion.

Jesus spoke about money often.
He spoke of treasure and wealth a handful of times throughout Matthew, Mark, Luke and John and Jesus mentions money matters in 11 of the parables.

Why does Jesus tell us we cannot serve two masters?

Serving money means we will be consumed with it; think about it all the time; bring it up often in conversation, or fear losing it.

Serving money means that money determines what we do instead of God. It calls the shots. It controls our lives. And it becomes an idol.

Jesus desires that we serve only God. He teaches us that our dependence should be completely on Him and His promise of provision for us.

One Minute Reflection
What master are you serving - God or Money?

"A life is either all spiritual or not spiritual at all. No man can serve two masters. The end you live for shapes your life. You are made in the image of what you desire."
(Thomas Merton)

Transfiguration

<u>Matthew 17:1-3</u>
"After six days Jesus took with him Peter, James and John the brother of James, and led them up a high mountain by themselves. There He was transfigured before them. His face shone like the sun, and His clothes became as white as the light. Just then there appeared before them Moses and Elijah, talking with Jesus."

The Transfiguration of Jesus is an event reported in the New Testament in which Jesus is transfigured (or metamorphosed) and becomes radiant upon a mountain. In the accounts of three of the gospels, Jesus and three of His apostles go to a mountain (the Mount of Transfiguration). On the mountain, Jesus begins to shine with bright rays of light. Then the prophets Moses and Elijah appear next to Him and He speaks with them. Jesus is then called "Son" by a voice in the sky, assumed to be God the Father.

What is so spectacular about this event is that it is the only time that there is a visual representation of the suffering servant and the glorious messiah blended as one being.

This event is a poignant foretaste of what is to come. It not only sheds light on who Jesus is but more importantly that God will fulfill His promises. Although Jesus will have to walk the path of rejection and crucifixion, God will not fail Him. Jesus will be raised from the dead and reign supreme forever.

However what is even more enlightening is that Moses and Elijah join Jesus. They represent both the law and the prophets of the Old Testament. Significantly, Jesus claimed He came to fulfill both the law and the prophets.

What does this mean?
By fulfilling the law, Christ satisfied all its requirements in our place. In other words, Christ has taken the punishment of sin in our place, and we now live under the grace of God.

<u>One Minute Reflection</u>
What is your new insight regarding the Transfiguration?

"Jesus Christ, the condescension of divinity, and the exaltation of humanity."
(Phillips Brooks)

Justification

<u>Romans 5:1</u>
"Therefore, being justified by faith, we have peace with God, through our Lord Jesus Christ."

One of the best ways to remember the meaning of justification is "just as if you were never guilty of any sin". In other words, once we declare with our lips and believe in our hearts that Jesus Christ is Lord and we accept the forgiveness of our sins because of His work on the cross, we are freely and eternally forgiven.

Brian Schwertly, a biblical expert, explains it this way
"The doctrine of justification deals with the question of how God, who is absolutely Holy and who demands ethical perfection in His creatures, can allow men who are guilty of breaking His law into His presence and fellowship. Christ's expiatory suffering delivers the believing sinner from the punishment which the law threatens, and Christ's perfect obedience establishes for him a right to the reward which the law promises."

When a person believes in Jesus Christ, God the Father in the heavenly court declares that that person is righteous solely on the basis of Christ's full satisfaction for sin and perfect obedience to the law.

We are justified, forgiven and back in right relationship with God because of what Christ has done.

Now, it is up to us to behave as if our new identity in Christ were true.

<u>One Minute Reflection</u>
Can you now explain justification?

"Justification is an act of God's grace wherein He pardons all our sins and accepts us as righteous in His sight only for the righteousness of Christ imputed to us and received by faith alone."
(Westminster Shorter Catechism)

Propitiation

Romans 3:25
"Whom God put forward as a propitiation by His blood, to be received by faith. This was to show God's righteousness, because in His divine forbearance He had passed over former sins."

"Propitiation" is used just four times in the Bible. It is a powerful word because it sums up just how strongly God feels about sin and justice. However, more importantly, it explains how strongly God feels about the love He has for mankind.

The word "propitiation" does not occur in the Old Testament. Instead the Old Testament word is "atonement". The Old Testament pre-illustrates the truth of the New Testament. It dramatically portrays propitiation and atonement in a ritual ceremony called Yom Kippur. Described in Leviticus 16, on this most holy day, two goats were presented to the High Priest. Lots were cast for which goat would be the sacrificial offering for the sins of the people, and the other goat was let go.

Today, God still demands payment for sin. However as God pronounces judgment against us for our sin, Christ steps forward and takes the punishment in our place. He is the Yom Kippur Goat for our sins. We who have accepted Him as our propitiation are like the goat that is allowed to escape. (FYI - That is where we get the word "scapegoat")

We might not like to talk about the word "sin". However, God is so offended by sin that His response is wrath. God feels betrayed about injustice caused by sin. The closest word we have in English to describe this emotion is wrath.

Propitiation is accomplished through Jesus Christ on the cross in His crucifixion or sacrifice, which was made possible through His sinless life. He accepted and fulfilled the wrath and indignation of God. 1 John 2:2 clarifies, *"He is the propitiation for our sins, and not for ours only but also for the sins of the whole world".*

One Minute Reflection
Can you now describe what the word "propitiation" really means?

"When sin is your burden, Christ will be your delight."
(Thomas Watson)

Regeneration

"He saved us, not because of works done by us in righteousness, but according to His own mercy, by the washing of regeneration and renewal of the Holy Spirit."

Paul writes the above Scripture passage in an epistle addressed to Titus. And though we know very little about Titus, the references to him in Paul's epistles (13 times) make it clear he was one of Paul's closest and most trusted fellow-workers in the gospel.

"Regeneration" is both a long and a big word in the Bible. It is one of the distinguishing hallmarks of Christianity.

Without being spiritually regenerated you cannot be a Christian.

Jesus conveyed the idea of spiritual regeneration when He told Nicodemus that he would have to be born-again. *Jesus replied, "Very truly I tell you, no one can see the kingdom of God unless they are born again (John 3:3)* In other words Nicodemus would have to be regenerated and renewed with the Holy Spirit.

Becoming a Christian is not merely an intellectual exercise. Neither is it merely turning over a new leaf morally. The Bible teaches that regeneration (or being born again) is not the result of anything we do. It is entirely the work of the Holy Spirit gracing a spiritually dead person. "Dead" in biblical terms doesn't mean, "ceasing to exist", rather it means, "separated" from one's life source. To be spiritually dead is to be separated from God.

If we want the best possible and fullest manifestation of a relationship with God, it will come through a personal relationship with Jesus Christ and the transforming and regenerative power of the Holy Spirit working in our life. We are all in need of spiritual regeneration.

One Minute Reflection
Is the work of the Holy Spirit being manifested through you?

"Faith does not proceed from ourselves, but is the fruit of spiritual regeneration." (John Calvin)

Grace

Ephesians 2:8
"For by grace are ye saved through faith; and that not of yourselves: it is the gift of God."

Grace is a simple word but one of the most significant in the Bible. One of the best ways to remember GRACE is - *God's Riches At Christ's Expense.*

Grace is God's unmerited favor. Grace is God bestowing good on us that we do not deserve. And we do not deserve it because we are continually turning away from God in thought, word and deed. God considers this the ultimate betrayal. It is like saying to God, "I know you gave me everything, but I don't care. You are inept at running the universe! I will run the show my way".

In the Bible, grace and mercy are like two heads of the same coin. Mercy is God withholding judgment that we deserve; grace is God giving us blessing or good that we do not deserve.

Because of God's mercy, we do not receive the judgment of God against our sins; because of God's grace, we receive glorious, eternal life. Both mercy and grace come to us through the Lord Jesus Christ.

You probably have heard the hymn "Amazing Grace" written by the English poet and clergyman John Newton (1725-1807). With a message that forgiveness and redemption are possible regardless of the sins people commit and that the soul can be delivered from despair through the mercy of God, "Amazing Grace" is one of the most recognizable songs in the English-speaking world.

"Amazing Grace, how sweet the sound,
That saved a wretch like me....
I once was lost but now am found,
Was blind, but now, I see."

One Minute Reflection
Do you experience God's grace in your own life?

"A state of mind that sees God in everything is evidence of growth in grace and a thankful heart."
(Charles Finney)

Overseer Of God's Household

<u>Titus 1:5-7</u>
"Since an overseer manages God's household, he must be blameless-not overbearing, not quick-tempered, not given to drunkenness, not violent, not pursuing dishonest gain. Rather, he must be hospitable, one who loves what is good, who is self-controlled, upright, Holy and disciplined."

The Book of Titus is a tiny chapter in the New Testament that introduces us to a new young pastor who was assigned the task of encouraging the Church in Crete. Titus was a friend and associate of the Apostle Paul. When Paul was compelled to ministry elsewhere, he invited Titus to stay and encourage struggling believers to obey the commands of God.

Paul proclaims: *"Since an overseer manages God's household, he must be blameless".*
The words have profound impact for us. We also are called to be overseers that manage God's household.

How exactly can we be "blameless"?

Paul lays out five negative qualities to be avoided and then moves to six positive qualities we need to embrace in our daily life. The ultimate object of Christianity is not simply to sin less, but to please and glorify God more in everything we do.

Qualities to avoid

Arrogance, overbearing attitudes, anger, drunkenness, violence and greed for dishonest gain

Qualities to embrace

Hospitality, devotion to what is good, self-control, uprightness Holiness and discipline

Titus is an example of a young man who served God with abandon. His mission went beyond the church door. We are also inspired to take God's transformational message back to our homes, sport's fields, shopping malls, neighborhoods and the world at large.

<u>One Minute Reflection</u>
What is one lesson you can take from Titus today?

"The motto for every missionary, whether preacher, printer, or schoolmaster, ought to be 'Devoted for Life.'"
(Adoniram Judson)

Jochebed - Mother Of Moses

Exodus 2:1-3

"Now a man of the tribe of Levi married a Levite woman, and she became pregnant and gave birth to a son. When she saw that he was a fine child, she hid him for three months. But when she could hide him no longer, she got a papyrus basket for him and coated it with tar and pitch. Then she placed the child in it and put it among the reeds along the bank of the Nile."

Jochebed's appearance in the Bible is short and sweet and although we are not told much about her, one trait stands out: trust in God.

We might remember the story: The Jews had been in Egypt 400 years and Pharaoh feared they would join a foreign army against the Egyptians or start a rebellion. He ordered all male Hebrew babies to be killed. To save her child, Jochebed set her baby adrift in the Nile River, hoping someone would find him and raise him to be their own.

Amazingly, at that same time, Pharaoh's daughter was bathing in the river. One of her maidservants saw the basket and brought it to her.

When she placed little Moses in the Nile River that day, Jochebed could not have known that he would grow up to be one of God's greatest leaders, chosen to rescue the Hebrew people from slavery in Egypt. However, by letting go and trusting God, an even greater dream was fulfilled.

The lesson for us
We may also have to turn our dreams over to God.
We may have desired a happy marriage, a successful career, a special talent, or some other worthwhile goal, yet circumstances have prevented it.

Like Jochebed, we won't always foresee God's purpose as we surrender our way, but we can trust that His plan is always be better than our own.

One Minute Reflection
Can you let go and let God into your life today?

"There is more power in a mother's hand than in a king's scepter."
(Billy Sunday)

The First Stone

John 8:7
"So when they continued asking Him, He raised Himself up and said to them, 'He who is without sin among you, let him throw a stone at her first.'"

Even if we haven't read every section of the Bible, we have all probably heard the story taken from the gospel of John, chapter 8. A very moral and religious group from Jesus' day, the Pharisees, bring a woman who has committed adultery before Jesus and ask if she should be stoned for her indiscretion which was against the law of day.

What does Jesus do?
He asks the men to consider their own sins before casting stones on hers.
In fact Jesus proclaims, *"He who is without sin among you let him throw a stone at her first."*

These men, so confident a moment earlier, were immediately struck by the realization of their own sins. Their hypocrisy was exposed in their own hearts; and as the story goes, one by one, they left the scene convicted by their own conscience.

This is the lesson that Jesus so cleverly teaches all of us.
When we judge others - we judge ourselves.

The sword of judgment is double edged because an unwillingness to judge ourselves undercuts our ability and right to pronounce judgment on others.

Today
Decide to reserve judgment
Keep the focus on yourself
Find a forgiving heart for those that fail you

One Minute Reflection
Could you revisit the last person you judged?

"Forgiveness is our command. Judgment is not."
(Neil Strait)

Water, Water, Everywhere

Mark 4:37-38

"A furious squall came up, and the waves broke over the boat, so that it was nearly swamped. Jesus was in the stern, sleeping on a cushion. The disciples woke Him and said to Him, 'Teacher, don't you care if we drown?' He got up, rebuked the wind and said to the waves, 'Quiet! Be still!' Then the wind died down and it was completely calm. He said to His disciples, 'Why are you so afraid? Do you still have no faith?'"

Today we will look at Jesus' calming of the storm.

The first mention of water in Scripture is found at the beginning of the Bible in Genesis and the last mention is found at the end in Revelation. In between water flows right through the pages of Scripture with hundreds of references. This demonstrates that there is a great spiritual significance than water and that we need to pay close attention to it.

According to the passage from Mark above, one evening Jesus and His disciples were crossing the Sea of Galilee in a boat when a furious storm came up. Jesus was in the stern, sleeping soundly, but the disciples woke Him and said, *"Teacher, don't you care if we drown?"*

Jesus got up, rebuked the wind and said to the waves, *"Quiet! Be still!"* Then the wind died down and it was completely calm. Jesus said to His disciples, *"Why are you so afraid? Do you still have no faith?"*

What can we learn and apply from this story?

This story is clearly meant to display Jesus' power over nature. However, our deeper teaching illustrates that Jesus has the power to save.

1) Jesus' power doesn't just comfort us, but fights for us also. He changes our natural circumstances with supernatural power.

2) We are much like the disciples, afraid even when Jesus is in our midst.

3) Jesus calms the storms in our lives. We need to have faith in His abilities.

One Minute Reflection
Are you focused on the storm of life or the saving faith of Christ?

"Profession and possession of faith are not the same thing."
(Tom Wells)

Living Water

John 4:13-14
"Jesus answered, 'Everyone who drinks this water will be thirsty again, but whoever drinks the water I give him will never thirst. Indeed, the water I give him will become in him a spring of water welling up to eternal life.'"

In our passage today from John 4, Jesus encourages us to remember that if we drink the water He gives us we will never thirst again.

What exactly did He mean?

Many of us know this story as the Woman at the Well. While Jesus was alone, a woman came to the well for water. It was not the usual time to go for water but she came then to avoid meeting people. We read that she had lived a tough life, been married to several men and now lived with a man who was not her husband. She was ashamed and considered an outcast. Jesus asks the woman for a drink and then offered this piece of wisdom:

Jesus answered, "Everyone who drinks this water will be thirsty again, but whoever drinks the water I give him will never thirst."

A drink of water will satisfy an immediate need but not our real need, which is spiritual. The only one who can satisfy our deepest desire is Christ Himself. The water that Jesus gives, He refers to as a *"spring of water"*. It is not a static or stagnant pond. It is alive, *"a spring welling up to eternal life"*.

The water Jesus offers:
cleanses
purifies
sustains
refreshes
regenerates
and lasts forever

One Minute Reflection
Do you understand why Jesus says we will never thirst again?

"Christ is not a reservoir but a spring. His life is continual, active and ever passing on with an outflow as necessary as its inflow. If we do not perpetually draw the fresh supply from the living Fountain, we shall either grow stagnant or empty, It is, therefore, not so much a perpetual fullness as a perpetual filling." (A. B. Simpson)

Walking On Water

Matthew 14:29-31

"Then Peter got down out of the boat, walked on the water and came toward Jesus. But when he saw the wind, he was afraid and, beginning to sink, cried out, 'Lord, save me!' Immediately Jesus reached out His hand and caught him. 'You of little faith,' He said, 'why did you doubt?'"

After feeding the 5000, Jesus sends His disciples ahead of Him in a boat to cross the Sea of Galilee. Several hours later in the night, the disciples encounter a storm. Jesus comes to them, walking on the water and He invites Peter to come.

We can see from the start of our passage today, Peter gets out of the boat and begins walking on the water toward Jesus. But when Peter takes his eyes off Jesus and sees the wind and waves, he begins to sink. Peter cries out to the Lord and Jesus immediately reaches out His hand and catches Peter. It is there and then that Jesus questions Peter about his faith.

We can learn three important lessons from this encounter.

1) Peter doesn't begin to sink until he focuses on the wind and the waves. Taking our eyes off Jesus will cause us to falter.

2) Peter starts out with good intentions. HIs faith has both high points and low points. This does not mean failure. Faith for all of us is a journey. Sometimes we are strong, and other times, we let fear take the best of us. Today's verse is a great reminder that Christ is just a call away.

3) We need to get out of our own boats and learn to depend on Christ.

One Minute Reflection
How do you relate to Peter in this story?

"Doubting does not prove that a man has no faith, but only that his faith is small. And even when our faith is small, the Lord is ready to help us."
(J.C. Ryle)

Root Of All Evil

<u>1Timothy 6:10</u>
"For the love of money is a root of all kinds of evil. Some people, eager for money, have wandered from the faith and pierced themselves with many griefs."

"Money is the root of all evil" could be the most misquoted verse in the entire Bible. As you can see from the passage above the verse actually reads
"For the love of money is the root of all kinds of evil."

But what exactly is God speaking about in our verse today?

There are 1600 verses in the Bible that have to do with money or finances and there are over 500 verses that include one of the words "money," "riches," or "wealth." God is definitely concerned with man's focus on money.

Our verse comes from the book of 1 Timothy. Interestingly enough Timothy means, "one who honors God". Timothy's mission was to serve God and have intimacy with God be his highest priority and he warns his readers about loving money more than loving God.

We need to ask ourselves, what is our highest priority?

Money is not, as it turns out, juxtaposed to spirituality. It is rather an instrument that expresses our spiritual selves because we become what we serve and love.

If we love money, our life will become about possessions, wealth, power, and seeking treasures for ourselves. If we love God, our life will be about becoming an ambassador of Christ and using our money to help others and enlighten them to the Glory of God. Our God has described Himself as a jealous God. He does not want to compete with earthly riches for first place in our life.

<u>One Minute Reflection</u>
Is your money is a testament to what you love?

"If a person gets his attitude toward money straight, it will help straighten out almost every other area in his life."
(Billy Graham)

Rejoice In Suffering

<u>1 Peter 1:6-7</u>
*"In all this you greatly rejoice, though now for a little while you may have
had to suffer grief in all kinds of trials. These have come so that the proven
genuineness of your faith-of greater worth than gold, which perishes even
though refined by fire-may result in praise, glory and honor when Jesus
Christ is revealed."*

The passage above is possibly the most important verses of Scripture in
the entire Bible if we want to understand suffering.

God is not interested in our circumstances, as much as He is interested
in the condition of our soul. When tragedy befalls us, we question why.
Why is this so hard?
Why am I facing this trial?
Why isn't God stopping this from happening?
Why is a loving God allowing this to happen?

The answer lies in the passage above from 1 Peter, which says:
*"These have come so that the proven genuineness of your faith-of greater
worth than gold, which perishes even though refined by fire-may result in
praise, glory and honor when Jesus Christ is revealed."*

God ultimately wants relationship with us. We need refining so that the
genuineness of our faith can be perfected. One of the most effective
ways to get us on our knees and into God's presence is through allowed
suffering. Through pain and trials we begin to yield to God's call, God's
ways and God's refinement. God always has a better plan in mind but He
needs us to cooperate.

And this is why we can rejoice in suffering.
As painful as it may be, trials always lead to a deeper understanding of
God's glory and a more profound revelation of Jesus Christ suffering and
resurrection.

<u>One Minute Reflection</u>
Do you see how suffering can lead you closer to God's glory?

"We always say 'make us partakers of your suffering' but when trials
come how quickly we forget to share this moment with Christ. We
forget it is an opportunity to do something beautiful for Christ."
(Mother Teresa)

Good Works

<u>Ephesians 2:8-9</u>
"For it is by grace you have been saved, through faith-and this is not from yourselves, it is the gift of God- not by works, so that no one can boast. For we are God's handiwork, created in Christ Jesus to do good works, which God prepared in advance for us to do."

One of the most widely misunderstood concepts of Christianity has to do with "good works".

Many people believe if we can just be good enough, kind enough, work in enough soup kitchens, say enough prayers, and do enough good deeds that they will be saved and gain eternal life.

However that reasoning is really the opposite of the Christian message. Our passage from Ephesians above carefully explains that *"it is by grace that we have been saved, through faith, and this is not from yourselves, it is a gift of God - not by works."*

In other words, being "saved" is not about doing enough good works to motivate God to love us because it never starts with us. Instead it all begins with God. God loves us first, and we accept by faith His generous gift of grace. Then as a response to His incredible and overwhelming love we offer good works in return.

The distinction is critical.

Our passage advises that *"no one can boast"* about our standing for we are God's handiwork. He has a plan for us that began before the creation of the world.

All we need to do is surrender our will to God, accept Christ as the Lord and Savior of our life, and then yield daily as we continue to conform to the likeness of Christ.

<u>One Minute Reflection</u>
Do you have a new understanding of good works?

"Good works do not make a good man,
but a good man does good works."
(Martin Luther)

Serving Each Other

Ephesians 4:11-13
"And He Himself gave some to be apostles, some prophets, some evangelists, and some pastors and teachers, for the equipping of the saints for the work of ministry, for the edifying of the body of Christ, till we all come to the unity of the faith and of the knowledge of the Son of God, to a perfect man, to the measure of the stature of the fullness of Christ."

Christians who discover their "calling" have a clearer, more focused understanding of God's will for their life. They also feel more energized, more productive and more connected to their spiritual selves.

Learning about spiritual gifts is both a spiritual and vocational issue. The Latin root of the word vocation is "vocare" meaning to "call".

The explanation of spiritual gifts is spelled out in the passage from Ephesians above:

Spiritual Gifts Are
for equipping saints for the work of ministry
for edifying the body of Christ
for building the unity of the faith
for deepening the knowledge of the Son of God
for attaining the full measure of Christ

The ultimate purpose of spiritual gifts is so that we can serve each other.

One Minute Reflection
Do you know which spiritual gift you have been given?

"In the New Testament, we don't find our gift through self-examination and introspection and then find ways to express it. Instead, we love one another, serve one another, help one another, and in so doing we see how God has equipped us to do so."
(Russell Moore)

Daniel In The Lions' Den

<u>Daniel 6:16</u>
"So the king gave the order, and they brought Daniel and threw him into the lions' den. The king said to Daniel, 'May your God, whom you serve continually, rescue you!'"

We find the story of Daniel in the Old Testament.
In 605 B.C., the Babylonians conquered Israel, taking many of its promising young men into captivity in Babylon. One of those men was Daniel.

When the lions' den event occurred, Daniel was in his 80s. Through a life of hard work and obedience to God, he had risen through the political ranks as an administrator. In fact, Daniel was so honest and hardworking that the other government officials wanted to remove him from office out of jealousy. They use Daniel's faith in God against him and ultimately he was thrown into a den of lions. We know from our passage today that the King mocked God's ability to save Daniel but Daniel is quoted as saying, *"My God sent His angel, and He shut the mouths of the lions. They have not hurt me, because I was found innocent in His sight".*

What lessons can we learn?

Grow in Faith
Daniel had spent almost 80 years of his life knowing God. He set aside regular times daily to spend with God in prayer. Daniel cultivated his relationship with God his entire lifetime so that when the ultimate test of his life came; his faith in God was complete.

Mature in Faith
Even though Daniel was an old man, he refused to abandon God. Even the threat of being eaten alive by lions did not change his trust in Him.

There may be times in our life when people try to get us to turn away from God. We can take encouragement from the story of Daniel and trust God for every circumstance of daily life.

<u>One Minute Reflection</u>
How does the life of Daniel inspire you today?

"Faith is to believe what you do not see;
The reward of this faith is to see what you believe."
(Saint Augustine)

Know God, Love God, Obey God

<u>Psalm 91:14</u>
"The LORD says, 'I will rescue those who love me. I will protect those who trust in my name'."

Today we are examining three powerful ways to connect ourselves to God.

1) Know God
We must read Scripture and meditate on His words.
We should take out our Bible, go to our favorite chapter and see what God has to tell us there. We can get into the habit of going deep into God's Word.

2) Love God
We can spend time in prayer, worship and praise.
We can declare our love of God to others. God desires a cheerleader.

3) Obey God
We should follow the prompting of the Holy Spirit. He might be inviting us to forgive someone who has betrayed us, reach out to an unloved person, admit we were wrong, or feed or clothe a homeless person.

Spend a moment rereading Psalm 91:14.
Recite it out loud and allow the words to take shape in your heart. Remember that God promises that He will rescue those that love Him and protect those that call on His name.

<u>One Minute Reflection</u>
How will you connect with God today?

"A thorough knowledge of the Bible is
worth more than a college education."
(Theodore Roosevelt)

The Words Of Jesus

<u>John 8:36</u>
"So if the Son sets you free, you will be free indeed."

Nothing compares to the pure, undiluted, powerful words of Jesus Christ. After all, He claimed to be the embodiment of all truth when He said, *"I am the way, the truth and the life."* Jesus claimed He, Himself, had come from God and that His mission was to reveal who God was and what God wanted.

The most important thing for us to remember here is that Christ invites us into a relationship with Him. He does not coerce us. The promises that Christ makes are only to those who accept His invitation and to those that abide in His Word.

Jesus is telling us that if He sets us free, we are free indeed

Through Jesus, these are the promises we can count on:
God will love us.
God the Father, Jesus the son, The Holy Spirit will be with us always.
We will receive a level of lasting joy we cannot attain on our own.
We will see miracles that others can't understand or explain.
We will avoid God's judgment.
We will be offered eternal life.
We will understand deep truths that will ultimately set us free.

The words of Christ have changed millions of lives - one life at a time. We can be transformed by the words of Christ as well today.

<u>One Minute Reflection</u>
Will you accept Jesus' declaration of freedom?

"A rule I have had for years is: to treat the Lord Jesus Christ as a personal friend. His is not a creed, a mere doctrine, but it is He Himself we have."
(Dwight L. Moody)

Pursuit Of Excellence

<u>Philippians 4:8</u>
"Finally, brothers and sisters, whatever is true, whatever is noble, whatever is right, whatever is pure, whatever is lovely, whatever is admirable-if anything is excellent or praiseworthy-think about such things."

We can set our minds on many things.
However, modern culture offers many distractions to fill our heads that are not always of a worthwhile endeavor. Video games, instant messaging, computer apps, smart phone access and reality based television are taking up too much of our precious time.

Our passage from Philippians reminds us to think on things that are excellent and praiseworthy as an intentional pursuit of admirable Christian living.

We live in a world that honors excellence.
But the world's view of excellence and God's view of excellence differ greatly.

The Greek Word translated "excellent" in the New Testament comes from "diapheor", which literally means "better thing" or the "highest and the best".

So biblically speaking, the pursuit of excellence refers to doing the best we can with the gifts and abilities God gives us, committing everything back to the glory of God. And ideally, it is done without the spirit of competition or seeking to excel simply to be better than others.

God is urging us to think about things that are noble, right, pure and lovely. We must be mindful of pursuing excellence in all of these things if we want to grow in Christian character and emulate Christ. We can also model for our children, spouses and friends that what we choose to think about matters!

<u>One Minute Reflection</u>
How much thinking do you devote to praiseworthy things?

"As the excellence of steel is strength, and the excellence of art is beauty, so the excellence of mankind is moral character."
(A. W. Tozer)

Heaven

John 14:1-3
"Do not let your hearts be troubled. You believe in God; believe also in me. My Father's house has many rooms; if that were not so, would I have told you that I am going there to prepare a place for you? And if I go and prepare a place for you, I will come back and take you to be with me that you also may be where I am."

When someone we love dies, it is a troubling time. We are not only grieving their loss but we are trying to come to terms with our own mortality. We want a clear picture of where exactly we are going when we go to Heaven.

Gratefully, we can get the answers we seek in our passage from John 14. Here, Jesus is comforting His own disciples about His impending death and resurrection. He wants them to understand there is nothing to fear.

We can take great comfort in what Jesus says.
He explains that Heaven is His Father's House – an actual place that is a home lovingly built and lavishly decorated with many rooms. He tells us that He has gone before us to prepare that specific place just for us, perfectly suited so we will be welcome upon our arrival.

Best of all Jesus reminds us that just as He goes ahead and prepares that place for us, He is also going to come back and take us to be with Him.

We will not be alone on the journey of death. Jesus is there every step of the way, loving us, guiding us and welcoming us into our eternal home in Heaven.

One Minute Reflection
Do Jesus' words help you be less troubled by death?

"Are you ready to go at once straight into Heaven, if the gates were thrown open? What manner of persons ought we to be to say it! Are we walking in a way perfectly consistent with stepping tonight at once into the glory, to be at home in the Father's house?"
(G.V. Wigram)

Divine Nature Of Sacraments

Matthew 26:26-27
"While they were eating, Jesus took bread, and when He had given thanks, He broke it and gave it to His disciples, saying, 'Take and eat; this is my body.' Then He took a cup, and when He had given thanks, He gave it to them, saying, 'Drink from it, all of you. This is my blood of the covenant, which is poured out for many for the forgiveness of sins.'"

So much of our spiritual and Christian life is of a solitary endeavor.
We pray, we study, and we meditate on Scripture.
But when we go to church, we participate in the body of Christ.
Nowhere is that more evident than in the communal nature of sacraments. St. Augustine defined a sacrament as "a visible sign of invisible grace."

Some of the most important sacraments are
Baptism
Confirmation
Reconciliation
Anointing of the sick
Matrimony
Holy Orders
Holy Communion

Every time we celebrate one of these - Christ offers Himself to us so that we might turn and offer ourselves back to Him.
It is during these sacraments that Jesus comes into the center of our lives.

Next time we participate in a sacrament, we can revel at the beauty, mystery and divine nature that God ordained in each of these prophetic symbols of His covenant. It is during these that we can make ourselves fully available to Christ.

One Minute Reflection
Which Sacrament means the most to you and why?

"Wherever we find the Word of God surely preached and heard, and the sacraments administered according to the institution of Christ, there, it is not to be doubted, is a church of God."
(John Calvin)

The Devil May Care

Peter 5:8
"Be alert and of sober mind. Your enemy the devil prowls around like a roaring lion looking for someone to devour."

It is easy to ridicule the existence of the devil. However, Jesus Himself was very clear that the devil exists, so we dare not feign ignorance or be unaware of his schemes and agenda.

The temptation of Christ is detailed in the Gospels of Matthew, Mark, and Luke. According to these texts, after being baptized, Jesus fasted for forty days and nights in the desert. During this time, the devil appeared to Jesus and tempted Him. Jesus refused each temptation, until the devil departed and angels came and brought nourishment. Just as the devil tempted Jesus, he can tempt us.

Satan is a serpent, and as such, he is not only deadly, but often is so well camouflaged we do not see him.

Satan always attacks the mind. That's his battlefield.

As we are told in the Scripture above, *"the devil prowls around like a roaring lion looking for something to devour"*.

Satan assaults our emotions and our minds. Temptation and discouragement are his greatest weapons. He used that same deceit to get Eve to doubt God's word.

How do we protect ourselves from the devil?

1) Surrender our life to God and walk in obedience to Him daily.

2) Be in the Word. The word of God is *"living and active, sharper than any two edged sword"*.

3) Invite God to protect us in any given situation.

One Minute Reflection
How seriously do you take the devil?

"I believe Satan to exist for two reasons: first, the Bible says so; and second, I've done business with him."
(D.L. Moody)

A Land Of Milk And Honey

Deuteronomy 6:2-3
"So that you may enjoy long life. Hear, Israel, and be careful to obey so that it may go well with you and that you may increase greatly in a land flowing with milk and honey."

Does God want us to truly enjoy this life?

The simple answer is yes.
This is well described in our passage today from the Old Testament as *"a land flowing with milk and honey".* However this promise of abundance has always been conditional upon obedience to the Lord Himself.

Our passage today proclaims: *"So that you may enjoy a long life, hear, Israel, and be careful to obey so that it may go well with you."*

"Milk and honey" originates in the Hebrew Bible in God's description of the country lying between the Mediterranean Sea and the Jordan River, namely, Canaan.
And it describes the best God has to offer:

As Jonathon Cohen explains:
"The biblical image of a perfect land so fertile its green hills flow with honey dripping from its hives, like liquid gold in the sunlight. A spacious land covered with pink hawthorn, red cyclamen, and white rockrose. There are the flowers of its myriad wild fruits, and the warm valley air smelling of their nectar. And gushing - somehow - from the land itself, there are springs of pure milk white as snow, and bright streams of it flowing through the hills, as if the milk of an eternally vibrant earth mother in her fruitful cycle of multiplication."

It is, according to the Bible, a paradise whose people would lack nothing. It is clear that the message is the same for us today. We can enjoy our life - but we must put God first, obeying His commands and giving Him the credit for every good thing.

One Minute Reflection
What do you need to hear from God and then obey?

"If God has given you the world's goods in abundance, it is to help you gain those of Heaven and to be a good example of sound teaching to your sons, servants, and relatives."
(Saint Ignatius)

A Narrow Gate

Matthew 7:13-14
"Enter through the narrow gate; for the gate is wide and the way is broad that leads to destruction, and there are many who enter through it. For the gate is small and the way is narrow that leads to life, and there are few who find it."

One of the most profound things you will notice if you read and study the teachings of Jesus Christ is that there is no comfortable middle ground. You and I are asked, and in fact, challenged to make a decision.

In our passage today from Matthew 7, Jesus is ending The Sermon On The Mount with a call to allegiance to Him and His Kingdom.

We are offered two different gates.

One gate is wide and we are warned it will lead to destruction.
The broad way is easy to find. In fact, unless you make a conscious choice to avoid it, you'll find yourself on it because it is what the world offers us and the entrances to the broad way are many and quite enticing.

The other gate is narrow and we are told to enter through it.
There is no room for ego, pride, clever dodging, human reasoning, or past baggage. However Jesus promises that this is the way that leads to life (peace, joy, abundance here on earth and eternal life in Heaven). Jesus tells us that very few find it.

What is this narrow gate and how do we enter it.
Christ is the gate. This is not about religion; it is about relationship with God, Himself. We are not meant to simply admire the teachings of Christ but challenged to make a choice about obeying them.

One Minute Reflection
Which gate will you choose?

"We must allow the Word of God to confront us, to disturb our security, to undermine our complacency and to overthrow our patterns of thought and behavior."
(John Stott)

Christ Has Overcome The World

"These things I have spoken to you, that in Me you may have peace. In the world you will have tribulation; but take heart, I have overcome the world."

What would Christ say about the world today?
The chaos, the unexpected tragedy, the school shootings, unprecedented climate change, hundreds of thousands of deaths due to starvation and political unrest, 9/11, Super Storm Sandy, Boston Marathon Bombing, massive crime, war and upheaval around the globe?

Jesus tells us in our Scripture passage from John 16.
"In the world you will have tribulation, but be of good cheer, I have overcome the world."

Jesus spoke these words originally to His disciples, as He knew they would be scattered after His arrest. He told them to have courage because although they would face terrible and inevitable struggles, they would not be alone. Christ would be with them even when they faced evil head on. He told them to take heart because the battle had already been won.

We can take Christ's words to heart today as well.
Thanks to the Bible, we know the end of the story.
The world is filled with tribulation, but Christ has overcome the world.

One Minute Reflection
How do Jesus' words give you courage to face today?

"The next time you find yourself alone in a dark alley facing the undeniables of life, don't cover them with a blanket, or ignore them with a nervous grin. Don't turn up the TV and pretend they aren't there. Instead, stand still, whisper His name, and listen. He is nearer than you think."
(Max Lucado)

Like A Thief In The Night

Matthew 24:42-44

"Therefore keep watch, because you do not know on what day your Lord will come. But understand this: If the owner of the house had known at what time of night the thief was coming, he would have kept watch and would not have let his house be broken into. So you also must be ready, because the Son of Man will come at an hour when you do not expect him."

We learn in the Bible is that there are certain events that will happen but that we will not be told the time or date they take place.

One of those events is mentioned in Matthew 24.
Jesus Himself makes an assertion about His second coming. He tells us to be watchful because He will come like a thief in the night. In fact He tells us *"the Son of Man will come at an hour when you do not expect Him"*. If we are not prepared, things will not go well for us. Jesus warns us to be ready; and He compares that preparation to the man who would have kept watch and would not have let his house been broken into.

How do we prepare for Christ's return?

Put a priority on heavenly matters

Create an urgency to work on becoming the person
that Christ has called us to be

Get our own "house" in order.

We can do so by repairing broken relationships, spending time understanding God's will for our life, and offering forgiveness and love to those in need

One Minute Reflection
If Christ returned tonight would you be prepared?

"Amid the thousands of shrill voices screaming for our attention, there is but one Voice we need to hear. The voice of the Lord Jesus Christ."
(David Jeremiah)

The Greatest

Matthew 18:4
"At that time the disciples came to Jesus, saying, 'Who then is greatest in the kingdom of Heaven?' Then Jesus called a little child to Him, set him in the midst of them, and said, 'Assuredly, I say to you, unless you are converted and become as little children, you will by no means enter the kingdom of Heaven. Therefore whoever humbles himself as this little child is the greatest in the kingdom of heaven.'"

Today we are looking at the question of who is the greatest in the kingdom of Heaven. As a matter of fact Jesus' own disciples ask Him this question at the start of our passage today in Matthew 18.

Jesus answers:
"Whoever humbles himself as this little child is the greatest in the Kingdom of Heaven."
Most of us want to be great at something but usually being humble has nothing to do with it. We might want to be the best at parenting, athletics, academics, a career, homemaking, decorating, cooking, finance, gardening or even a life of faith. However, in today's world to be the greatest we often have to boast, push, brag, connive, outsmart, outmaneuver and outwit everybody else to get ahead.

Jesus turns our secular values on their head.
He tells us the greatness He values is not found in working harder to get ahead. Instead, Jesus illustrates greatness as it is demonstrated in the humble nature of a child. In the same way, we need to express and offer our lives in a spirit of deference to God.

In what ways can we take on this mindset?
We acknowledge that we have nothing to offer Jesus but our sin and need for salvation. We recognize our complete inability to save ourselves and yield to His wisdom and strength to accomplish all things.

<u>One Minute Reflection</u>
In what way can you humble yourself like a little child?

"The problem with those who are not humble is that they spend much of their lives hunting wealth, possessions and qualifications for their own sake, hoping it will give them the status and self-esteem they crave. However God has already given them the highest status in the world - children of the living God."
(S.D. Gordon)

Too Busy For God

<u>Luke 10:38-40</u>

"As Jesus and His disciples were on their way, He came to a village where a woman named Martha opened her home to Him. She had a sister called Mary, who sat at the Lord's feet listening to what He said. But Martha was distracted by all the preparations that had to be made. She came to Him and asked, 'Lord, don't you care that my sister has left me to do the work by myself? Tell her to help me!'"

Today we are looking at the life of Martha.
Martha of Bethany is one of the most memorable characters in Scripture, and we can learn valuable lessons from studying her life.

The story from Luke above begins when Jesus is visiting the home of Martha and her sister Mary. Martha has many things to do in anticipation of Jesus' visit. Who can blame her? She wants her home just right for this important visit. She is the perfect hostess, cook, cleaner, and table setter, as she prepares to welcome the Lord.

Martha is very, very busy. She is distracted with the details but also overly concerned that her sister is not helping her. She asks Jesus why He does not seem to care.

And here is the paradox for all of us. We can make ourselves crazy, worried about everything being perfectly in its place, but then miss the most important thing this life has to offer. God is not interested in the circumstances of our lives being neat and tidy, all wrapped up with a pretty bow, He is interested in the condition of our souls.

How to calm our Martha tendencies?

1) Realize God wants our companionship more than our perfection.
2) Surrender every burden over to Jesus
3) Take a day off from a perfected routine - spend time with God instead.

<u>One Minute Reflection</u>
In what ways are you like Martha??

"It is not enough to be busy. So are the ants.
The question is: What are we busy about?"
(Henry David Thoreau)

Extravagant Intimacy

Luke 10:41 -42
"Martha, Martha," the Lord answered 'you are worried and upset about many things, but few things are needed-or indeed only one. Mary has chosen what is better, and it will not be taken away from her.'"

Today we are looking at the life of Mary of Bethany.

And as we read the passage above from Luke 10, we discover that while Jesus visits the home of two sisters, they each react quite differently to His presence. Martha was completely preoccupied with making everything perfect, while Mary simply sat at Jesus' feet.

Jesus says: *"Martha, Martha, you are worried and upset about many things, but few things are needed - or indeed only one. Mary has chosen what is better."*

What can we learn from this encounter?
Only one thing is needed.

Mary is sitting at the feet of Jesus absorbing every profound word He utters. Her sole focus is on Him; learning from Him; studying Him and loving Him.

This is the challenge for us as well.
How do we find real, intimate time for Jesus?
Over 70% of us now work outside the home. We have errands to run, children to raise, households to organize. We need time for our marriages, friendships, aging parents and neighbors in need.

However we must decide that Jesus is our # 1 priority.

Let us all learn to choose *"what is better"* and know that Jesus Himself promised that it will not be taken away from us.

One Minute Reflection
It what ways can you emulate Mary's attitude toward Jesus?

"To fall in love with God is the greatest of all romances; To seek Him, the greatest adventure; To find Him, the greatest human achievement."
(Augustine)

Reconciliation

2 Corinthians 5:18-19
"All this is from God, who through Christ reconciled us to Himself and gave us the ministry of reconciliation; that is, in Christ God was reconciling the world to Himself, not counting their trespasses against them, and entrusting to us the message of reconciliation."

Today we are looking at why Christ voluntarily went to the cross.
The answer is about reconciliation with God.

Since God is Holy, sin separates us from Him and makes us His enemies, whether we feel we are or not. Jesus came to bind us back together with God. Christ came to earth as Deity clothed in human flesh, and He paid the penalty for our sins by dying in our place...because the penalty of sin is death.
This is God's system of atonement.

John Stott explains it this way in his book The Cross of Christ, "God took His own loving initiative to appease His own righteous anger by bearing it His own self in His own Son when He took our place and died for us. There is no crudity here to evoke our ridicule, only the profundity of Holy love to evoke our worship".

God created a rescue plan to put us back in right relationship with Himself. He acted out of pure love.
For God is love.

Reconciliation is initiated by God and mediated through Christ.
We are forgiven because of what Christ did on the cross, now we have to learn to act reconciled and forgiven in our day-to-day life.

One Minute Reflection
Do you feel reconciled to God and therefore your fellow man?

"The number one problem in our world is alienation, rich versus poor, black versus white, labor versus management, conservative versus liberal, East versus West.. But Christ came to bring about reconciliation and peace."
(Billy Graham)

Why Do We Need A Savior?

John 4:10
*"This is love: not that we loved God, but that He loved us and
sent His Son as an atoning sacrifice for our sins."*

In John 4:10 we are reminded that God loved us so much that He sent
His son as an atoning sacrifice for our sins. But the question we are
reviewing today is why do we really need a Savior?

We need a Savior for our past
Sin is our greatest problem and it is universal to the entire world.
All of us sin every day in thought, word or deed.
The result of that sin is worry, regret, anger, addictions, guilt, insecurity,
resentments, broken relationships, wars, crime, and unforgiving hearts.
We can't save ourselves so we need a Savior to take care of our past sins.

We need a Savior for our present
Jesus sets the example on how to live now. Our job is to conform to the
likeness of Christ as He invites us to follow Him. However, what is even
more exciting is that when we place our faith in Him, He sends His Holy
Spirit to live and dwell in our hearts. This enables us to do things now
that we could not do by our own strength before.

We need a Savior for the future
Jesus offers us eternal life and a place with Him in Heaven.
Romans 6:23 says, *"For the wages of sin is death, but the gift of God is
eternal life in Christ Jesus our Lord."*

Jesus handles our past sins, enables our present life with the Holy Spirit
and offers us a future that is eternally secure in Heaven.

<u>One Minute Reflection</u>
Do you need a Savior?

"Jesus is the only Savior, but not everybody who is saved by Him is
aware that He is the one doing the saving."
(Tony Campolo)

Defining Prayer

<u>Matthew 6:7-13</u>
"And when you pray, do not keep on babbling like pagans, for they think they will be heard because of their many words. Do not be like them, for your Father knows what you need before you ask Him. This, then, is how you should pray: 'Our Father in heaven, hallowed be Your name.'"

What is Prayer?

Prayer is primarily communion with God. It is the interaction of the human mind, heart, and soul with God, not only in contemplation or meditation, but also in direct address to Him. Prayer may be oral or mental, occasional or constant, formal or informal. It is the place where we find common ground with God.

Some Reasons to Pray

To spend time with God and enjoy His companionship
To access the will of God to find the purpose of our lives
To give thanks and demonstrate respect and devotion
To ask for help, express concerns or seek forgiveness

Where is the Lord's Prayer found in the Bible?

Matthew chapter 6, verses 9 - 13
Luke chapter 11, verses 1 - 4

What can we learn by studying The Lord's Prayer?

If you read the passage above from Matthew 6, Jesus gives us some important insight into prayer in general and why, more specifically, the Lord's Prayer is so important. He tells us not to babble on with many words because it will not be meaningful or impressive. God knows what we need before we ask. Jesus then goes on to give us what we now refer to as the Lord's Prayer. There are only 57 words in this prayer and all of them are significant.

<u>One Minute Reflection</u>
Have you contemplated all the words in the Lord's prayer?

"The Lord's Prayer, which is so familiar to all of us, is much more than a liturgy to recite or even pattern to copy. It gives us a profoundly satisfying philosophy in which the essentials of the Christian faith and the Christian life are clearly set forth."
(John Stott)

Lord's Prayer

Matthew 6:9-15
"Our Father, who art in heaven, hallowed be thy name; thy kingdom come; thy will be done on earth as it is in Heaven. Give us this day our daily bread; and forgive us our trespasses as we forgive those who trespass against us; and lead us not into temptation, but deliver us from evil. For the kingdom, the power, and the glory are yours now and forever. Amen."

The most important prayer in the Bible is, of course, The Lord's Prayer. Jesus Christ gave this prayer to the world, as an example of what genuine Christian prayer should be like.

We have all probably said the Lord's Prayer thousands of times at church, the dinner table, weddings and funerals.
The Lord's Prayer is found in two Gospels

Luke: 11:1
One day Jesus was praying in a certain place.
When He finished, one of His disciples said to Him, "Lord, teach us to pray, just as John taught his disciples."

Matthew 6:7-9
"And when you pray, do not keep on babbling like pagans, for they think they will be heard because of their many words. Do not be like them, for your Father knows what you need before you ask Him. This, then, is how you should pray:"

The Lord's Prayer is hugely significant because every single line of it challenges our assumptions about who we are, who God is and what the world should be like.

One Minute Reflection
What is one new insight you can take away from this prayer today?

"We start with an invitation into the Father's presence and then the prayer makes three petitions about God and His glory followed by three petitions about ourselves. The order is significant. God our heavenly father, His name hallowed, His kingdom extended, His will done. Our needs supplied, our sins forgiven and our temptations overcome...what a prayer and all in 57 words."
(John Stott)

Our Father

Matthew 6:9
"Our Father in Heaven, hallowed be Thy name."

Jesus Christ gave the Lord's Prayer to the world, as an example of what genuine Christian prayer should be like.

Today we are looking at the first line of the Lord's Prayer. The fundamental difference between various kinds of prayer is the different images of God that lies behind them. We often ask of God what we believe He is capable of providing. Jesus called Him, Father, who resides in Heaven and whose name is to be hallowed.

"Our Father"
"Our" father connotes that God is the father to the whole world not just for us alone. We are meant to approach God as a child approaches a father; with respect, love and a certain trust that He will provide and protect. Jesus is also telling us that although God created the entire universe, He desires to have an intimate, personal relationship with us as a father does to a child.

"In Heaven"
God resides in a place called Heaven, which is a spiritual realm. When God created the earth, He spoke it out of this spiritual realm called Heaven and He manifested the world into the physical realm called earth. Everything that was created in this earthly realm came from Heaven. God resides in Heaven and when we put our trust in Christ, we are guaranteed a place there with Him.

"Hallowed be thy name"
Jesus is reminding us that God is sovereign, majestic and omnipotent. His name is meant to be "hallowed" meaning "regarded as Holy; venerated; and sacred."
This is why taking the Lord's name in vain is such an offense. God is Holy, set apart and He deserves our deepest respect.

<u>One Minute Reflection</u>
Do you respect God's name?

"We must begin our prayers with praising God, and it is very fit He should be first served, and that we should give glory to God, before we expect to receive mercy and grace from Him."
(Matthew Henry)

Thy Kingdom Come

Matthew 6:10
"Thy kingdom come, Thy will be done, on earth, as it is in Heaven."

We are examining the second line of The Lord's Prayer where Jesus mentions a kingdom. What does He mean?

"Thy Kingdom Come"
Jesus said, *"My kingdom is not of this world"* (John 18:36) Jesus is talking about a radical, new way of living that you and I can be part of. It is a place where things operate differently than the world's way of doing things. He said *"the last will be first"*, *"the first will be last"*, "the poor will be blessed", *"sinners are forgiven"*, *"the self-righteous are chastised"* and *"the lost will be found"*. Moreover, He commanded us to love our enemies and turn the other cheek.

When we say *"thy kingdom come"* in the Lord's Prayer, we are not making a request, instead we are declaring a vow pledging God's kingdom to be established through us.

"Thy Will Be Done "
Once we have established God's Kingdom, then we need to submit to the will of God. It is the "king" of the kingdom to whom we give allegiance. God's kingdom is not a democracy where the will of the people reign. It is about following Christ and obeying His will in our marriage, family, career, ministry, money, body, thoughts, words, and conduct.

"On Earth As it is In Heaven"
This line is a reference to the fact that God is in charge in Heaven and He also wants to be in charge on earth; not by force but by invitation and devotion. God longs for restored fellowship with the men and women He created in His very own image. He wants us to follow His lead not because we have to but because it leads to the most prosperous outcome for our lives.

One Minute Reflection
What is your definition of God's kingdom?

"There are two kinds of people: those who say to God,
"Thy will be done," and those to whom God says,
"All right, then, have it your way."
(C.S. Lewis)

Our Daily Bread

Matthew 6:11-12
*"Give us this day our daily bread.
And forgive us our debts, as we forgive our debtors."*

"Give us this day, our daily bread"

Here Jesus is asking us to recognize that we are in need of daily sustenance and our very existence is dependent on Him. Jesus said, *"I am the bread of life".* The definition of bread used here consists of both the needs of body and the soul. When we ask God to *"give us this day our daily bread"* we are requesting that God provide bread for our physical hunger and bread for spiritual poverty as well.

"Forgive us our debts, as we forgive our debtors"

There are two distinct elements in this statement regarding forgiveness. First, we are asking for God's forgiveness. Second, we are asking for forgiveness in relation to how we in turn are forgiving those who are indebted to us.

The word "as" is a very significant word. Translated from the Greek word it means "in proportion to". We desire God to forgive us, but we must also be willing to forgive others by the same measure. This ultimately demonstrates that we love and honor God more than we hate the offense of another.

We all have daily needs, but first and foremost we need forgiveness so we can be back in right relationship with God, our Creator.

<u>One Minute Reflection</u>
What do you need for your daily bread?

"Grace is available for each of us every day - our spiritual daily bread - but we've got to remember to ask for it with a grateful heart and not worry about whether there will be enough for tomorrow."
(Sarah Ban Breathnach)

Deliver Us

Matthew 6:13
"And lead us not into temptation, but deliver us from the evil one".

Today we finish with the last line of the Lord's Prayer.

"Lead us not into temptation"
Temptation is everywhere but we don't have to allow it to take root in our lives. Most temptation starts with a suggestion, however we need to cut it out before it descends from our minds into our hearts. Temptation is not by itself sinful. It becomes sin when we allow the temptation to become action, even in our minds.

What are we tempted by?
It could be pride, greed, popularity, lust, arrogance, drugs, money, fame, gossip, cheating, lying, coveting...just to name a few. Some are sins of the mind such as envy and some of them are sins of action such as murder. In this petition we are asking God to lead us away from all of those temptations.

"But deliver us from the evil one"
Satan himself is a master of suggestion and temptation. Genesis 3:1 reminds us, *"Now the serpent was more cunning than any beast of the field which the LORD God had made".* Evil exists as a real force in the universe. However The Lord's Prayer points to God's ability to be victorious to deliver us from that evil. God has the final authority on every matter and He will provide ultimate protection.

"For thine is the kingdom, and the power, and the glory forever."
We often end the Lord's Prayer with this line, which is not found in original Scripture because it was a later addition. None of the earliest biblical manuscripts have this closing refrain. But it does remind us once again of God's kingdom, God's power and God's Glory which reigns forever.

"Amen"
When we say "amen" we are not just closing the prayer, instead we are agreeing with what we just recited and claiming it to be true.

One Minute Reflection
What temptation can God help you overcome?

"For prayer is nothing else than being on terms of friendship with God."
(Saint Teresa of Avila)

Approval Rating

<u>Galatians 1:10</u>
"Am I now trying to win the approval of human beings, or of God? Or am I trying to please people? If I were still trying to please people, I would not be a servant of Christ."

When Oprah Winfrey was asked to give the commencement speech at Harvard University, she made a staggering admission about the mindset of most people she interviewed over the years. This is what she said:
"The single most important lesson I learned in 25 years talking every single day to people, was that there's a common denominator in our human experience. The common denominator I found in every single interview is we want to be validated. We want to be understood. I've done over 35,000 interviews in my career. And as soon as that camera shuts off, and inevitably in their own way, everyone asks this question: 'was that okay?"

Why do we all need validation?
Too often our self-worth is based on what other people tell us about ourselves and not what God declares to be true. In marked contrast to the world, our passage today from Galatians 1:10 reveals two life-changing facts which, if embraced, can provide each of us with a sense of purpose, excellence and acceptance.

Man possesses dignity by virtue of his divine creation. We were created in the image of God and are worthy of all good things because God declares we are worthy. The glory goes to God. There is only one, true authority on our self-worth and that is Jesus Christ. Since He gave His own life up for us that should tell us just how valuable we really are to Him, to the world and to each other. We don't have to earn our value; we simply have to accept it based on faith in Christ.

<u>One Minute Reflection</u>
Where do you gain your self-worth?

"Self-image, the concept we have of ourselves, must begin not by looking in the mirror but by looking into the face of God."
(Sam Storms)

Meeting Our Needs

Philippians 4:19
"And my God will meet all your needs according to the riches of His glory in Christ Jesus."

The Bible reveals God as our provider. Throughout the pages of Scripture, God is portrayed as the one who sees and cares for all of our needs.

Today we are examining the wisdom we can extract from Paul's New Testament letter to the church in Philippi, which was founded around 50 AD. Paul is sharing four important truths about having our needs met by Christ, Himself.

What can we learn from Philippians 4:19?

One
Paul uses the words "*my God.*" We can take comfort in the fact that God knows us intimately and deeply and is our personal provider.

Two
Paul tells us, "my God shall supply." If we seek God, we can allow Him to supply whatever we need.

Three
Paul reports that God shall meet *"all your needs."* This is where we have to separate out our desires from our needs. God will give us what we need to develop into the persons He originally created us to be.

Four
Finally Paul asserts that God meets our needs *"according to the riches of His glory in Christ Jesus."* God's giving is not merely giving from His riches, but according to His riches. In other words, Christ, Himself, is the prize, not what we can gain from Him. It is a critical distinction.

<u>One Minute Reflection</u>
What do you need out of God's riches today?

"All of God belongs to me, and the whole wealth of His aggregated perfections is available for stopping the crannies of my heart and filling its emptiness. My emptiness corresponds with His fullness as some concavity does with the convexity that fits into it, and the whole that He is waits to fill and to satisfy me."
(Alexander McLaren)

Are You A Good Samaritan?

<u>Luke 10: 36-37</u>
*"Which of these three do you think was a neighbor to the man who fell into
the hands of robbers?" The expert in the law replied, 'The one who had
mercy on him.'"*

One of the parables most well known to us is the story of The Good
Samaritan. It is so famous that its main character is now an entry in the
English dictionary.

This parable points to more than a simple lesson on being helpful to
those who are down and out, defenseless and forgotten. The
real question that we are meant to ponder is: whom do we perceive as
our "neighbor" and what are our prejudices about helping them?

For a deeper understanding - read the entire parable in Luke 10.

The question is would we stop, go out of our way, minister to and take
care of any of the following people who Christ would consider our
neighbor?

Someone who does not understand or respect us
Someone we don't know and have no responsibility to help
Someone who is hard or inconvenient to love
Someone who can't say thanks or pay us back
Someone who may have betrayed us
Someone who has caused us harm or hurt us

Jesus is asking us to consider that He is revealing Himself in every single
person we encounter. When we extend ourselves out of selflessness and
God's love, we are doing the work that God has called us to do. The key
to being a Good Samaritan is that we need to "be Christ" and to minister
"as Christ" to the world around us.

<u>One Minute Reflection</u>
Are you a Good Samaritan?

"On the parable of the Good Samaritan: I imagine that the first question
the priest and Levite asked was: 'If I stop to help this man, what will
happen to me?' But by the very nature of his concern, the good
Samaritan reversed the question: 'If I do not stop to help this man, what
will happen to him?'"
(Martin Luther King, Jr.)

The Time Will Come

<u>Mark 13:32-33</u>
"But about that day or hour no one knows, not even the angels in Heaven, nor the Son, but only the Father. Be on guard! Be alert. You do not know when that time will come."

There is a clear difference between how we view time and how God explains time in the Bible. If we can change how we understand time, it will become our friend instead of our foe.

You and I are concerned with the "passage of time" yet there is no word in Hebrew for the chronological time in the abstract. Instead the emphasis is on the "providence" of timing or the "purpose" of a certain time.

This is especially clear when we listen to the words of Jesus Himself. They can all be found in the New Testament. He often used words such as *"day"*, *"age"* *"generation"* *"hour"*. He spoke of "my hour has not yet come", *"the signs of the times"*, and *"no one knows the time"*.

But in every occasion Jesus's reference to time has to do with something significant or the importance of a specific event. Jesus is never concerned with controlling time or getting more of it. He is only concerned with aligning with His father's perfect timing.

In today's passage, Jesus tells us that no one knows the time when God will intervene in human history. As Christians we need to think differently about time. Here are several things we can do.

Be prepared - we need to be alert and ready to present ourselves to God

Be patient - we need to trust that God's timing is perfect in all matters

Be priority driven - we need to pursue all accomplishments great and small with the sole purpose of knowing God, loving God and displaying God's infinite glory

<u>One Minute Reflection</u>
In what way will you consider time differently?

"Every moment comes to us pregnant with a command from God, only to pass on and plunge into eternity, there to remain forever what we have made of it."
(Francis de Sales)

Overflowing Bounty

<u>Ephesians 3:20</u>
"Now to Him who is able to do immeasurably more than all we ask or imagine, according to His power that is at work within us."

Most of us tend to have a scarcity mindset. We operate from a vision of insufficiency with our own time and resources and talents.

Why do we buy into the myth that there is not enough to go around? After all we serve a God of abundance. He created the entire universe out of nothing. The challenge for all of us is to replace a "scarcity" mindset with a "more than enough" mindset.

"Test me in this," says the LORD Almighty, "and see if I will not throw open the floodgates of heaven and pour out so much blessing that there will not be room enough to store it."
(Malachi 3:10)

We may experience lack in the natural realm but there's nothing that prayer and seeking the face of God can't change things in the Heavenly realm.

Believe God for a spiritual abundance of love, joy, peace, happiness and health. Believe God for abundance in every area of your life.

<u>One Minute Reflection</u>
Do you have a scarcity or abundance mindset?

"Whatever the blessing in your cup, it's sure to run over. With Him the calf is always the fatted calf, the robe is always the best robe, the joy is unspeakable, the peace passes understanding. God's way is always characterized by overflowing bounty."
(F. B. Meyer)

Stepping Into Faith

Joshua 3:14

"So when the people broke camp to cross the Jordan, the priests carrying the Ark of the Covenant went ahead of them. Now the Jordan is at flood stage all during harvest. Yet as soon as the priests who carried the ark reached the Jordan and their feet touched the water's edge, the water from upstream stopped flowing."

Most of us know the story of the original Crossing of The Red Sea where the Israelites were escaping from the pursuing Egyptians in the book of Exodus. Tragically, however this generation of Israelites angered the Lord so often by their unbelief and disobedience that He consigned almost all, except for a remnant, to roaming the wilderness for 40 years until they died, never inheriting the Promised Land.

In today's passage from Joshua above we see that God's people are finally going to get to cross into the Promised Land after all.

The two crossings are very alike but have one critical difference

When crossing the Jordan this time, God's leaders had to physically step into the water before the water stopped flowing. Notice what the Scripture above notes, *"Yet as soon as the priests who carried the ark reached the Jordan and their feet touched the water's edge, the water from upstream stopped flowing."*

This time God called upon His people to literally make a *"step into faith"* before He would deliver them. God required His people to demonstrate their trust in Him.
God may be waiting for us to take a valiant first step of faith as well.

One Minute Reflection
Is there an area of your life where you could step out in faith?

"Faith don't come in a bushel basket, Missy. It comes one step at a time. Decide to trust Him for one little thing today, and before you know it, you find out He's so trustworthy you be putting your whole life in His hands."
(Lynn Austin)

Be A Burden Bearer

<u>Romans 15:1-2</u>
"We who are strong ought to bear with the failings of the weak and not to please ourselves. Each of us should please our neighbors for their good, to build them up."

We know a lot about each other's strengths, mostly because that is what we are willing to share with each other. Personal victories are what we talk about, celebrate and even envy in each other.

However, God calls us to bear each other's burdens and be compassionate with our weaknesses and failings as well. If we are willing to bear each other's burdens - we will discover the secret that there are many more blessings bestowed as we climb down the "ladder" of life.

How do we start being a "burden bearer"?

Awareness
We have to be sensitive to those around us. Everyone is carrying some degree of difficulty. Open your eyes and see who might be in need today. We won't have to travel far.

Availability
Everyone is so "busy" now that we believe that no one has the time or energy to care. However, availability is a matter of choice and priority. We can make ourselves available to sit, listen, share, pray, offer assistance, or step in where God is calling us.

Alignment
Bearing someone else's burdens means we have to align ourselves with Christ. We must learn to demonstrate His compassion, His love, His gentleness, His mercy, His forgiveness, and His desire to truly care for those in need.

<u>One Minute Reflection</u>
Whose burden could you bear today?

"I used to think that God's gifts were on shelves one above the other and that the taller we grew in Christian character, the more easily we should reach them. I find now that God's gifts are on shelves one beneath the other and that it's not a question of growing taller, but of stooping lower and that we have to go down, always down to get His best ones."
(F. B. Meyer)

Do Not Dare To Compare

2 Corinthians 10:12-13

"We do not dare to classify or compare ourselves with some who commend themselves. When they measure themselves by themselves and compare themselves with themselves, they are not wise. We, however, will not boast beyond proper limits, but will confine our boasting to the sphere of service God Himself has assigned to us."

The Apostle Paul is reminding us to never compare ourselves to other people.

Why?
The definition of "comparing" means examining the similarities and differences of two or more things, ideas or people. When we compare ourselves with others, it always results in us either believing that we are better than the other person or that we are worse off. Either state corrupts our thinking.

If we believe we are better - the result is pride.
If we believe we are not as worthy - the result is jealousy or despair.
This kind of emotional baggage can have debilitating ramifications in every area of life.

**The only question we need to be asking ourselves is
how am I doing measuring up to God's standard for my life?**

We are reminded today to keep the focus on ourselves in the sphere of service that God Himself has assigned to us. We need to be grateful for all we have and boast only about what God has done.

One Minute Reflection
Can you stop comparing yourself to other people?

"Humility is not thinking less of yourself but thinking of yourself less. Humility is not thinking that others are better than you or more intelligent, nicer, or more deserving. They may be. They may not be. Humility is when you consider other people's interests before your own."
(C.S. Lewis)

Waiting On The Lord

<u>Lamentations 3:25</u>
"The Lord is good to those who wait for Him, to the soul who seeks Him."

Today we are offered one of the great secrets of the Bible.
Those who wait on the Lord - will be blessed!!!

Waiting on God is one of the hardest ways to spend our time! But it is also one of the most valuable. We live in a time where we desire and demand instant answers. God does not operate on our time-line, nor is He even concerned with it. God is eternal and therefore He has set an appointed time for all things!

Waiting on God is not passive time but ACTIVE time.
It is a time to direct our attention to God and search for what He is telling us.

God uses waiting time for several reasons
He has things to teach us - if we pay attention
He wants us to get in step with His timing
He wants us to fully trust His plan for our life
He wants to sift our true motives for wanting something
He wants us to stand completely on His promise that all things will work for good for those that love God and are called according to His purpose!

A lot happens when we actively wait on God
God always uses waiting time to mold us and shape us into the persons He desires us to be. Then He graciously renews our strength and perspective so that we can accomplish all things through Him.

In other words: waiting on the Lord prepares us fully and perfectly for God's plan in our life!

<u>One Minute Reflection</u>
What will you do with your waiting time?

"Timing is so important! If you are going to be successful in dance, you must be able to respond to rhythm and timing. It's the same in the Spirit. People who don't understand God's timing can become spiritually spastic, trying to make the right things happen at the wrong time."
(T.D. Jakes)

Success God's Way

*"Commit to the Lord whatever you do,
and He will establish your plans."*

Is success a legitimate goal for Christians?
The answers depend upon your definition of success. Our culture defines "success" as the achievement of wealth, possessions, status, celebrity or fame. Much of the world's definition has to do with being "self-made". We have self-made moguls, self-made millionaires, and self-made celebrities.

However God looks at success very differently.

His goal for us is ongoing growth in Christ-like character, conduct and conversation. God is desperately in search of people who will be ambassadors for His set of values here on earth.

But that's not all.
God also "calls" all believers to specific tasks designed for their personality, talents, abilities, and spiritual gifts which no one else can fulfill except that specific person. We must make sure not to waste our time filling up on the world's definition of success and missing out on the treasure God has in store.

We are told today to *"commit to the Lord"* and
that He will then establish our plans.

We are stewards of the resources that God has entrusted to us while we're on the earth. Success in God's kingdom is best illustrated when we are fulfilling the words from Proverbs 16:3 above, *"Commit to the Lord whatever you do, and He will establish your plans."*

One Minute Reflection
Will you be "God-made" instead of "self-made"?

"It seems that our society has confused success with fulfillment, accomplishment with satisfaction and achievement with peace."
(Myles Munroe)

Finish Well

"For I am already being poured out like a drink offering, and the time for my departure is near. I have fought the good fight, I have finished the race, I have kept the faith."

Here in the 2 Timothy, Paul is imprisoned in Rome writing to his pastor friend, Timothy. Paul was more than a mentor to Timothy; he was like a father as well. Clearly feeling lonely and abandoned; Paul realizes that his earthly life is coming to an end as he pens this Scripture passage above.

The Book of 2 Timothy is essentially Paul's "last words."

Paul encourages Timothy to remain passionate for Christ and to remain firm in sound doctrine. Paul states that he has fought the good fight, finished the race and kept the faith. He tells us his life was *"poured out like a drink offering"*.

We need to ask if our lives have been poured out like a drink offering as well.

There is a wealth of potential in each of us. We have dreams, talents and resources that God has given us. Our passage is a wonderful reminder to live everyday giving ourselves away. We must decide if we will rob the world of our potential or bless it with the rich, valuable, untapped resources that lie deep within us.

Becoming a Christian is relatively easy, however staying the course for Christ for the long haul is tough. We can invite the Holy Spirit to give us the strength to finish. The real test of our faith is if we can and will endure.

Will we fight the good fight?
Will we finish the race?
Will we keep the faith?

One Minute Reflection
What part of your life is God asking you to finish well?

"When we make progress quickly, it feeds our emotions. Then when there's a period of waiting or we hit a plateau, we find out how committed we really are and whether we're going to see things through to the finish or quit."
(Joyce Meyer)

God's Purpose

Exodus 9:16
"But I have raised you up for this very purpose, that I might show you my power and that my name might be proclaimed in all the earth."

Every single person on this earth is in search of his or her purpose. Purpose is the key to life. Our happiness in life is dependent on our becoming and doing exactly what we were born to do.

God is very clear throughout the entire Bible about what our purpose is for our life on earth. If we reread the Scripture passage above and pay close attention to the words written there, they speak for themselves: God declares, *"I raised you up for this very purpose, that I might display my power in you and that my name might be proclaimed in all the earth".*

Here in Exodus 9, the Israelites have been enslaved in Egypt for about 400 years, and during that time, they had lost faith in God. There were ten plagues sent upon Egypt by God to convince Pharaoh to free the Israelite slaves. However God reminds Pharaoh that his real purpose was that God's power would ultimately be displayed through him in all the earth.

What does this mean for us?

Our purpose here on earth is also to reflect God's greatness in all we do and say so that His name will be proclaimed in all the earth. There are many ways, and various paths to take but the destination is always the same. We were born to reflect God's glory.

One Minute Reflection
In what way is God raising you up for His namesake?

"You cannot fulfill God's purposes for your life while focusing on your own plans."
(Rick Warren)

Bless The Broken Road

<u>James 1:2-4</u>
"Consider it pure joy, my brothers and sisters, whenever you face trials of many kinds, because you know that the testing of your faith produces perseverance. Let perseverance finish its work so that you may be mature and complete, not lacking anything."

Meaningless suffering is intolerable but understanding what Scripture says about God's permissive will for suffering helps us see the overall goal for some of our troubles.

**If we study the passage from James above, we notice
four reasons that we can consider trials, *"pure joy".***

The testing of our faith
Each adversity is an opportunity to believe God for His promises

Producing endurance
We need to abide with the Lord in good times and bad and to abide with each other for the long haul.

Developing maturity and completeness
The goal of the Christian life is to conform to the likeness of Christ

Not lack anything
All our needs will be met when we surrender to Christ

Brokenness is often the path God uses to accomplish His goals. We can rejoice in our trials because God always has something better in mind.

**<u>One Minute Reflection</u>
Will you allow God to bless your broken road?**

"Jesus said, 'Blessed are the poor in spirit' - contrary to what we would expect, brokenness is the pathway to blessing!"
(Nancy Leigh DeMoss)

A Good Life Motto

<u>Micah 6:8</u>
"He has shown you, O mortal, what is good. And what does the LORD require of you? To act justly and to love mercy and to walk humbly with your God."

Above is one of the most well known and often quoted lines of Scripture from the Old Testament.

The author is "Micah of Moresheth", one of the Old Testament Prophets. The word "Micah" means, "Who is like Yahweh."

Micah prophesied during a period of upheaval and crisis, spiritual lethargy, apostasy and hypocrisy. The people still worshiped Yahweh, but it had become a ritual without devotion or practical life-changing reality.

People's hearts had become hardened and it showed in their treatment of each other, which violated the basic tenants of the Mosaic covenant. Their society failed to practice justice or forgiveness and their pursuit of idolatry became supreme.

Our modern, self-seeking society mirrors these Old Testament times because we also live in a time of upheaval and crisis. This is a time where "might makes right" and the pursuit of creation takes precedence over our allegiance to our Creator.

However God's requirements for all of us are still the same.

Act Justly
Love Mercy
And Walk Humbly with Your God

It is a good life motto!

<u>One Minute Reflection</u>
What is one way you could act on our Scripture passage today?

"Give the world the best you have and it may never be enough. Give your best anyway. For you see, in the end, it is between you and God. It was never between you and them anyway."
(Mother Teresa)

Surrender

Psalm 37:7
"Surrender yourself to the Lord and wait patiently for Him; do not fret when people succeed in their ways, when they carry out their wicked schemes."

It was C.S. Lewis who said; *"the more we surrender ourselves to God, the more we truly become ourselves because He made us".*

Surrendering is one of the most significant Christian concepts you can undertake if you want to have a deeper relationship with Jesus Christ. To surrender means, "to relinquish possession or control to another, to submit to the power, authority, and control of another".

Surrendering is not a popular concept because most of us think of it in terms of losing control or personal power. However, surrendering to God is actually the way to a full, abundant life. Remember Jesus told us - *"we must lose our life to find it".*

God has a plan for our lives, and surrendering to Him means we set aside our own plans and eagerly seek His. The good news is that God's plan for us is always in our best interest and far exceeds anything we can imagine.

Surrendering our life means:
Following God's lead
Waiting for God's timing
Obeying God's commands
Expecting All Good Things
And
Trusting God's purpose and will for our life

The supreme example of self-surrender is Jesus. The night before His crucifixion Jesus surrendered Himself to God's plan. He prayed, *"Father, everything is possible for you. Please take this cup of suffering away from me. I want your will, not mine."*

One Minute Reflection
What are you willing to surrender to God?

"The greatness of a man's power is the measure of his surrender."
(William Booth)

Christ In Me

<u>Galatians 2:20</u>
"I have been crucified with Christ and I no longer live, but Christ lives in me. The life I now live in the body, I live by faith in the Son of God, who loved me and gave Himself for me."

One the most radical verses in the Bible is Galatians 2:20.

The Apostle Paul is giving us a foundational truth that once we are united to Christ through faith and acceptance of what He did on the cross for us, we are never the same. We are forever changed.

The Bible reminds us: *"I no longer live but Christ lives in me".*

Paul describes this as a "death" and a "resurrection" which we share with Christ. In Christ the old things pass away and new things have begun, therefore our old life is finished and we have risen to a new life.

What does this new life look like?
We can sin, but we no longer want to
We can swear, but we know it won't please God
We can gossip, but we don't really enjoy it
We can envy others, but we know God has a great plan for us too
We can steal, but we understand we reap what we sow
We can punish our enemies but Christ has asked us not to
We can be sarcastic and mean, but we reach for compassion and trust

We decide to choose differently and we invite the Holy Spirit to enable us to do better in every area of our life.

<u>One Minute Reflection</u>
What does Christ in you look like?

"A Christian reveals true humility by showing the gentleness of Christ, by being always ready to help others, by speaking kind words and unselfish acts."
(Ellen G. White)

Widow's Story

Luke 21:1-4

"And He looked up and saw the rich putting their gifts into the treasury, and He saw also a certain poor widow putting in two mites. So He said, 'Truly I say to you that this poor widow has put in more than all; for all these out of their abundance have put in offerings for God, but she out of her poverty put in all the livelihood that she had.'"

Today we are looking at the Widow's Story. Here a poor widow gives out of her poverty and God views her trivial amount with more regard than the large offerings of the rich.

The purpose of the passage appears to explain what true discipleship for Jesus looks like. It is being willing to give everything you have, even your livelihood, for the sake of God. Those who merely contribute from their own surplus really aren't sacrificing anything at all. By giving all she had, the widow showed utter devotion to God.

What is relevant to Jesus' moral evaluation is not how great the gift is but our motivation behind our giving.

Luke 21:1-4 reminds us that we can either give out of devotion or we give out of duty.

This story is about the heart of the giver.

Our giving should be out of love for God not self-gratification
Our giving should demonstrate our trust in God who supplies all our needs
Our giving should be unto God cheerfully, generously and confidently
Our giving should be our first fruits, not the crumbs that are leftover

One Minute Reflection
Do you check your heart or bank balance when you give to God?

"God doesn't need us to give Him our money. He owns everything. Tithing is God's way to grow Christians."
(Adrian Rogers)

True Prosperity

"When daybreak came, Jesus stood on the shore. However, the disciples did not know it was Jesus. Jesus called to them, 'you don't have any fish, do you?' 'No,' they answered. 'Cast the net on the right side of the boat,' He told them, 'and you'll find some.' So they did, and they were unable to haul it in because of the large number of fish. Therefore the disciple, the one Jesus loved, said to Peter, 'It is the Lord!'"

One of the greatest lessons on true prosperity comes from the exchange of Jesus and the fishermen here in John 21.

You may know the story. The fisherman fish all night, they are cold, wet and discouraged because they have caught nothing. Then God asks them to do something completely unreasonable. Throw their nets on the starboard side of the boat, in shallow water and at the wrong time of the day.

None of it makes any sense.
Why would the fish be out now?
Why would the fish only be on one side of the boat?

However, these fishermen do as the Lord says and they haul in an unthinkably huge load of fish.

Same skills, same boat, same nets,
Yet under the instruction of Jesus they have a completely different experience.

We know our own "fishermen" experience. Too often when we feel stuck, poor, incapable, not worthy, and unsuccessful and we assume our empty nets mean we are a failure. However, this story illustrates the only thing we are failing to do is listen to God.

As the fisherman realize that all they needed was to be obedient to God, the fish are no longer important because the presence of the Lord trumps their abundant haul.
Now that is true prosperity!

One Minute Reflection
What is God asking you to do that might seem unreasonable?

"Christ is wont to catch every man in the way of his own craft -
magicians with a star, fishers with a fish."
(John Chrysostom)

Let Down Your Net

<u>Luke 5:4-6</u>
"When He had finished speaking, He said to Simon, 'Put out into deep water, and let down the nets for a catch.' Simon answered, 'Master, we've worked hard all night and haven't caught anything. But because you say so, I will let down the nets.' When they had done so, they caught such a large number of fish that their nets began to break."

You might know the story above from the Gospel of Luke. Here Jesus has been standing on the lake preaching to the crowds. He sees two boats near the shore and asked Simon to take Him out into the sea and when He finishes speaking, He invites Simon to put down his nets for a catch.

Simon is a fisherman. He knows that no fish are caught during this time of day and Simon also has the proof that no fish were caught all night either. However instead of continuing on with his protest, Simon answers Jesus with these words:
"Because you say so, I will let down the nets."

Well clearly this story is not about fishing and ultimately it is not about scarcity and abundance. However, it is about having faith in the power of Jesus Christ. When Jesus is instructing us and we are listening and obeying Him, things turn out better than the plan we had originally depended on. We need to get the focus off our own empty nets, and instead look to God who will fill them to over flowing.

Jesus goes on to call these fishermen to be His first disciples. Later in Luke 5:10, Jesus says to Simon, *"Don't be afraid; from now on you will fish for people."*

Jesus is always on the lookout for faithful, obedient men and women who He can bless with the fruit of His kingdom.

<u>One Minute Reflection</u>
Where is God telling you to let down your nets?

"Faith never knows where it is being led,
But it loves and knows the One who is leading."
(Oswald Chambers)

Works Of God

John 9:1-3
"As He went along, He saw a man blind from birth. His disciples asked Him, 'Rabbi, who sinned, this man or his parents, that he was born blind?' 'Neither this man nor his parents sinned,' said Jesus, 'but this happened so that the works of God might be displayed in him.'"

In our passage today, we come across a discussion between Jesus and His disciples regarding a man who had been blind since birth.

It was a common belief in Jewish culture of this time period that personal suffering was the result of some great personal sin. However Jesus states that this man's suffering is neither because of him or his parents' sin but instead happened so that the works of God might be displayed in him.

We live in a fallen world. Although God's creation is beautiful and mysterious it is also filled with turmoil, evil and destruction. However even in the midst of trying circumstances, Jesus is clear that He does not want us following Him because of comfort or convenience. Instead He demands our love and devotion based on faith in Him alone.

Jesus wants us to know that everything and anything that we surrender to Him is a divine appointment to display the works of God.

Jesus is going to heal this man's physical sight, however is also going to heal his spiritual sight. This blind man is being given the greatest gift of his life, which is to know that God loves him, and used him for the ultimate purpose of displaying the works of God.

One Minute Reflection
Do you see suffering as a problem or a possibility?

"A season of suffering is a small price to pay for a clear view of God."
(Max Lucado)

A Call To Action

Matthew 28:18-19

"Then Jesus came to them and said, 'All authority in Heaven and on earth has been given to me. Therefore go and make disciples of all nations, baptizing them in the name of the Father and of the Son and of the Holy Spirit, and teaching them to obey everything I have commanded you".

Christians have a very specific call to action, which has come to be called the Great Commission. Found in Matthew 28 above, it is one of the most significant passages in the Holy Bible.

The resurrected Jesus appeared to His disciples in Galilee and gave them the instructions above.

What is important to know

These words are the last recorded personal instruction given by Jesus to His disciples. This is a special calling from Jesus Christ to all His followers (including us) to take specific action while here on this earth.

The instruction

There are a lot of modern-day believers who are distracted, complacent and laboring for every reason but the right one. Christ needs enthusiastic followers to make disciples of all nations.

We must know what we are talking about

We need to be ready to give an account. As 1 Peter 3:15 states: *"But in your hearts revere Christ as Lord. Always be prepared to give an answer to everyone who asks you to give the reason for the hope that you have. But do this with gentleness and respect".*

Christ calls us to tell others how He has transformed our lives. People won't know unless we tell them.

One Minute Reflection
How will you be part of Christ's Great Commission today?

"We know exactly what needs to be done to advance the Gospel and fulfill the Great Commission. The question is will we do it?"
(David Jeremiah)

The Great Flood

<u>Genesis 7:1</u>
"The Lord then said to Noah, 'Go into the ark, you and your whole family, because I have found you righteous in this generation.'"

The story of Noah and the Flood, Genesis Chapters 6-9, is one of the best-known stories in the Bible. God tells Noah to build an ark and fill it with every species on the earth. When the ark is full, a flood inundates the earth. Only Noah and those on his ark survive because God found him the only righteous man of his generation.

The Bible says that the time of Noah was a wicked time. God saw the evil thoughts of man's heart were steering him away from God so He declared that He would destroy man from the earth everyone except for Noah and his family.

We know from a later biblical account that
God makes a covenant with humanity to never destroy the world again. The rainbow is given as a reminder of this covenant.

What does this all mean for us today?

It is easy to see the comparison of the saving ark with Jesus Christ as the saving Redeemer. In Noah's day people were called to turn from their sins and return to God. When they refused to trust in God, they were destroyed in the flood. In the same way today, we are called to repent of our sins and accept Christ as our Savior. We are to enter into Him; our righteousness comes not by our own deeds but only by faith in a Holy God.

<u>One Minute Reflection</u>
Would God call you righteous in your generation?

"We often think of great faith as something that happens spontaneously so that we can be used for a miracle or healing. However, the greatest faith of all, and the most effective, is to live day-by-day trusting Him. It is trusting Him so much that we look at every problem as an opportunity to see His work in our life."
(Rick Joyner)

Miracles

John 2:11
"What Jesus did here in Cana of Galilee was the first of the signs through which He revealed His glory; and His disciples believed in Him."

The author of the 4th gospel was one of Jesus' closest companions. John wrote the gospel to convince his readers that Jesus was, in fact, God. John points to astonishing miracles and amazing teachings in order to convey that Jesus is the eternal God who became fully human and lived here on earth where many could see Him and all could be forgiven for their sins and have eternal life.

John's account of Jesus' public ministry is organized around 7 miracles. We need to recognize two basic types of miracles - miracles of creation and miracles of providence.

The miracles should not distract us, but instead, we should revel in the manifestation of the glory of God.

Here are the 7 Miracles discussed in John's Gospel:

Miracle 1 (Water Into Wine)

Miracle 2 (Healing the Official's Son)

Miracle 3 (The Healing at the Pool of Bethesda)

Miracle 4 (The Feeding of the 5000)

Miracle 5 (Walking on the Water)

Miracle 6 (Healing The Man Born Blind)

Miracle 7 (Raising Lazarus From The Dead)

One Minute Reflection
Do you believe in miracles today?

"Our first concern about the gospel miracles should be not to "defend" them but to understand them. And when we have learned to do that, we shall find that their defense can take care of itself."
(F. F. Bruce)

Accept Correction

<u>Proverbs 19:20</u>
*"Hear counsel, receive instruction, and accept correction,
that you may be wise in the time to come."*

We all want to be the best versions of ourselves that God created us to be.

Proverbs 19, which can be found in the Old Testament, tells us one specific way to be wise in the eyes of God. A good definition of a biblical proverb is "a short saying that expresses a general truth for practical, godly living." The purpose of a proverb is to present wisdom in a short, memorable format.

We all know how easy it is to blame other people for our problems. However to truly grow and evolve we must keep the focus on what we can do to improve our own situation.

Proverbs 19:20 gives us a three-step strategy:

**First we have to *"hear counsel"*
then we must *"receive instruction"*
and finally we have to *"accept correction"*.**

Ultimately the result will make us wise and therefore transform our beliefs and ultimately our behavior.

Of course the best place to find instruction is in God's Word.

As 2 Timothy 3:16 reminds us, *"every Scripture passage is inspired by God. All of them are useful for teaching, pointing out errors, correcting people, and training them for a life that has God's approval."*

<u>One Minute Reflection</u>
How will you make time to hear God's counsel?

"Being open to correction means making ourselves vulnerable, and many people are not willing to do that."
(Myles Munroe)

Heavenly Calling

<u>Hebrews 3:1</u>
"Wherefore, holy brethren, partakers of the heavenly calling, consider the Apostle and High Priest of our profession, Christ Jesus."

Today we learn about our identity in Christ.

We are sacred
Our passage is addressed to the "holy brethren". This is anyone who has placed his/her trust in Jesus Christ as Lord and Savior. The word "Holy" means that we have been "set apart"; dedicated or consecrated to God and therefore sacred. When we start to identify ourselves as sacred, everything else changes; our thoughts, our words and our deeds.

We have a heavenly calling
To *be "partakers of the heavenly calling"* means that although we reside here on earth, our home is in Heaven. This is an important distinction because no matter what happens during our very temporary life on planet earth, we can remain joyful knowing our place is with God and He guarantees a happy ending.

Today's passage teaches us that Christ is both an "Apostle" signifying that Jesus represents the full manifestation of God to us. And He is also a "High Priest" signifying that Jesus intercedes for us to God. Therefore, Jesus is the bridge between man and God. To consider Jesus Christ seriously, we must spend time not only reading the Bible about Christ, but also meditating on who He is and what He claimed about Himself.

<u>One Minute Reflection</u>
Do you know what your heavenly calling is?

"Nothing makes God more supreme and more central in worship than when a people are utterly persuaded that nothing - not money or prestige or leisure or family or job or health or sports or toys or friends - nothing is going to bring satisfaction to their sinful, guilty, aching hearts besides God."
(John Piper)

Do Not Forsake Wisdom

Proverbs 4:6-7

"Do not forsake wisdom, and she will protect you; love her, and she will watch over you. Wisdom is supreme; therefore get wisdom. Though it cost all you have, get understanding."

This century has produced an information explosion unparalleled in human history. We have instant access to volumes of knowledge at the click of our mouse. Yet with all we have learned, man is still not able to answer the most basic spiritual questions of how did we get here; where do we go when we die; and what is the meaning of life.

God is the only one who can give us the answers we seek because He is the creator and source of everything.

In the Biblical sense, wisdom is the ability to judge correctly and to follow the best course of action, based on knowledge and understanding. Our passage from Proverbs 4 today tells us several important things.

1) Get Wisdom

The Bible tell us that we must look to God for wisdom. God provides all the knowledge we need to be wise. We can meditate on His word and study the commands of His son, Christ.

2) God Supplies Wisdom to those who ask

God is the source of wisdom. Wisdom is a divine gift. We don't get it by living a long life, traveling the world or receiving higher education. We receive wisdom from God when we ask in faith.

3) Wisdom is Supreme

A wise person aligns his or her life to God's purposes. Since God created us out of love, He has established His principles and commands to serve our highest interests. To live wisely, we need to understand that the search for self-fulfillment begins and ends with fulfilling God's will for our life.

One Minute Reflection
How can you make the pursuit of wisdom a priority today?

"Wisdom in Scripture is, broadly speaking, the knowledge of God's world and the knack of fitting oneself into it."
(Cornelius Plantinga, Jr.)

The Gift Of Peace

John 14:27

"I am leaving you with a gift--peace of mind and heart. And the peace I give is a gift the world cannot give. So don't be troubled or afraid."

In our passage today from John 14, Jesus speaks of two kinds of peace.

The world's peace

The only peace the world offers is shallow and fleeting. Most people's pursuit of peace is merely an attempt to get away from problems. However problems will always exist. The fact is, apart from God, there is no real peace in this world.

The peace Christ offers

The biblical concept of peace does not focus on the absence of trouble. Biblical peace is unrelated to circumstances; it is a goodness of life that is not touched by what happens on the outside. You may be in the midst of great trials and still have the peace of Christ.

Jesus is actually offering us two kinds of peace

First there is a peace born out of friendship with God through our having faith in His atoning work on the cross. Secondly, there is the peace that comes from that relationship - a peace of sweet enjoyment and quiet rest in the confidence that God has our best interests at heart.

How do we get peace?

Jesus said, *"I am leaving you with a gift"*. This is the secret to peace; it is a supernatural gift from God. The peace Jesus gives has to be received and applied in our lives. We must pursue peace by pursuing Christ as the highest priority.

<u>One Minute Reflection</u>
Will you accept the gift of peace today?

"Christ's life outwardly was one of the most troubled lives that was ever lived: tempest and tumult, tumult and tempest, the waves breaking over it all the time. But the inner life was a sea of glass.
The great calm was always there."
(Henry Drummond)

The Helper

"But the Helper, the Holy Spirit, whom the Father will send in My name, He will teach you all things, and bring to your remembrance all things that I said to you."

Today's lesson is about God's gift of the Helper, the Holy Spirit.

Jesus assured His disciples during His earthly ministry that although He would leave them; He would not leave them alone. He promised that He would give them the gift of the Holy Spirit for fellowship, guidance, comfort, and strength.

This is an important revelation for us today because the Holy Spirit is a gift that we can use in our daily life also. First we must understand several biblical facts about the Holy Spirit.

The Holy Spirit is God - One full part of the Trinity

The Holy Spirit is a Person

The Holy Spirit gives wisdom, power and gifts

The Holy Spirit is active, creative and powerful

The Holy Spirit has been around since the beginning of time and has moved powerfully throughout history

The Holy Spirit is available to each and every believer of Jesus Christ

Why is this important for us to know?
The Holy Spirit enables followers of Christ to live their lives empowered to do things they could never do by their own strength or ability. Jesus said those who receive the Holy Spirit, receive power. This is power for living, power for witness, power for prayer, power to perform miracles, power to love, power to forgive, power to change the hearts and minds of a broken world.

One Minute Reflection
How will you use the gift of the Helper today?

"Earthly wisdom is doing what comes naturally. Godly wisdom is doing what the Holy Spirit compels us to do."
(Charles Stanley)

Obedience And Blessings

Deuteronomy 28:1
"If you fully obey the LORD your God and carefully follow all His commands I give you today, the LORD your God will set you high above all the nations on earth."

Our passage today is a great reminder that if we obey God, we can expect His blessings. However, at the same time need to remember that His choice of blessing may be different from ours. If we walk in His will, He will bless us in ways we never imagined.

One of the great things about the Bible is that it is replete with stories and examples from other people's lives. Below is a list of biblical figures whose obedience became a blessing.

Noah's obedience saved his family from the flood.

Abraham's obedience resulted in his becoming the father of a great nation, God's chosen people, Israel.

Moses led the Israelites out of Egyptian bondage.

Joshua won the battle of Jericho by following God's strategy.

David refused to harm Saul.
He was a shepherd boy who became King

Peter obeyed Jesus' command to fish in the heat of day.
He became the rock on which the church was built.
Paul followed God's will and took the gospel further than anyone else.
He is the most prolific writer of the New Testament epistles.

One Minute Reflection
In what specific way is God calling you to be obedient?

"You can only learn what obedience is by obeying."
(Dietrich Bonheoffer)

Giving It Up For God

Luke 9:23-24

"Then He said to them all, 'If anyone desires to come after Me, let him deny himself, and take up his cross daily, and follow Me. For whoever desires to save his life will lose it, but whoever loses his life for My sake will save it.'"

For every human being, when faced with the decision of following Christ or not, there will always be something to give up. Because we are giving up ourselves, we will be giving up one or more things that we love in order to make the love of God our first priority.

Jesus explained this Himself in the above passage when He said, *"If anyone desires to come after Me, let him deny himself."*

All four gospel accounts, Matthew, Mark (8:34-35), Luke, and John (12:25) record Jesus saying this. In Matthew (10:39-39; 16:24-25) Jesus says it twice; and in Luke (9:24; 14:26-27; 17:33) He says it three times. No other saying of Jesus is given such emphasis in the gospels.

What we need to give up will not be the same thing for each person. For some of us it might be our preoccupation with money, fame or the perfect home. Others it might be a past grievance, prejudice or toxic friendship. Some of us it may be pride and arrogance.

God invites each of us daily to deny ourselves and come after Him. He wants open hearts, minds and souls for His sake.

One Minute Reflection
If you had a face to face with Christ, what would He ask you to give up?

"Self-denial is a practice which lies very near to the heart of true religion. Without its exercise there can be no conversion to Christ. Qualities most basic to a Christian frame of heart - notably humility and meekness - would dissolve without its active expression."
(Walter J. Chantry)

Letting Go Of The Past

<u>Philippians 3:13-14</u>
"One thing I do, forgetting those things which are behind and reaching forward to those things which are ahead, I press toward the goal for the prize of the upward call of God in Christ Jesus."

One of the most important things we can give up for God is our past.

No one can speak from experience more than the Apostle Paul, the author of our passage today. He speaks of forgetting those things, which are behind, and reaching forward to those things, which are ahead.

With a deep, peaceful, joy Paul writes his Epistle to the Philippians while imprisoned in Rome. He is residing in circumstances, which would lead most of us to misery and discouragement. However, Paul considered himself the Lord's prisoner, placed there by divine wisdom for the purpose of carrying out God's will and work.

If Paul focused his life on the past, the things he did before he was saved, it would have incapacitated him for his present work. Paul had been a persecutor of Christians, dragging them out of their homes, arresting them, even consenting to their death. But Paul left the past behind and pressed toward his new goal of the upward call of Christ.

Paul tells us to forget the past and lay hold of a much brighter future that God Himself has planned and created for us.

<u>One Minute Reflection</u>
What are the things of my past I can leave behind?

"We are products of our past, but we don't have to be prisoners of it."
(Rick Warren)

Forgiveness - Set Yourself Free

Matthew 5:23-24
*"And when you stand praying, if you hold anything
against anyone, forgive him, so that your Father in Heaven may forgive
you your sins."*

The Bible is replete with statements and teachings on
forgiveness. Our passage today is another great reminder that if we
hold anything against anyone we must forgive him so that God will
continually forgive us.

In our hearts we may be ready to forgive but often we are not
sure how to proceed.

Steps to Forgiveness

1) We recognize that all of us are sinners in need of forgiveness.

2) We believe and experience Christ's loving forgiveness in our own
lives.

3) We make the decision to offer the same forgiveness God has granted
us to others.

4) We surrender to Christ the pain and inability to forgive if the betrayal
is too deep.

5) We pray for those that hurt us.

6) We trust that God will judge all the wrongs in the world, so we don't
have to.

7) We reconcile to others with humility.

One Minute Reflection
What step could you take today toward forgiveness?

"It is in pardoning that we are pardoned."
(St. Francis of Assisi)

Maximize Your Spiritual Potential

Isaiah 55:11
"So shall My word be that goes forth from My mouth; It shall not return to Me void, But it shall accomplish what I please, And it shall prosper in the thing for which I sent it."

Potential is that which exists in possibility and has the capability of manifesting into actuality. God created every single one of us with unlimited potential. We each have dormant abilities, untapped power, unused talents and latent success.

The first place we can develop our potential is in the spiritual realm and one of the best and most efficient ways to do this is to memorize Scripture.

God Himself explains the reason through His prophet Isaiah. God promises to bless His word not ours, so it benefits us to know His word, memorize it and develop our ability to call on it.

As God proclaims:
"So shall my word that goes forth from My mouth; it shall not return to me void, But it shall accomplish what I please."

Isaiah teaches us to maximize our potential in all situations by understanding God through His word. The truth is when our mind is infused with Scripture; God's Word and not other sources will inform our consciousness.

Why memorizing Scripture matters
There is a profound difference between reading the Bible and investing time in Scripture memorization. The discipline of memorization allows us to meditate and absorb the passage itself. God's Word gives us unlimited power and ability in every situation of our life.

One Minute Reflection
Will you write down a passage of Scripture and memorize it today?

"Bible memorization is absolutely fundamental to spiritual formation. If I had to choose between all the disciplines of the spiritual life, I would choose Bible memorization, because it is a fundamental way of filling our minds with what it needs"
(Dallas Willard)

Words Of My Mouth

Psalm 19:14
"May these words of my mouth and this meditation of my heart be pleasing in your sight, LORD, my Rock and my Redeemer."

In the most direct terms with clear illustrations God explains to us the power of our every word - either for building up or tearing down, for sidelining or for moving forward, for despair or for great destiny.

As Psalm 19:14 reminds us we want the words of our mouth to be pleasing to God.

How we speak to ourselves
We have been declared loved and deserving by a powerful, personal God. We should be kind, gentle and speak only encouraging words to ourselves, as God Himself would speak with us.

How we speak to others
We can either contribute or contaminate any conversation by a simple choice of words. We can work on not gossiping, not maligning and not ridiculing. Instead we should insert a Christ centered consciousness into every discussion.

How we speak to God
God wants to speak with us daily. We can choose our words carefully and ask God to show us how to communicate with Him.

Today's lesson is a good reminder for all of us that we need to hold ourselves accountable to a higher authority when it comes to the words of our mouth and the mediations of our heart.

<u>One Minute Reflection</u>
Are your words are pleasing to God?

"I know nothing in the world that has as much power as a word."
(Emily Dickinson)

Confidence In Christ

<u>Hebrews 10:35-36</u>
"So do not throw away your confidence; it will be richly rewarded.
You need to persevere so that when you have done the will of God, you will
receive what He has promised."

If we study the Bible long enough - the one thing we will come to know beyond a shadow of a doubt is that when God makes promises, He always fulfills them.

Today's passage from Hebrews describes one of the most important promises of all.

If we remain confident in Christ - we will be richly rewarded

Hebrews is a book of the Bible that demonstrates through its writing that Jesus Christ is superior to everyone and everything. Jesus is God's final word to humanity and everything God wants to accomplish, He has already spoken through Christ.

God is telling us, in fact declaring to the human race, that we must be confident in Christ. We must persevere through doubt, despair, obstacles, persecution, trials, tribulations and anything that gets in the way so that we can do the will of God and be rewarded richly for our faith.

It is easy to be complacent in the Christian faith. There are so many distractions and desires to tempt us and draw us back into a comfortable, secular life.

God is in search of those men and women who will display the ultimate obedience to Christ.

<u>One Minute Reflection</u>
In what specific way are you confident in Christ?

"Going to church does not make you a Christian,
Any more than standing in a garage, makes you a car."
(Billy Sunday)

Hope And A Future

"For I know the plans I have for you," declares the Lord, "plans to prosper you and not to harm you, plans to give you hope and a future."

Hope is both a strong belief and the anticipation that something good is going to happen. In Scripture, according to the Hebrew and Greek words translated by the word "hope" and according to the biblical usage, hope is an indication of certainty.

Hope in Scripture means "a strong and confident expectation."

When circumstances overwhelm us, we can always shift our focus to the promise In Jeremiah 29:11. God avows that He has a plan to prosper us and to give us hope and a future. Knowing this does three things.

It shifts how we see ourselves.
We are aware now that everything here on earth is temporary but we are guaranteed an inheritance that will neither fade nor spoil in Heaven, our destiny and our future.

It changes what we value.
The passage reminds us to be more concerned with God's will, timing and ways than our own way of seeing things. God is a planner and has us in mind even though we can't always understand the path before us.

It gives us confidence in the greatness of God
Even though our lives may lie in ruins, God has promised to never leave or forsake us. His promise is that we will prosper and have peace even when the physical world tells us something different.

We must remember to live by faith, not by sight.

One Minute Reflection
What is the hope for your future?

"Most of the important things in the world have been accomplished by people who have kept on trying when there seemed to be no hope at all."
(Dale Carnegie)

My Help

Psalm 121:1-4
"I will lift up my eyes to the hills-From whence comes my help? My help comes from the Lord, Who made Heaven and earth. He will not allow your foot to be moved; He who keeps you will not slumber. Behold, He who keeps Israel Shall neither slumber nor sleep."

Are there any words more beautiful, confirming, assuring and majestic than those of Psalm 121? Psalms express the deepest passions of humanity. Men and women throughout history have used the psalms to express God's mercy and provision.

The Book of Psalms, commonly referred to simply as Psalms, is a book of both the Hebrew and Christian Bible. Taken together, its 150 poems express the full range of human emotion and faith.

We don't know who wrote all of the Psalms but most are attributed to the authorship of King David. David is known as the "sweet psalmist of Israel." This is the same David we know as a shepherd tending his sheep and the David of "David and Goliath".

Our psalm today reminds us to look to the Lord for help. He made the heavens and the earth and therefore is grand enough to not allow our foot to be moved. We are reminded He will neither slumber nor sleep as He watches over us.

Read today's psalm out loud and allow the words to come alive in your own life. Psalms will impart a language full of depth, hope and possibility.

One Minute Reflection
Do you have a favorite psalm?

"With God our trust can be abandoned, utterly free. In Him are no limitations, no flaws, no weaknesses. His judgment is perfect, His knowledge of us is perfect, His love is perfect."
(Eugenia Price)

Believe It Or Not

"And without faith it is impossible to please God, because anyone who comes to Him must believe that He exists and that He rewards those who earnestly seek Him."

There is one central message of the Book of Hebrews, which is that Jesus Christ, is superior to everyone and everything else life has to offer. What we learn in our Scripture passage today from Hebrews 11:6 is that a life of faith is pleasing to God. This is not a passive faith but a faith built upon intentional will of the heart.

We are given three specific insights

1) Without faith - it is impossible to please God

2) We must believe that God is who He says He is

3) God will reward those who seek Him

We are responsible for maintaining our fellowship with God by doing the works that He has commanded us to do. There must be continuous exercise of faith through prayer, study into His Word, and seeking to be like Him by conforming to His Son Jesus Christ.

To walk by faith is not just an intellectual exercise. We have been given a serious responsibility to believe in God's character and His works as revealed in His Holy Word. We must trust God and submit to His commands in every area of life.

Our Scripture emphasizes that God rewards those who earnestly seek Him and consistently walk with Him by faith. It is up to us to make faith our way of life so that we can enjoy God forever and benefit from His everlasting mercy.

One Minute Reflection
How will you please God today?

"Trust the past to God's mercy, the present to God's love and the future to God's providence."
(Augustine)

Endless Possibilities

<u>Matthew 19:26</u>
"And looking at them Jesus said to them, 'With people this is impossible, but with God all things are possible.'"

All things are possible with Christ.

With Christ
We will have forgiveness for our sins
We will have the security of eternal life
We will have rest for our weary soul
We will have victory over defeat
Healing when we are sick
Strength when we are weak
Friendship when we are lonely
Consolation in times of sorrow
Hope and encouragement in times of defeat
Workable answers when we think none are left
Peace in the midst of chaos
Prosperity regardless of our bank account
Purpose for every day
Abiding joy in all occasions

But most of all we will have love, for God is love.
A deep abiding, never leave you, never disappoint you, always on your side, kind of love.

Jesus reminds us today – with God all things are possible.

<u>One Minute Reflection</u>
What do you need from Christ today?

"Jesus says, I love you just the way you are.
And I love you too much to let you stay the way you are."
(Chris Lyons)

Abraham - Our Role Model

Genesis 12:1-3

"The LORD had said to Abram, 'Leave your country, your people and your father's household and go to the land I will show you. I will make you into a great nation and I will bless you; I will make your name great, and you will be a blessing. I will bless those who bless you, and whoever curses you I will curse; and all peoples on earth will be blessed through you'."

Abraham, the founding father of the Jewish nation of Israel, was a man of great faith and obedience to the will of God. His name in Hebrew means "father of a multitude."   As we read in our passage today from Genesis 12, he was originally called Abram, or "exalted father," then God changed his name to Abraham as a symbol of the covenant promise to multiply his descendants into a great nation that God would bless and call his own.

What can we learn from the life of Abraham?

1) Abraham's life shows us the blessing of simple obedience. When asked to leave his family, Abraham left. When asked to sacrifice Isaac, Abraham *"rose up early the next morning"* to do so.

2) We learn from Abraham that God can and will use us in spite of our weaknesses. God is greatly pleased by faith and a willingness to obey Him regardless of our status, wealth or position in society.

3) Abraham came to the full realization of God's purpose and promise only over a long period of time through a process of revelation. God's calling will usually come to us in stages and we need to be patient, trusting in God's timing not our own.

One Minute Reflection
How can Abraham be your role model this week?

"Instant obedience is the only kind of obedience there is; delayed obedience is disobedience."
(Thomas a Kempis)

John The Baptist

John 1:31
"I myself did not know Him; but for this I came baptizing with water, that He might be revealed to Israel."

John the Baptist is one of the most distinctive characters in the New Testament. We learn of his mission in John 1:31 above which was to be a forerunner and precursor to Jesus Christ, Himself.

John tells us, *"I myself did not know him"*. In other words John was not personally acquainted with Jesus. Though they were remotely related to each other, it seems they had no personal acquaintance until Jesus came to be baptized by him.

When John began final preparations for his mission to announce Jesus to the world, he withdrew into the harsh, rocky desert to fast and pray. We are told that he kept himself alive by eating locusts and wild honey and wore a rough garment of camel's hair, tied with a leather girdle.

Through God's direction, John challenged people to prepare for the coming of the Messiah by turning away from sin and being baptized as a symbol of repentance.

How Is John the Baptist A Role Model For Us?
John's adult life was characterized by blind devotion and utter surrender to Jesus Christ and His kingdom. He demonstrated how to unabashedly share the good news of Jesus Christ. He was a man filled with faith who preached the need for a Savior and he claimed that the Kingdom of God was at hand.

One Minute Reflection
Is there someone you could share the Gospel with this week?

"John's baptism was a radical act of individual commitment to belong to the true people of God, based on personal confession and repentance."
(John Piper)

Goal Setting

<u>Proverbs 21:5</u>
*"Good planning and hard work lead to prosperity, but hasty shortcuts
lead to poverty."*

We all want to improve our lives and the fastest way to do that is
through planning and hard work. Many of us feel as if we are adrift in
the world. We are not always sure which way to go or what decisions to
make to fulfill our personal accomplishments.

A key reason for this is that we haven't spent enough time thinking
about what we really want from life, and we haven't set formal goals.

The writer of Proverbs reminds us in our text today that goal setting is
of paramount importance. A goal is a predetermined purpose, pursued
according to a specific set of planned action steps.

God created us with several parts. Like a pie with separate pieces, each
part is critical to who we are; and all of these parts must be considered
when you set goals.

The five parts of a person include:
Spiritual Family Social Physical Work

Setting goals aligns priorities. We know our first priority must be
God. Jesus reminds us to *"Seek first the kingdom of God and His
righteousness and all things will be added unto to it".* (Matthew 6:33)

The best way to goal set is:
Pray
Invite God to guide you
Write down specifically what you want to accomplish
Be positive
Start with one step toward your goal and then add on daily
Always align your goals with the Word of God

<u>One Minute Reflection</u>
Is there a goal you would like to commit to today?

"You are never too old to set another goal or to dream a new dream."
(C.S. Lewis)

Free From Worry

Matthew 6:25
"Therefore I tell you, do not worry about your life, what you will eat or drink; or about your body, what you will wear. Is not life more than food, and the body more than clothes?"

To have a life free from worry, we must trust in the Lord.

It sounds simple enough but it isn't.

The poet Robert Frost (1874-1963) wrote, "The reason why worry kills more people than work is because more people worry than work." Seriously, worry has become an American pastime. For many people, worry has become so ingrained in their personalities that once the old worries are gone they search for new ones.

Jesus is offering us the answer for all our burdens - Himself. This expresses the desire and compassionate heart of the Savior and His appeal for people to come to Him as a relief from oppression. It is a call to turn from whatever we are presently depending on and instead yield to Him.

Christianity is a relationship with the person of Jesus Christ. It is not a call to a program, a system of religion, or to a church.

It is an invitation by Christ to Christ.

One Minute Reflection
How will you respond to Jesus' invitation for trust in Him?

"Thou hast created us for thyself,
and our heart is not quiet until it rests in Thee."
(Augustine)

Now Faith

Hebrews 11:1-3

"Now faith is confidence in what we hope for and assurance about what we do not see. This is what the ancients were commended for. By faith we understand that the universe was formed at God's command, so that what is seen was not made out of what was visible."

The theme of Hebrews Chapter 11 is "faith".
The English word "faith" is written most often in Hebrews. Faith occurs 24 times in Hebrews chapter 11, and the expression "by faith," which first occurs in Hebrews 11:3 is found 19 times in this chapter also.

The verse we are studying today tell us three significant things:

1) Christian Faith is Confident
Our faith is not just hope, optimism or a good sense about the future. Our faith is an absolute utter certainty about the things for which we believe, and the things which God has promised to bestow upon us in the future.

2) Christian Faith is Confident in Unseen Things
An invisible spirit kingdom surrounds us and there are realities, which cannot be seen, touched, tasted, weighed, or measured. Just as we analyze the physical world by our senses, we can also communicate with the spirit world through our faith.

3) Christian Faith is Confident in a God Who Created The Universe
In other words, our faith is not blind. We are confident in God not because our faith is strong enough but because the object of our faith is a mighty, steadfast and all loving God. We trust in a God who created the entire universe and everything in it. Moreover, we trust in a God who has embraced us in His loving, saving power, and will sustain us into eternity and beyond.

One Minute Reflection
How would you describe your own "faith"?

"Faith is trusting God to do what He has promised because we are convinced by His provisions that God is both willing and able to keep His Word."
(Scott Hafemann)

God's Presence In Worship

<u>Colossians 1:10</u>
"Then you will live a life that honors the Lord, and you will always please Him by doing good deeds. You will come to know God even better."

Many of us want to know God at the deepest possible level. One of the best ways to experience God's presence is in worship.

By definition, worship is: "To pay great honor and respect to".

In the First book of Colossians, verse 10 above, Paul explains, *"live a life that honors the Lord, we will come to know God even better."*

Today's church culture suggests that worship is predominantly something related to music. This is not what is meant by praise and worship in the Bible, at least not in the New Testament. The word 'worship' is never used in the Bible in the context of Christians meeting together.

Fundamentally, authentic worship is about pursuing things, which please God, not us. It is about living our life in service to God and therefore to each other.

How can we authentically worship God?
Worship is living every moment of the day to please God by our obedience to His Spirit in thought, word and deed. We honor God and demonstrate our love for Him by doing good deeds and following the example that Jesus set.

<u>One Minute Reflection</u>
How will you worship God today?

"It is in the process of being worshipped that God communicates His presence to men."
(C.S. Lewis)

Equipped By God

Exodus 4:10-12

"Moses said to the Lord, 'Pardon your servant, Lord. I have never been eloquent, neither in the past nor since you have spoken to your servant. I am slow of speech and tongue.' The Lord said to him, 'Who gave human beings their mouths? Who makes them deaf or mute? Who gives them sight or makes them blind? Is it not I, the Lord? Now go; I will help you speak and will teach you what to say.'"

Surveys about our fears commonly show fear of public speaking at the very top of the list. The fear of standing up in front of a group and having to convince others of our ideas is so great that many people say they fear it more than death. Interestingly enough, we learn from our passage today from Exodus 4:10, that Moses also had a fear of public speaking.

Moses had been called by God to lead the Israelites out of slavery. However we read above that he complained to God that he was the wrong person to deliver God's message because he *was "slow of speech and tongue".*

How does God respond?

God graciously promises Moses to be His helper, His teacher, and to supply him with exactly the right words.

By extension, this is true for us as well. When God calls us to do something, He will also equip us for the task at hand. God is always sufficient, no matter what real or imagined inadequacies we might possess.

Three significant truths are made clear in our Scripture passage:

1) God uses sinful and common people to accomplish His purposes

2) God's message is powerful and He will perfect its delivery

3) When God calls us, He also equips us

<u>One Minute Reflection</u>
What do you need God to equip you to do?

"We may be sure that if God sends us on stony paths He will provide us with strong shoes, He will not send us out on any journey for which He does not equip us well."
(Alexander MacLaren)

Who Are You Becoming?

2 Corinthians 4:7
"But we have this treasure in jars of clay to show that this all-surpassing power is from God and not from us."

Many people believe that the Christian life is only about doing things to please God. They think Christianity is an endless to do list of going to church, reading the Bible, working at missions, reflecting at retreats, praying regularly, tithing and sharing the gospel message.

However the truth is that authentic Christianity is about *becoming* rather than *doing*. The life of faith that God designed involves receiving Jesus into our hearts and allowing Him to change our habits, mindset, beliefs, interests, and concerns so we become more and more like Him.

We are reminded in our verse today that we have God's treasure in jars of clay so that all-surpassing power is from God and not us. The Christian life is about allowing God to remove everything within us that relies on "self." And instead live moment by moment, in full dependence on Him.

The challenge is to continually aware of God's presence.

God wants to do an "inside job" on us and we need to give Him access to our hearts. The true Christian life is about surrendering our lives to Him all while inviting His searching Spirit to transform us into the people He would like us to become.

One Minute Reflection
What is your plan to become like Christ?

"The steady discipline of intimate friendship with Jesus results in men becoming like Him."
(Harry Emerson Fosdick)

Be Thankful

<u>Colossians 2:6-7</u>
"So then, just as you received Christ Jesus as Lord, continue to live your lives in Him, rooted and built up in Him, strengthened in the faith as you were taught, and overflowing with thankfulness."

One of the most notable things about Christianity is the emphasis on being thankful in all things. In the passage above from Colossians, The apostle Paul is writing to a church of Christians who needed encouragement because they were under attack. Paul could not visit them because he, himself, was in chains in a Roman prison.

The lesson is clear in today's passage - we can and should be thankful in all things because we are rooted and built up in Christ Jesus. In other words, we can fully trust that God has our situation covered and will plan for a perfect outcome.
Therefore even during our trials, we can be grateful.

Just imagine how different our lives would be if *"overflowing with thankfulness" was* our intention for each and every day.

Gratitude does several things.
First, we acknowledge that God is in control of our lives during the bad times as well as the good.

Second, we realize that God is greater than any problem we face. Therefore we can trust that He always has the best intentions in mind no matter what our circumstances tell us. We must live by faith not sight.

Finally we should never make idols out of our problems. We do not need to over think our dilemmas or obsess about obstacles because we know what we focus on expands. Instead, God wants us to put our attention fully on Him.
God has a miraculous plan for our life - our job is to be thankful for it!

<u>One Minute Reflection</u>
Can you list three things to be thankful for right now?

"Begin by thanking Him for some little thing, and then go on, day by day, adding to your subjects of praise; until you see in everything some cause for thanksgiving."
(Priscilla Maurice)

Don't Forfeit Your Soul

Matthew 16:26-27

"What good will it be for someone to gain the whole world, yet forfeit their soul? Or what can anyone give in exchange for their soul? For the Son of Man is going to come in His Father's glory with His angels, and then He will reward each person according to what they have done."

In our passage today from the Gospel of Matthew,
Jesus offers two rhetorical questions to consider.

The first question has to do with the significance of the soul in comparison to gaining the entire world. The second question emphasizes the supreme value of one's soul against anything we can exchange for it in this life.

Jesus is chronicling the relative value of our temporary, physical lives compared to what awaits us in His eternal kingdom.

In short, there is no comparison!

So if Jesus' words are true, why do we spend so much time in search of gaining our part of the "whole world"? Whether our hungers are physical (for food, alcohol, drugs, sex, wealth) or mental (for position, control, power, vengeance), it seems we get sidetracked searching for satisfaction in earthly treasures.

Jesus tells us He is going to come again in His Father's glory and He will reward each of us according to what we have done. We are going to spend a lot more time in eternity than our lifetime here on earth.

We should start to notice how much time, conversation, and focus we spend on the things of this earth and how much time, conversation and focus we spend on God.
The results may surprise you.

One Minute Reflection
How much are you investing in your soul?

"The greatest enemy to human souls is the self-righteous spirit which makes men look to themselves for salvation."
(Charles Spurgeon)

Beauty From Ashes

Isaiah 61:3
"To provide for those who grieve in Zion-
to bestow on them a crown of beauty instead of ashes,
the oil of joy instead of mourning, and a garment of praise
instead of a spirit of despair."

Today's passage from Isaiah, found in the Old Testament,
is one of the most visually beautiful verses in the whole Bible.
It is Scripture we can read and grab onto in the midst of great despair.

What does this passage tell us??

God is going to provide!

During Old Testament times of mourning, Jews put on sackcloth, and
spread dust and ashes on their heads as a symbol of debasement,
mourning, or repentance. Additionally, someone wanting to show a
repentant heart would often wear old raiment clothing, sit in ashes, or
put ashes on top of their head. This was an outward sign of an inward
condition.

However we are reminded in this passage that God can provide for
those that grieve. Although we see lives reduced to ashes, God can
bestow a crown of beauty. When we endure mourning, God provides oil
of joy and when we experience despair God will exchange it for a
garment of praise.

Isaiah reminds us to call on God because with Him all things are
possible.

One Minute Reflection
What condition can God help you exchange for a crown of beauty?

"We want gain without pain; we want the resurrection without going
through the grave; we want life without experiencing death; we want a
crown without going by way of the Cross. But in God's economy, the way
up is down."
(Nancy Leigh DeMoss)

Christ Has Set Us Free

<u>Galatians 5:1</u>
"It is for freedom that Christ has set us free. Stand firm, then, and do not let yourselves be burdened again by a yoke of slavery."

Freedom is a subject that Christ was very concerned about and the Apostle Paul discusses in his passage above from Galatians.

Paul pens these words because he is worried about man's perspective and confusion regarding freedom. To the world, freedom means the right to be and do as you please; it means doing your own thing and being your own boss. However, the Bible teaches that this kind of freedom ultimately leads to a life of bondage to sin.

True freedom is the willingness and ability to allow God to be in control of our life.

Jesus said that He had come to earth to *"proclaim freedom"* (Luke 4:18). And told His followers, *"If the Son sets you free, you will be free indeed"* (John 8:36).

Jesus was not setting us free to do whatever we want; He was freeing us to do what we should do. He understood that we are inherently tied to sin and so He created a rescue plan to save us from ourselves. Jesus wants to liberate us to walk in relationship with God and to be the kind of people He created us to be.

God created us in His image. Therefore, when we follow His commands, it always serves our best interest.

This is true freedom indeed.

<u>One Minute Reflection</u>
What is your definition of Freedom?

"To serve God, to love God, to enjoy God,
is the sweetest freedom in the world."
(Thomas Watson)

Environment For Eden

Genesis 2:15
"The Lord God took the man and put him in the Garden of Eden to work it and take care of it."

All living creatures need the right environment to survive and ultimately thrive. And the best environment for man is in the presence of God. Men and women were created in the image of God and placed in the Garden of Eden, which was the perfect environment for them to live. Eden was not only a physical, geographical location but it was also a place where man and God were one. There was no separation.

The Bible declares that sin separated man from God and got us all thrown out of the garden and whether we are aware of it or not, we have been trying to find our way back ever since. This is why most of are never quite satisfied with the ways things are now and always in search of something better.

Eden is our true home and the place we all ultimately belong. It is the only place where we can fully function at top capacity because we were created to live there.

Jesus provides the way back to Eden and that way is Himself.
If we want to recreate Eden, we must continually remain and abide in Christ Jesus.
This is how God intended for us to live and Jesus now provides the perfect environment for us to live joyful, purpose-driven, abundant lives.

One Minute Reflection
In what way can you put yourself back in Eden this week?

"The Bible is the story of two gardens: Eden and Gethsemane. In the first, Adam took a fall. In the second, Jesus took a stand. In the first, God sought Adam. In the second, Jesus sought God. In Eden, Adam hid from God. In Gethsemane, Jesus emerged from the tomb. In Eden, Satan led Adam to a tree that led to his death. From Gethsemane, Jesus went to a tree that led to our life."
(Max Lucado)

Importance Of Praise

<u>Psalm 34:1</u>
"I will bless the Lord at all times;
His praise shall continually be in my mouth".

Christians often speak about praising God but we don't always think about the benefit of practicing it. Praise is when we acknowledge the supreme excellence of God's being.

In Church we often say or sing the doxology. The word "doxology" literally means a study of praise. The traditional doxology used in Protestant churches was written in 1674 in England.

Praise God, from Whom all blessings flow
Praise Him, all creatures here below
Praise Him above, ye Heavenly Host
Praise Father, Son, and Holy Ghost. Amen.

It is important to understand the difference between gratitude and praise. Being thankful describes our attitude toward what God has done, while praise is offered for who God is in His being. Praise is not about an outward performance. It is born out of the intentions of the heart.

All believers are commanded to praise God!
In fact, Isaiah 43:21 explains that praise is one reason we were created. It states; *"the people I formed for myself that they may proclaim my praise."*

When we praise God we invite His presence into our lives. This is why our Psalm today tells us to praise God continually because in this way we can at all times be in the presence of almighty God.

There are several reasons and benefits to practice praise.
1) Praise allows and invites God's presence
2) Praise puts God in first place in our lives
3) Praise reminds us that God is capable of all things

<u>One Minute Reflection</u>
Will you praise God for who He is as opposed to what He has done?

"My satisfaction in Him is incomplete until expressed in praise of Him for satisfying me."
(Sam Storms)

The Word Is Alive

Hebrews 4:12
"For the word of God is alive and active. Sharper than any double-edged sword, it penetrates even to dividing soul and spirit, joints and marrow; it judges the thoughts and attitudes of the heart."

Hebrews 4:12 could be the most important explanation in the Bible regarding God's word. It tells us many significant things.

1) God's Word is alive.
Did you know the Library of Congress contains 150 million items on approximately 838 miles of bookshelves with more than 32 million books and yet only one book claims to be "alive"? That book is the Holy Bible.

2) God's Word is active.
God's Words is intentional. The Word of God is continually at work transforming us into the people God calls us to be.

3) God's Word is sharp and penetrating.
God's Word is sharp as a surgeon's scalpel, cutting through everything and laying us bare before our Creator. No one is impervious to God's Word because it exposes our real desires, our deepest thoughts, our shifting motives and our sinfulness. God's Word penetrates into the innermost recesses of our being.

4) God's Word will judge our thoughts and attitudes of the heart.
This verse plainly tells us that there is a reckoning upon which we must give account. God's Word discerns and judges, leads and guides, separates right from wrong and ultimately leads us to our own holiness.

If we are in search of real transformation; serious, personal growth; a deep and abiding authenticity; a knowledge of our true selves; an understanding of why we were created and what our purpose is; and blessings beyond anything we ever imagined possible, then we must consider a serious study of God's word.

One Minute Reflection
How will you commit to applying God's Word daily?

"We must allow the Word of God to confront us, to disturb our security, to undermine our complacency and to overthrow our patterns of thought and behavior."
(John Stott)

Why Pray?

Colossians 4:2
"Devote yourselves to prayer, being watchful and thankful."

Today we are looking at the question of why we should devote ourselves to prayer.

1. God's Word Calls Us to Pray

One key reason to pray is because God has commanded us to pray. If we are to be obedient to His will, then prayer must be part of our life in Him. Our passage today from Colossians reminds us to devote ourselves to prayer.

2. Jesus Prayed Regularly

The Bible also offers glimpses into Jesus' prayer life.
There are at least three reasons that Jesus prayed.
First, Jesus prayed as an example to His followers.
Second, He found answers, power, and instruction during prayer.
Third, He demonstrated the Trinity at work. As God the Son, Jesus could pray to God the Father with help from God the Holy Sprit.

3. Prayer Can Succeed Where Other Means Have Failed

When trouble or trials come our way, we often use our own wisdom, effort and cunning to solve our problems. Prayer can assist with guidance, a new perspective, power to proceed, and supernatural strength to do what normally might be impossible.

4. Answered Prayer Provides Hope to Others

When our prayer is answered, it can serve as a potential witness for those who need confidence or hope. We can lead the way in how to pray, when to pray and demonstrate how a great and mighty God has answered our prayers.

<u>One Minute Reflection</u>
How will you develop a devoted prayer life?

"Prayer does not change the purpose of God.
But prayer does change the action of God."
(Chuck Smith)

Testing...1,2,3

<u>James 1:3-4</u>
"Because you know that the testing of your faith produces perseverance. Let perseverance finish its work so that you may be mature and complete, not lacking anything."

James is one of the earliest writings of the New Testament probably when the original followers of Jesus were still alive. James was the half-brother of Jesus. The central message of James is that faith in Jesus will be reflected in a life obedient to Him as Lord.

Our passage today reveals that there is testing in life.
However the testing is not so God can see how we
Will respond because He already knows everything.

The testing is so that we can see how we respond.

God is only interested in the salvation and completeness of our souls. James reminds us that testing produces perseverance, and perseverance finishes its work so that we will not be lacking in anything.

This is good news for us because every trial has the ultimate purpose to lead us to a more genuine faith. God wants to mature us, complete us, and prepare us for meaningful work in His Kingdom.

If we are not lacking in anything, the result will be:
A genuine faith, which inspires us to endure trials
A genuine faith that manifests itself in action
A genuine faith, which humbly looks to God for answers

<u>One Minute Reflection</u>
When was the last time your faith was tested?

"Trust the past to God's mercy, the present to God's love
and the future to God's providence."
(St. Augustine of Hippo)

Full Armor Of God

"Finally, be strong in the Lord and in His mighty power. Put on the full armor of God, so that you can take your stand against the devil's schemes."

The Apostle Paul is making many claims in this important piece of Scripture but the main emphasis is on the fact that all of us are going to face many attacks in this lifetime and we must be prepared to use every piece of God's armor to prepare for battle.

He tells us that the enemy we face is real and that a healthy respect for his power is necessary. The evil we are fighting has three main characteristics.
1) It is powerful   2) It is wicked   3) It is cunning

Paul was very familiar with the Roman soldiers and was eventually chained to one by his wrist. He details six main pieces of a soldier's equipment that is an analogy to things we can use as God's full armor to stave off daily spiritual attacks.

the belt,
the breastplate,
the boots,
the shield,
the helmet,
and the sword

He uses them as pictures of
truth, righteousness, good news of peace, faith, salvation
and the word of God

These pieces of armor equip us in our fight against negative powers.
We are reminded here of the balanced teaching of Scripture.
We need a proper coupling of divine help from God and our own
preparation to stand firm in our daily life.

One Minute Reflection
What piece of armor do you need to put on to face today?

"In heaven we shall appear, not in armor, but in robes of glory. But here these are to be worn night and day; we must talk, work and sleep in them, or else we are not true soldiers of Christ."
(William Gurnell)

The Spoken Word

"And Jesus answered them, 'Have faith in God. Truly, I say to you, whoever says to this mountain, Be taken up and thrown into the sea, and does not doubt in his heart, but believes that what he says will come to pass, it will be done for him.'"

Most of us read God's Word, study God's Word, meditate on God's Word and memorize God's Word.

However, one of the most powerful ways to interact with Scripture, is to speak the Word of God out loud.

Scripture itself is full of instances that illustrate the power of speaking the words of God aloud. Moreover, we know from Genesis that all of existence came into being when God spoke.

Here are just a few examples:
And God said, "Let there be light," and there was light.
And God said, "Let there be an expanse in the midst of the waters."
And God said, "Let the waters swarm with swarms of living creatures."
Then God said, "Let us make man in our image, after our likeness."

God's words are so powerful that they actually manifest into physical reality. Everything we experience today is the result of words that were spoken by God.

A degree of that same creative power has been given to us.
Jesus urges us to speak our words with faith and believe what we say to be true.

Confessing the Bible aloud and hearing ourselves speak the Scripture plants a foundation of faith. The more we become established in the Word of God, the more we will produce the desired result.

One Minute Reflection
Will you start to speak favorite passages of Scripture out loud?

"Sometimes you need faith and victory spoken over your life. Words have created power. When you receive them into your spirit, they can ignite seeds of increase on the inside."
(Joel Osteen)

Wilderness Wandering

<u>Numbers 32:13</u>
"The Lord's anger burned against Israel and He made them wander in the wilderness forty years, until the whole generation of those who had done evil in His sight was gone."

The Bible tell us that nearly 3,500 years ago, God delivered His people from Egyptian bondage as described in Exodus, Chapters 1-12. They were to take possession of the land God had promised their forefathers, a land *"flowing with milk and honey."*

Prior to entry, however, they took a vote amongst each other and decided it was too dangerous to enter the land even though God told them they could. Their lack of belief in God's promises brought forth His wrath and as we see in our passage today from Numbers, God cursed them with forty years of wilderness wandering until the unbelieving generation died off.

Sadly, they never stepped foot into the Promised Land.

What lesson can we take from biblical history?

All the Israelites had to do was trust God's Word and obey God's instruction. Instead, they missed an incredible blessing. This is the same God who had delivered them from Egypt, opened up the Red Sea, and gave them commands at Mt. Sinai. However even with all the evidence of God's provision and love, they still allowed their fear and lack of trust in God's Word to thwart their entrance to the Promised Land.

We should not make the same mistake.
God always has the best in mind for us.
We must take God at His word, regardless of the circumstances before us and then obey what He tells us to do.

<u>One Minute Reflection</u>
Will you take God at His word today?

"You can only learn what obedience is by obeying."
(Dietrich Bonheoffer)

A Lamp

Psalm 119:105
"Your word is a lamp for my feet, a light on my path."

Psalm 119 is one of the most well known among all the Psalms. It is also the longest psalm in the longest chapter of the Bible containing 176 verses.

Simply put, this psalm underlines the concept of spiritual illumination. We are told God's word is a *"lamp for our feet"*.
A lamp, by implication, indicates just enough light for the immediate area. We need to recognize that God's word, as a lamp, will shed sufficient light so that with each step in our walk with God, we are equipped with just what is necessary and no more.
In this way we are always dependent on God's daily provision.

God's Word as a lamp shows us the way. It lights the path to prevent our stumbling in the darkness, bumping into unexpected obstacles, or wandering off in dangerous directions, which would lead us away from God altogether.

How do we ensure God's Word will be a lamp for our feet and a light on our path?

Be prayerful before reading Scripture

Be prudent in how we interpret God's word

Be practical in making sure we apply God's commands

Be patient in waiting on the Lord's response

Be passionate about sharing God's wisdom with the rest of the world

One Minute Reflection
How is God's word a lamp onto your feet?

"The Word of God well understood and religiously obeyed is the shortest route to spiritual perfection. And we must not select a few favorite passages to the exclusion of others. Nothing less than a whole Bible can make a whole Christian."
(A.W. Tozer)

God's Voice

John 10:27
"My sheep hear my voice; I know them, and they follow Me."

Life presents a never-ending series of decisions to be made. And we usually want definitive answers. We ask the experts, check in with friends, consult family members, write out a pros/cons list or simply go with our intuition.
However, wouldn't it be better to just hear directly from the voice of God?

The Bible tells us there are several ways to hear God's voice!

Fix Our Receptivity
Without great antennae, we won't get clear insight. The Lord is always speaking to us but we are not always hearing what He is saying. It is impossible to hear God's still, small voice if we have busy, noisy, distracted lives.

Know God's Character
God speaks primarily through His written Word. His character and ways are all spelled out for us in the Bible. If we want to understand who God is and how He operates, we must put in the time to get to know Him on the most intimate and personal level.

Consult the Counselor of Truth
Jesus told His disciples that He would give them an advocate of truth. In John 14:16-17, He said; *"And I will ask the Father, and He will give you another advocate to help you and be with you forever- the Spirit of truth."* That same counselor is available to us as well.

God wants us to hear His voice so that we can apply His principles to every area of our life.

One Minute Reflection
How will you hear God's voice today?

"God's voice is still and quiet and easily buried under an avalanche of clamor."
(Charles Stanley)

What's In A Name?

Isaiah 42:8
"I am the LORD; that is my name! I will not yield my glory to another or my praise to idols."

Today, most people choose names for children based on their preferences, but in ancient times, a name characterized the person.

When God spoke, He identified Himself, *as "I am the LORD."*

Why did God choose this name for Himself?

It may seem like a strange name to us, but in reality, it's the most effective way to describe someone who is completely self-existent.

We know the rendering of God's name as Jehovah or Yahweh. In most versions of the Bible, it is usually translated as "LORD" in capital letters.

So what does "I am who I am" mean for us?

God is exactly who He says He is.
He is the same yesterday, today and tomorrow.
God is the sovereign force of the entire universe.
God is omnipresent, omnipotent, and omniscient.
He will never leave or forsake us.
He is present and available in every situation.
God desires our fellowship and allegiance.
His promises and unfailing love endure forever.

One Minute Reflection
What does I AM mean to you?

"'I am that I am - This explains His name Jehovah, and signifies, that He is self-existent; He has His being of Himself, and has no dependence upon any other. And being self-existent He cannot but be self-sufficient, and therefore all-sufficient, and the inexhaustible fountain of being and bliss."
(John Wesley)

Sheer Delight

"Many, LORD my God, are the wonders you have done, the things you planned for us. None can compare with you; were I to speak and tell of your deeds, they would be too many to declare."

We all want to celebrate the wonders of God.
Psalm 40:5 conveys the deep expression of being overwhelmed by all that God has done.

How do we declare for ourselves all that God has done?

Use Our Minds to Know Him

We can study Him, explore His ways and investigate His will. We can become a student of the character of God. He is so mysterious, complex and riveting - it is hard not to be deeply curious about the ways of God.

Learn to adore God's beauty

To delight in God is to behold His beauty in all its infinite handiwork. We can start by taking a closer look at the world around us. Literally stop to smell the roses. Everywhere we look we should be simply amazed at the depth of His attributes; from a child's tiny finger to a star streaking across a moonlit sky. God's manifestation is everywhere and we as humans are the only creatures that have been given the capacity to delight in it.

Be exhilarated by the depth of God's love

We can revel daily in the simple message that God sent His only son into this world so that we could know Him and Love Him more deeply and that we could have God reveal Himself most fully to us.

One Minute Reflection
How will you declare your delight in God today?

"The universe must exist for the self-expression of God
and the delight of God."
(Ernest Holmes)

Truth About Thanksgiving

Psalm 100:4-5
"Enter into His gates with thanksgiving, and into His courts with praise; be thankful unto Him, and bless His name. For the Lord is good."

God has always been at the center of Thanksgiving. President Abraham Lincoln officially set aside the last Thursday of November, in 1863, "as a day of thanksgiving and praise to our beneficent Father." In 1941, Congress ruled that after 1941, the fourth Thursday of November be observed as Thanksgiving Day and be a legal holiday.

It is important to remember Thanksgiving is about God.

Throughout the Bible, there are numerous references to giving thanks. In the Old Testament, individuals offered up sacrifices out of gratitude. The Israelites sang a song of thanksgiving as they were delivered from Pharaoh's army after the crossing of the Red Sea and later, the Mosaic Law set aside three times each year when the Israelites were to gather together to give thanks for God's provision and grace.

In the New Testament, there are repeated admonitions to give thanks to God as well. The passage above from Psalms reminds us to be thankful because God has the best in mind for us and the Lord is good. We are counseled to "bless" His name.

As we prepare for Thanksgiving, let's remember to be intentionally thankful for all that God has done.

One Minute Reflection
What are you most thankful for this Thanksgiving?

"Whereas it is the duty of all Nations to acknowledge the providence of Almighty God, to obey His will, to be grateful for His benefits, and humbly to implore His protection and favor- and whereas both Houses of Congress have by their joint Committee requested me to recommend to the People of the United States a day of public thanksgiving and prayer to be observed by acknowledging with grateful hearts the many signal favors of Almighty God especially by affording them an opportunity peaceably to establish a form of government for their safety and happiness."
(Opening quote from the Thanksgiving Proclamation signed by George Washington, President of the United States of America, October 3, 1789)

A Higher Way

Isaiah 55:8-9

*"For my thoughts are not your thoughts, neither are your ways my ways,"
declares the Lord. 'For as the heavens are higher than the earth, so are my
ways higher than your ways and my thoughts than your thoughts.'"*

Isaiah is one of the most significant books of the Bible for many reasons.
Isaiah was a prophet whose ministry spanned the reign of five kings
from 739 to 686 B.C. Isaiah's collected writings can be viewed as the
Bible in miniature. Isaiah has 66 chapters just as the Bible has 66 books.

What makes Isaiah even more remarkable is that there are two major
sections of Isaiah. The first section has 39 chapters just like the Old
Testament and the second section has 27 chapters like just the New
Testament. Moreover the themes are alike as well. Isaiah opens with the
story of rebellion and sin and ends with the announcement of God's
promised deliverer.

**Today's passage reminds us of a very important truth.
God's Ways are Higher Than Our Ways**

Isaiah 55:8-9 tells us why we often don't understand what God is doing:
*'For my thoughts are not your thoughts, neither are your ways my ways,'
declares the Lord."*

God sees the whole picture because He has an eternal point of view.
We must approve of God's ways, even when we can't comprehend them.
To trust in the Lord with all our heart means we need to accept that God
is in charge and surrender in faith to His promise for a happy ending.

One Minute Reflection
Do you need to surrender control of something over to God's ways?

"I know God won't give me anything I can't handle.
I just wish he didn't trust me so much."
(Mother Teresa)

Fulfilling The Law

"Think not that I have come to abolish the law and the prophets; I have come not to abolish them but to fulfill them."

Matthew 5:17 is perhaps one of the most significant lines of Scripture in understanding moral law as explained in the Old Testament compared to the New Testament. Jesus tells His disciples: *"I have not come to abolish the law and prophets, but to fulfill them."*

What does this mean?
The phrase "the law and the prophets" refers to the whole teaching people received about God's character and purposes presented during the time of the Old Testament. Jesus is explaining that He is not doing away with God's system of moral law but instead He is going to help man by fulfilling it.

The key to understanding this Scripture
Jesus came to earth to fulfill all righteousness. He alone shows us what true righteousness is and therefore what the whole Old Testament law was about. We need to put the legal requirements contained in the law and prophets into the larger context of Jesus' own relationship to God.

In Christ, we see what righteousness actually is
In Christ, we are able to see what true humanity looks like without the effects of sin.
God's aim is for all of us to be made right - Holy in fact - so that we can be back in right relationship with Him.

The entire system is turned upside down
We don't try and please God (keep the law) to be good enough for God to love us.
Instead, God loves us first so much that He sends His own son to die for our sin, and as a response to that love, we desire to please God and conform to the likeness of Christ. Thus fulfilling the law.

One Minute Reflection
Are you still trying to be "good enough" for God?

"There is always the danger that we may just do the work for the sake of the work. This is where the respect and the love and the devotion come in - that we do it to God, to Christ, and that's why we try to do it as beautifully as possible."
(Mother Teresa)

Lesson From Locusts

Joel 2:12-13

"Even now," declares the Lord, "return to me with all your heart, with fasting and weeping and mourning. Rend your heart and not your garments. Return to the Lord your God, for He is gracious and compassionate, slow to anger and abounding in love, and He relents from sending calamity."

Today's passage comes from the Old Testament book of Joel. Little is known about this man who was a prophet in the southern kingdom of Judah. The Book of Joel was written around 850 B.C., and its overriding theme is that God will reveal His wrath, power and holiness when His people need correction.

During this time, the land of Israel had been invaded by millions of locusts that had stripped the earth of its vegetation. Joel warned that this event was designed by God as a wakeup call, and he appealed to all the people of the land to *"fast and weep and mourn"* with a repentant heart so there would be renewed material and spiritual blessings for the nation.

Why is this important for us to know?

God conveys the same message today as He did thousands of years ago. We need to repent and return to God.

Joel declared, *"Rend your heart not your garments"*.
The word "rend" determines the seriousness of this statement. To rend means, "to tear apart or lacerate".

Joel uses this illustration of ripping open garments to invite us to do the same things with our heart. True repentance involves a complete and total change in one's life. True repentance will be seen in our actions. Fasting, weeping, and mourning are all evidence of true, genuine repentance.

"Return to the Lord your God" - our verse tells us that that God is gracious and compassionate, slow to anger, abounds in loving kindness, and will relent of all calamities.

One Minute Reflection
What do you need to repent of and return to God?

"How else but through a broken heart may Lord Christ enter in?"
(Oscar Wilde)

A New Covenant

Matthew 26:27-28
"Then He took a cup, and when He had given thanks, He gave it to them, saying, 'Drink from it, all of you. This is my blood of the covenant, which is poured out for many for the forgiveness of sins.'"

We don't hear a lot about covenant in our modern day life however covenant is how God chose to communicate to us, redeem us, and to guarantee us eternal life in Jesus Christ. This truth is revealed in the Bible and is the basis of Christianity.

The Bible is a covenant document. The first mention of the word "covenant" can be found in Genesis 6:18 when God spoke with Noah. He said, *"But I will establish my covenant with you and you will enter into the ark"*. A covenant presupposes two or more parties who come together to make a contract, agreeing on promises, stipulations, privileges, and responsibilities.

Why is understanding covenant so important for us today?
We need to look at what God had in mind from the start. The story of the covenant begins with God's heart being broken when He saw the destruction of humanity as they turned away from Him. By initiating a covenant with mankind, God would bind Himself to us and ask us to bind ourselves to Him.

God had this plan from the very beginning and He pre-ordained that a new covenant would be established. This is the covenant you and I now benefit from when we put our faith in the body and blood of Jesus Christ.

Thousands of years earlier in the Old Testament Book of Jeremiah 31:31-33, Scripture states, *"The days are coming," declares the Lord, "when I will make a new covenant with the people of Israel and with the people of Judah..... declares the Lord. "I will put my law in their minds and write it on their hearts. I will be their God and they will be my people."*

<u>One Minute Reflection</u>
How will understanding covenant deepen your faith in God?

"There is no more blessed way of living, than the life of faith based upon a covenant-keeping God."
(Charles Spurgeon)

Prepare For A King

<u>Matthew 4:17</u>
"Repent for the KINGDOM of Heaven is near."

In the New Testament, Jesus is referred to as the King;
This happens at the beginning of His life and then again at the end.

Jesus is the King who rules over a Kingdom.
Over 66 times in the New Testament - a "kingdom" is mentioned.

Jesus did not come to introduce us to a religion but to a kingdom

Fundamentally, the idea of Jesus being "King of kings" and "Lord of lords" means that there is no higher authority. His reign over all things is absolute and inviolable.

We learn today that God's kingdom is available to us in Jesus Christ. We must repent and offer ourselves back to God to gain entrance onto His kingdom.

God's kingdom is not a physical place with a specific and limited location, for the rule and reign of God cannot be contained to time and space. This is not a natural kingdom, but a spiritual kingdom where Christ resides in the hearts of His people with His authority guiding and directing our lives.

This Christmas we are reminded to celebrate the birth of a King.

<u>One Minute Reflection</u>
How will you prepare to welcome the King?

"The Bible tells us that Jesus Christ came to do three things. He came to have my past forgiven, give me a purpose for living now and the promise of a home in Heaven."
(Rick Warren)

Nothing Can Separate Us
<u>Romans 8:38-39</u>
"For I am convinced that neither death nor life, neither angels nor demons, neither the present nor the future, nor any powers, neither height nor depth, nor anything else in all creation, will be able to separate us from the love of God that is in Christ Jesus our Lord."

The passage above from Romans 8 is one of the most profound, powerful and positive verses in the entire Bible because it is a guaranteed promise that no matter what you are facing - the love and power of God is available. We are assured that nothing in all of creation can create a chasm between God and us once we are securely anchored by faith to Jesus Christ.

No Circumstance
Nothing we have gone through in the past, are dealing with at present, or will encounter in the future can take us away from Christ. No storm, no devastation, no fire, no flood. He is with us in life's victories and life's defeats.

No Evil Powers
The unseen powers of evil that try to deceive and ensnare us with discouragement, temptation or negative influences can never separate us from God who holds us securely in His loving grasp.

No Person
Once you put your full Trust in Christ, nothing and no one--not even you--can break that relationship. God calls you by name and has adopted you as one of His own.

This promise of security should motivate us to have a keen awareness of gratitude even in the worst times of our lives. God is greater than anything we face. His love for us will overcome any personal defeat we are facing. God is good and His love is great. We never have to be alone.

<u>One Minute Reflection</u>
How can God fill an empty place in your life today?

"Men have presented their plans and philosophies for the remedying of earth's ills, but Jesus stands alone in presenting not a system, but His own personality as capable of supplying the needs of the soul."
(A.C. Dixon)

Authentic Self

Psalm 139:23-24
"Search me, O God, and know my heart! Try me and know my thoughts! And see if there be any grievous way in me, and lead me in the way everlasting!"

If we desire spiritual transformation, we must understand our two selves.

The Outer Self

The outer self is the person we present to the world. The one whom we believe will be pleasing to others. We create an identity of who we think we should be instead of who we really are. We might demonstrate that we are clever, funny, charming, smart, successful, endearing, confident, or attractive. We do this because we learn from experience that we can gain love and acceptance by presenting a made up and often better version of ourselves to the world. Unfortunately the result is that we are always trying to be something other than who we truly are.

The Inner Self

The other self is who we truly are before God; it is the good, the bad and the ugly parts of ourselves that make up our authentic self. The journey of transformation in our own life starts with how God sees us and not just with how we identify ourselves.

The Bible says we are both deeply flawed but also deeply loved.

Understanding who God says we are is the beginning of our true purpose and ultimate destination. If we want to live a life of true joy and peace, then we must know and love our authentic selves so that we can begin to conform to the person that God has called us to be.

Our passage today from Psalm 139 tells us that genuine positive change begins and ends in God. We must be courageous enough to ask God to search us, to know our hearts and minds and to bring to the forefront any grievous ways so that we can be led in His way everlasting.

It is only in the discovery, awareness, and acceptance of our true selves that we can honestly begin a life of spiritual transformation.

One Minute Reflection
What would you discover if you invited God to search you?

"The problem of sanctity and salvation is in fact the problem of finding out who I am and discovering my true self."
(Thomas Merton)

Take Delight

Psalm 37:4
"Take Delight in the Lord and He will give you the desires of your heart."

What a wonderful phrase: *"take delight".*
To delight means to "take extreme satisfaction from something that gives great pleasure". Wouldn't it be wonderful to greet each morning with real delight in the Lord and wonder and amazement for the day ahead?

You will notice in our passage today from Psalm 37 that there is a very close and intimate connection between the principle and the promise.

The Principle: First we must delight ourselves in the Lord
The Promise: God will give us the desires of our heart.

Here's how Matthew Henry, minister and Bible commentator, explains it: *"He has not promised to gratify all the appetites of the body and the humors of the fancy, but to grant all the desires of the heart, all the cravings of the renewed sanctified soul. What is the desire of the heart of a good man? It is this, to know, and love, and live to God, to please Him and to be pleased in Him."*

Could there be any better ending? Ultimately, the desires of our heart grow into the same desires as the Lord's heart as we delight in Him. He promises to fulfill our heart's desire until it overflows.

One Minute Reflection
How will you delight in the Lord today?

"The universe must exist for the self-expression of God and the delight of God."
(Ernest Holmes)

Get Happy

Luke 11:28

"Jesus replied, "But even more happy are all who hear the word of God and put it into practice."
What is happiness? Why is everyone in search of it? And can you really find the secret to a happy life? These are the questions everyone wants the answers to.

If you search for books about happiness on Amazon, over 70,000 entries come up. That is a lot of books on happiness. There is the *Art of Happiness, Authentic Happiness* and *The Architecture of Happiness.* You can find *Happiness Now, The History of Happiness* or *Happiness in a Storm.* Even Anna Quindlen wrote a book called *A Short Guide to a Happy Life.*

As a country, we have always been interested in happiness. In our own Declaration of Independence it is written, "*We hold these truths to be self evident, that all men are created equal and are endowed by their Creator with certain inalienable Rights, that among these are Life, Liberty and the Pursuit of Happiness*".

Lifelong happiness is what most of us are searching for. We want to find a way to enjoy every single day of our lives regardless of our circumstances. It is a state of well being, serenity and blissful peace we want to capture and keep.

Our passage today gives us the one true key to happy life.
"*Jesus replied, "But even more happy are all who hear the word of God and put it into practice."*

This life is not a dress rehearsal. If we want to enjoy every moment, all we need to do if follow the prescription given by our Lord, Jesus Christ, above.

One Minute Reflection
What will you do today to practice happiness?

"Seek to do good, and you will find that happiness will run after you."
(James Freeman Clarke)

Giving Is Receiving

Acts 20:35
"In everything I did, I showed you that by this kind of hard work we must help the weak, remembering the words the Lord Jesus Himself said: 'It is more blessed to give than to receive.'"

Most of us have all heard the saying; *"It is more blessed to give than to receive"*. However we may not know that the original words can be found in Acts 20:35 above. It turns out that none of the four canonical Gospels record this saying of Jesus. However it eventually made it to Paul who included it in the text above.

Paul wanted to express something profound about giving.
For Paul, the author of Acts, giving was more than a monetary offering; giving meant extending himself as an act of deep love for Christ. Paul manifested his giving in three ways; through extensive traveling at a time when traveling was a hardship; through proclaiming a message to people who often didn't want to hear it; and through exhausting himself as a tent maker so he could fund his missionary calling.
Paul reminds us that:

Giving is a privilege
We can give out of gratitude toward God

Giving is one dimension of stewardship
We can give of our time, treasure or talents

Giving is an act of worship
Sacrificing our possessions is a way to honor God

Giving is an investment
Jesus encouraged believers to give things away in order to *"lay up treasure in heaven"*.

Giving always leads to a blessing
Christ tells us; *"It is more blessed to give than to receive"*.

One Minute Reflection
Is there something of value you could give away for Christ's sake?

"We make a living by what we get, but we make a life by what we give."
(Winston Churchill)

Home Is Where The Heart Is

John 1423

"Jesus answered him, 'If anyone loves me, he will keep my word, and my Father will love him, and we will come to him and make our home with him.'"

We tend to put a lot of emphasis on our temporary homes.

The Rev Charles Hoffacker believes we may be dangerously preoccupied. He illustrates his points in the following sermon.

"There are reasons to believe that Americans are growing more and more preoccupied with their homes. Some people claim that we have gone from simply cocooning in our homes to burrowing into them, and thus shutting out the world far more successfully. No longer is our home just our castle; it has become our fortress.
The message sounds forth from every direction. Decorate your home! Equip your home! Maintain your home! Enjoy your home! Worry about your home! Your home reveals who you are, and who you want to be. First, make your home in your image, and then let it return the favor: you are made over in the image of your home. You own it; it owns you."

In our passage today, Jesus speaks of our true home. He tells His disciples about making our home with God. It is solely secured in Christ.

There is an old saying that "home is where your heart is". Jesus is asking us, reminding us and warning us to be preoccupied with Him instead of our temporary homes.

Having a heart for God and His Son, Jesus Christ will guarantee that we have an eternal home in Heaven we can count on.

One Minute Reflection
Do you spend more time on your earthly home or your Heavenly home?

"My home is in Heaven. I'm just traveling through this world."
(Billy Graham)

Friend Of God

John 15:15
"No longer do I call you servants, for the servant does not know what his master is doing; but I have called you friends, for all that I have heard from my Father I have made known to you."

Jesus' words above from John 15 invite us to reexamine the sometimes-casual way we refer to Jesus as our friend. The mark of friendship with Jesus is not only what Jesus does for us, but also what we can do for Him.

The concept of friendship is best seen in the Trinity. God is a being of three persons existing in a community of love and friendship. Each member of the Trinity; Father, Son, and Holy Spirit, loves and serves the other working together toward a common purpose.

Friendship with Jesus can serve us the same way.
However, we are as close to God as we choose to be.

Friends get to know each other. How well do we know God?

Friends enjoy each other's company. How much time are we spending with God and are we having fun while doing it?

Friends are honest about who they really are.
Are we forthright with God about our feelings, shortcomings and concerns?

Friends care about issues their friends care about.
Have we made it our business to delve into matters that are important to God? Christ cared about Scripture, obedience to God's commands, feeding the poor, and bringing glory to God in all things.

Friends demonstrate their love for one another.
We must love generously without counting the personal cost.

One Minute Reflection
How good a friend are you to Jesus?

"By friendship you mean the greatest love, the greatest usefulness, the most open communication, the noblest sufferings, the severest truth, the heartiest counsel, and the greatest union of minds of which brave men and women are capable."
(Jeremy Taylor)

Thanks In Everything

1 Thessalonians 5:18
"Give thanks in all circumstances, for this is God's will for you in Christ Jesus."

Today's verse from Thessalonians is one of those verses of the Bible where we may wish to respond:

"Are you kidding me?"
"Why would I give thanks in everything?"
"Clearly you don't know the problems endure."
"I have no intention of giving thanks when things have not gone my way."

However, the Apostle Paul states very directly, *"In everything give thanks."*
There are no exceptions or excuses; we must give thanks in everything. No matter what circumstance, regardless of trial, testing, loss, pain, betrayal, poverty, disappointment, we must give thanks.

In fact we are being told that giving thanks in all circumstances is a duty not a preference. Paul tells us that thankfulness should be an intentional way of living.

Thanksgiving is the essence of Christian living and attitude. It is God's will for us in Christ.

God is the ultimate provider, protector and benevolent source of everything. We are reminded here to thank Him in all things.

One Minute Reflection
What is one thing you could be thankful for now?

"Thankfulness acknowledges that God is our provider.
Thankfulness prevents a complaining spirit.
Thankfulness creates a positive outlook on life.
Thankfulness invites joy to dwell in our hearts."
(Kent Crockett)

Everything Is Beautiful

Ecclesiastes 3:11
"He has made everything beautiful in its time. He has also set eternity in the human heart; yet no one can fathom what God has done from beginning to end."

God has declared everything beautiful in its time. We are reminded of this in the Hymn *All Things Bright and Beautiful* by Cecil Frances Alexander.

All things bright and beautiful,
All creatures great and small,
All things wise and wonderful,
The Lord God made them all.

Each little flower that opens,
Each little bird that sings,
He made their glowing colours,
He made their tiny wings.
The purple-headed mountain,
The river running by,
The sunset and the morning,
That brightens up the sky;

The cold wind in the winter,
The pleasant summer sun,
The ripe fruits in the garden,
He made them every one;
The tall trees in the greenwood,
The meadows for our play,
The rushes by the water,
To gather every day;
He gave us eyes to see them,
And lips that we might tell
How great is God Almighty,
Who has made all things well.

One Minute Reflection
How will you appreciate God's beauty today?

"Never say there is nothing beautiful in the world anymore. There is always something to make you wonder in the shape of a tree, the trembling of a leaf."
(Albert Schweitzer)

Who Are We Feeding?

2 Corinthians 13:5-6
"Examine yourselves to see whether you are in the faith; test yourselves. Do you not realize that Christ Jesus is in you—unless, of course, you fail the test? And I trust that you will discover that we have not failed the test."

An old Cherokee told his grandson about a battle that goes on inside people; he entitled it The Story of Two Wolves. He said, "My son, the battle is between two "wolves" inside us all.

One is Evil
It is anger, envy, jealousy, sorrow, regret, greed, arrogance, self-pity, guilt, resentment, inferiority, lies, false pride, superiority, and ego.

The other is Good
It is joy, peace, love, hope, serenity, humility, kindness, benevolence, empathy, generosity, truth, compassion and faith.

The grandson thought about it for a minute and then asked his grandfather: "Which wolf wins?" The old Cherokee simply replied, "The one you feed."

The Story of Two Wolves might just be a Cherokee legend but for a Christian, this story could be an illustration of the Christian's conflict and struggle between the two natures - the old and the new nature. Our passage today explains that as a Christian our lives are no longer worldly; they are now spiritual. We are told to examine ourselves. Our old nature refers to everything that is part of our natural pride, especially the supreme love of self and with it self-righteousness, self-promotion, and self-justification.

Jesus now resides in us. We can feed our new selves by meditating on the Word of God, modeling Christ and inviting the Holy Spirit to inform our hearts and minds daily.

One Minute Reflection
Which self are you feeding?

"If conversion to Christianity makes no improvement in a man's outward actions - if he continues to be just as snobbish or spiteful or envious or ambitious as he was before - then I think we must suspect that his 'conversion' was largely imaginary."
(C.S. Lewis)

Character

Romans 5:5
"We also glory in tribulations, knowing that tribulation produces perseverance; and perseverance, character; and character, hope."

Today we are examining how we build
Character for Christ.

Character is the springboard to a successful life. Developing biblical character in the face of our daily struggles is essential to having a growing relationship with Christ. Character is not just having integrity or being honest or even doing the right thing. A person's character is the sum of his or her disposition, thoughts, intentions, desires, and actions. It is good to remember that character is developed over many experiences, not on the basis of a few isolated actions.

We are told in Romans 5:5 above that building and developing character is a process that comes from experience and often that experience can be one of conflict or tribulations. Since, it is the Lord's purpose to develop character within us, He will use trying times for our ultimate good.

Moreover, we are reminded in Scripture that we can actually rejoice in trials because trials produce perseverance and perseverance produces Christ-like character and Christ-like character is proven character, which leads to eternal hope.

Proven character comes from the word "dokime" in secular Greek. It was used to describe metals that had been tested and determined to be pure. The idea behind "dokime" is that when metal is put through a fiery test and it comes out on the other side "persevering and enduring", you call the metal proven, authentic or genuine.

The exact same thing happens when our faith is tested. If we persevere and hold up under the heavy load of difficult circumstances, we have "proven" that our faith is authentic and genuine.

One Minute Reflection
What tribulation is God using to lead you?

"The measure of every man's virtue is best revealed in time of adversity - adversity that does not weaken a man but rather shows what he is."
(Thomas a Kempis)

Joseph - A Godly Man

Matthew 1:20

" But after he had considered this, an angel of the Lord appeared to him in a dream and said, 'Joseph son of David, do not be afraid to take Mary home as your wife, because what is conceived in her is from the Holy Spirit. She will give birth to a son, and you are to give Him the name Jesus, because He will save His people from their sins.'"

Joseph does not get much play in the Christmas story because the spotlight is most clearly pointed at Mary and the magnificent birth of the baby, Jesus.

However there is actually a lot all of us can learn about this very godly man. Joseph first appears in the Bible in the gospels of Matthew and Luke, Joseph was a carpenter whose lineage is traced back to King David.

Joseph was also a man of strong conviction who lived out his beliefs in his actions. He was described in the Bible as a righteous man who was chosen by God to be the earthly father of Jesus Christ.

Imagine God looking down to choose a man to raise His own son? Joseph clearly had God's endorsement.

We can only imagine he must have been shocked when Mary informed him that she was pregnant. We know from Matthew 1:20 that God was good enough to send an angel to set the record straight and let Joseph in on the events that were about to take place.

What was Joseph's response?
He never doubted God's will in choosing him to watch over Mary and her son. He remained faithful to both of them and to God as well.
He showed courage in believing the angel.
He showed faithfulness in believing God's plan over his own.
He remained open to the promptings of the Holy Spirit.
But mostly he honored God by obeying His word.

One Minute Reflection
What lesson on faith can you take from Joseph?

"God foretold various signs through His prophets and one of them was the birth of a savior. These prophets spoke of things that mankind should watch for so that the Messiah would be recognized and believed." (Lucinda Franks)

The Good Shepherd

Luke 2:8
*"And there were shepherds living out in the fields nearby,
keeping watch over their flocks at night."*

The angels reserved the most magnificent announcement
about the birth of Jesus for the least likely recipients - the shepherds.

Who were shepherds, and why did they deserve such a privilege?

Shepherds are reflections of each one of us
Shepherds have been around since the beginning of the Bible. Abel was
called a "keeper of the sheep", and other experienced shepherds
included Jacob, Moses, and David who ultimately became King of Israel.
However shepherds were also despised and unwanted.   They were not
considered important - not personally, politically, or economically. If
God chose to reveal His glory first to them, then God is making an
important statement to each one of us.   We are never out of God's reach,
He deems each of us worthy to be called His own as well.

Jesus is the ultimate Good Shepherd
Jesus identifies Himself as the Good Shepherd (John 10:1-18). In His own
words, Jesus tells us in verse 11: *"I am the good shepherd. The good
shepherd lays down his life for the sheep."* And in verses 14-15: *"I am the
good shepherd. I know my own sheep, and they know me just as my Father
knows me and I know my Father. And I lay down my life for the sheep."*

Jesus knows us and cares for us as a Shepherd does for his sheep.
So when the glory of Jesus' birth was announced to the shepherds, it
was a pronouncement of the one glorious Shepherd still to come.

One Minute Reflection
In what way do you experience Jesus as the Good Shepherd?

"Christ proclaimed: 'I am the Good Shepherd.' He then further showed,
and with eloquent exactness, the difference between a shepherd and a
hireling herder. The one has personal interest in and love for his flock,
and knows each sheep by name."
(James Talmage)

The Glory Shone

<u>Luke 2:9</u>
"And, lo, the angel of the Lord came upon them, and the glory of the Lord shone round about them."

The one thing we know for sure is that during the birth of Christ, God's glory was on display.

What is Glory?
Glory is the full manifestation of God expressing Himself. God's glory is His splendor and His majesty. The glory of God summarizes the seriousness, the weightiness, and the infinite significance of all of the attributes of God. It sums up who He is in His perfection.

The Hebrew word for "glory" is Kabod; it basically means weight.

The Bible teaches that throughout history, all the works of God have as their ultimate goal, the display of God's glory.

God's glory is the ultimate Christmas Lesson

Jesus Christ is the full manifestation of God's glory and God chose to redeem us through Christ so that we would manifest His glory as well. As Christians we need to be manifesting Christ's glory in all we do and there is no better time to start than right now during this Christmas season.

<u>One Minute Reflection</u>
How do you describe glory?

"The supreme goal of God in history from beginning to end is the manifestation of His great glory. Accordingly our duty is to bring our thoughts, affections, and actions into line with this goal. It should become our own goal. To join God in this goal is called glorifying God. The way we glorify God is first to delight in His glory more than in anything else and be grateful for it."
(John Piper)

Wonderful Counselor

"For to us a child is born, to us a son is given, and the government will be on His shoulders. And He will be called Wonderful Counselor, Mighty God, Everlasting Father, Prince of Peace."

Isaiah is often referred to as "The Messianic Prophet", because of his many prophecies that were fulfilled in Jesus. The New Testament quotes more Scriptures from the book of Isaiah than any other Old Testament prophet.
Today's passage is a prophecy about the reign of Jesus Christ
It is quite remarkable that Isaiah declared Christ to be true 800 years before His actual birth. What does Isaiah tell us about Jesus Christ?

He will be called Wonderful Counselor
When Isaiah calls Jesus the *"Wonderful Counselor"*, he indicates the kind of character this coming King will embody. The word wonderful in this passage literally means "incomprehensible."

He will be called Mighty God
As a powerful and mighty warrior, Jesus, the Mighty God, will accomplish the destruction of God's enemies. Remember that Jesus said; *"the world is full of tribulation, but I have overcome the world".*

He will be called Everlasting Father
God's nature is without beginning or end. He is the Alpha and the Omega and resides outside of time, as we understand it. He is an Everlasting Father.

He will be called Prince of Peace
In a world filled with war and violence and sin, Jesus acts in human history as the embodiment of peace. He enables us to have peace with God, peace with others and peace within ourselves.

One Minute Reflection
How does biblical prophecy impact your faith?

"Understanding Bible prophecy encourages in two unique ways. First, it serves as a reminder that God controls history. Second, understanding God's promises for the future provides a solid foundation to which you can anchor your hope - a sturdy shield with which you can deflect your doubts and fears about tomorrow."
(John MacArthur)

Be Wise

Matthew 2:10-11
"When they saw the star, they were overjoyed. On coming to the house, they saw the child with His mother Mary, and they bowed down and worshiped Him. Then they opened their treasures and presented Him with gifts of gold and of incense and of myrrh."

Although many nativity scenes depict the Wise Men as being present at the birth of Christ, the truth is they visited Him much later when Jesus was about two years old.

We learn in Matthew 2 above that these men recognized Jesus Christ as the long awaited Messiah. Once they saw the star and were overjoyed, they traveled thousands of miles to worship Him. On coming to the house they bowed down and opened their treasures and presented Him with gifts of gold, incense and myrrh.

Their gifts symbolize Christ's identity and mission:
Gold points to His majesty ... for He was king.
Frankincense illustrates to His deity ... for He was God.
Myrrh demonstrates His Humanity ... for He was destined to die.

What does this story mean for us today?
It is a very simple message.
The Magi responded to the revelation God had given them.
In other words, they believed God and they obeyed God.
These wise men demonstrated true, deep, abiding faith.

The God we serve is a God of revelation.
He wants us to know Him and so therefore He reveals Himself to us.
We find God in nature, in creation, in prayer, in His Holy Word and most significantly in the birth and person of Jesus Christ.
That is why we celebrate Christmas!!!

One Minute Reflection
What part of the Wise Men's story resonates with you today?

"I heard the bells on Christmas Day
Their old, familiar carols play,
And wild and sweet
The words repeat
Of peace on earth, good-will to men!"
(Henry Wadsworth Longfellow)

Power Of The Most High

"The angel answered, 'The Holy Spirit will come on you, and the power of the Most High will overshadow you. So the Holy one to be born will be called the Son of God.'"

One important but often forgotten piece of the Christmas story is just how important the Holy Spirit is to the birth, life and resurrection of Jesus Christ.

This is the same Holy Spirit who brooded over the waters at Creation, inspired the Old Testament prophets and empowered the first disciples at Pentecost. The Holy Spirit is still performing miracles today and plays a significant role in the life of every believer.

As Luke 1:35 above reminds us, Gabriel, the angel, spoke with Mary about the miracle of her virgin birth. He explains that it will come about because of the power of the Holy Spirit.

Who Is The Holy Spirit?
The Holy Spirit is God, One full part of the Trinity
The Holy Spirit is a person
The Holy Spirit creates, teaches, speaks, and has feelings
The Holy Spirit gives wisdom, power and gifts

Why is this important for us to know?
The Holy Spirit enables followers of Christ to live their lives empowered to do things they could never do by their own strength or ability. The Holy Spirit is the one that draws us to Christ. He is the one who baptizes us in the spirit, and He is the one who gives us our spiritual gifts to advance God's kingdom here on earth.

The Holy Spirit longs for us to know Him, love Him and serve Him. As you reflect on the season - consider the Holy Spirit and invite Him into your heart as you prepare to celebrate Christmas.

One Minute Reflection
How will you honor the Holy Spirit this Christmas Season?

"There is not a better evangelist in the world than the Holy Spirit."
(C. L. Moody)

Do Not Be Afraid

<u>Matthew 1:20</u>
"But after he had considered this, an angel of the Lord appeared to him in a dream and said, 'Joseph son of David, do not be afraid to take Mary home as your wife, because what is conceived in her is from the Holy Spirit.'"

The Christmas story is filled with phrases to "fear not" and "do not be afraid". We need to pay close attention to this for God is telling us something profound. His message about fear is perfectly timed around the birth of Christ.

To Joseph
"Joseph, son of David, do not fear to take Mary as your wife, for that which is conceived in her is from the Holy Spirit." Matthew 1:20

To Zechariah
"Do not be afraid, Zechariah, for your prayer has been heard, and your wife Elizabeth will bear you a son, and you shall call his name John." Luke 1:12-13

To Mary
"Do not be afraid, Mary, for you have found favor with God." Luke 1:29-30

To the Shepherds
"And the angel said to them, 'Fear not, for behold, I bring you good news of great joy that will be for all the people.'" Luke 2:10

As it turns out almost every book of the Bible contains a "fear not" suggestion or command. Even Jesus Christ asked His disciples; "You of little faith, why are you so afraid?"

With Christ being for us, nothing can be against us.
The Christmas message tells us in no uncertain terms that with Christ there is no reason to be afraid.

<u>One Minute Reflection</u>
What fear could you surrender to Christ this Christmas Season?

"Have no fear for what tomorrow may bring. The same loving God Who cares for you today will take care of you tomorrow and every day. God will either shield you from suffering or give you unfailing strength to bear it. Be at peace, then, and put aside all anxious thoughts and imaginations."
(Francis de Sales)

Good News Of Great Joy

<u>Luke 2:10</u>
"But the angel said to them, 'Do not be afraid. I bring you good news that will cause great joy for all the people.'"

One of the most famous passages regarding the subject of "joy" is found in the Bible directly related to the Christmas message. It comes from Luke 2:10 when the angel of the Lord announces the coming birth of Jesus Christ.

The incarnation of Christ is considered "good news of great joy".

The word "incarnation" comes from the Greek word keno which refers to an "emptying." It describes someone of great position who is brought low, voluntarily laying aside his high rank and becoming as nothing in comparison with his prior dignity. Jesus, God from all eternity, left behind His infinitely glorious state by choice and became man.

That is a reason for Joy. But what does this mean for us personally?

We can now know with certainty that God loves us and wants to be in a deep, abiding relationship with mankind. Consider that no one in all of history has ever given up more or gone to such lengths for the sake of you and me.

We can also know with certainty that God is with us. Because of Christ and His promise of the Holy Spirit we can live knowing that the spirit of God resides in our hearts and will never leave or forsake us.

Finally, God has offered us eternal life with Him in Heaven.
The birth, life, death and resurrection of Jesus Christ are a reason to celebrate.

<u>One Minute Reflection</u>
Where will you find the most joy this Christmas season?

"Christmas is most truly Christmas when we celebrate it by giving the light of love to those who need it most."
(Ruth Carter Stapleton)

Magnificat

Luke 1:46-49

"And Mary said, 'My soul magnifies the Lord, and my spirit rejoices in God my Savior, for He has looked on the humble estate of His servant. For behold, from now on all generations will call me blessed; for He who is mighty has done great things for me, and Holy is His name.'"

Today we are studying a portion of *The Magnificat*, taken from Luke's Gospel. This is the Blessed Virgin Mary's hymn of praise to the Lord. Mary is so moved by a vision of God, that she breaks out in song that has come to be known as *The Magnificat*.

Although the Magnificat has had numerous musical settings from such composers as Palestrina, Bach and Mozart, it can be recited as well as sung. Its name comes from the first line of its text in Latin ("Magnificat anima mea Dominum") translated in the first line above *"My soul magnifies the Lord"*.

Mary was a righteous woman and was favored by God because she gave herself in complete faith to be used by God for His purposes. In this regard, Mary reminds us about the essential link between humility and holiness that we all seek.

The great lesson for each of us is that putting aside our own agendas and being open to God's will is the one essential ingredient needed to allow God's holiness to dwell in and shine through us.

Mary is a lasting example this Christmas season of true humility and divine holiness being offered and reflected through faith in God.

One Minute Reflection
What part of Mary's story resonates with you?

"We never give more honor to Jesus than when we honor His Mother, and we honor her simply and solely to honor Him all the more perfectly. We go to her only as a way leading to the goal we seek - Jesus, her Son." (Saint Louis Marie de Montfort)

Angels

Matthew 1:20-21
"But after he had considered this, an angel of the Lord appeared to him in a dream and said, 'Joseph son of David, do not be afraid to take Mary home as your wife, because what is conceived in her is from the Holy Spirit. She will give birth to a son, and you are to give Him the name Jesus, because He will save His people from their sins.'"

Angels are mentioned over 300 times in the Bible. Throughout Scripture we are told that God created angels; angels were present at the creation of the world; and angels live for eternity. We also learn that angels are wise, intelligent and very interested in the affairs of humanity. They were created to worship and glorify God and help mankind.
The Bible tells us that angels serve, minister, praise, worship, deliver, announce, provide, protect, guide, encourage and are often present with believers at their time of death.

Angels are present throughout the Christmas Story. We learn that on three separate occasions angels brought the announcement of the birth of Christ to Mary, to Joseph and to the shepherds.

Angels have been immortalized by Hymn writers with such memorable phrases as' *"Angels from the realms of Glory"*, *"Angels we have heard on High"* and *"Hark the Herald Angels Sing"*.

The word "angel" actually comes from the Greek word "aggelos", which means, "messenger."

Angels are part of human history and may be part of our modern life as well. Hebrews 13:2 says, *"Keep on loving each other as brothers. Do not forget to entertain strangers, for by so doing some people have entertained angels without knowing it"*.

One Minute Reflection
What do you believe about angels?

"Angels - like all other intelligent creatures - were designed to render worship to God, not to receive worship themselves. In fact, in every case in Scripture, whenever angels are offered any form of worship, they always rebuke the worshiper and redirect all worship to God alone."
(John MacArthur)

Peace On Earth

Luke 2:14
"Glory to God in the highest, and on earth peace, good will toward men."

All we need to do is turn on the evening news to know how much conflict there is throughout the world. However God has a plan that can change all of that.

One of the most important Christmas messages we can reflect on is that Jesus came to earth as the "Prince of Peace". Luke 2:14 elaborates, *"Glory to God in the highest and on earth - peace, good will toward men."*

What does this mean?
Jesus' birth, life and death are about reconciliation and the restoration of peace that was once enjoyed by God in fellowship with His creation.

Jesus came to insure we would have peace in three areas of our lives.

Peace with God
Jesus came to bind us back together with God.

Peace with Others
Christ not only reconciled us to God, but He also made it possible for us to enjoy harmonious relationships with others. Jesus can heal our emotional wounds and conflicts that keep us from loving each other.

Peace within Ourselves
The peace that Jesus gives us is an internal calm, which produces confidence no matter what is going on around us. God's peace is superior to anything the world can offer, because it is based on a relationship with Christ and has nothing to do with our circumstances.

One Minute Reflection
How will you give and receive peace this Christmas season?

"We make war that we may live in peace."
(Aristotle)

O Holy Night

"And she brought forth her firstborn son, and wrapped Him in swaddling clothes, and laid Him in a manger; because there was no room for them in the inn. And in the same region there were shepherds out in the field, keeping watch over their flock by night."

Christmas Eve is the evening or entire day preceding Christmas Day. One reason celebrations occur on Christmas Eve is because the traditional Christian liturgical day starts at sunset - an inheritance from Jewish tradition.

Since Christian tradition holds that Jesus was born at night as seen in our text from Luke 2:8 above telling us that the Shepherds were watching their flock by night, Midnight Mass is celebrated on Christmas Eve, traditionally at midnight, in the commemoration of His birth.

"O Holy Night" is a well-known Christmas carol composed by Adolphe Adam in 1847 which was later changed to a singing edition by Unitarian minister John Sullivan Dwight.

The text reflects on the birth of Jesus and of mankind's redemption.

O holy night! The stars are brightly shining,
It is the night of our dear Saviour's birth.
Long lay the world in sin and error pining,
'Til He appear'd and the soul felt its worth.
A thrill of hope the weary world rejoices,
For yonder breaks a new and glorious morn.
Fall on your knees! O hear the angel voices!
O night divine, O night when Christ was born;
O night divine, O night, O night Divine.

One Minute Reflection
What makes Christmas Eve Holy for you and your family?

"Without holiness on earth we shall never be prepared to enjoy Heaven. Heaven is a Holy place. The Lord of Heaven is a Holy Being. The angels are Holy creatures. Holiness is written on everything in Heaven... How shall we ever be at home and happy in Heaven if we die unholy?"
(J.C. Ryle)

A Sign To You

Luke 2:12
"This will be a sign to you: You will find a baby wrapped in cloths and lying in a manger."

Is there anything more precious and hopeful than a newborn baby? In the recounting of the Christmas Story in the Bible from Luke 2, we are told that the baby lying in a manger will be a sign to us.

A sign of what?
Hope; and not just any hope but hope in a God who keeps His Word and fulfills His promises.

God foretold numerous signs through His prophets, which are recorded in the Old Testament. The most important one was the birth of a savior. These prophets spoke of things that mankind should watch for so that the Messiah would be recognized and believed.

In general, a sign, in the sense that it is used here in Luke 2:12 is a visible and physical reminder of a verbal promise that God has made. All signs are proof given to strengthen our faith in God's Word, to remind us that whatever God has promised will in fact happen.

Christ is a sign of hope.
If we have Jesus, we have hope. And more than hope for life now, but also hope for a glorious and eternal future.

This Christmas while we are racing around buying gifts, attending parties and feeling the pressure of an already too busy season, remember our real hope is in a baby who grows up to be the Savior of the entire world.

Let's make sure not to leave Christ out of the "Christ"mas celebration.

One Minute Reflection
What hope can Christ bring you today?

"God foretold various signs through His prophets and one of them was the birth of a savior. These prophets spoke of things that mankind should watch for so that the Messiah would be recognized and believed."
(Lucinda Franks)

What Next

"When they had seen Him, they spread the word concerning what had been told them about this child, and all who heard it were amazed at what the shepherds said to them. But Mary treasured up all these things and pondered them in her heart. The shepherds returned, glorifying and praising God for all the things they had heard and seen, which were just as they had been told."

The Christmas Eve services are over, Santa has come and gone and the gifts have been torn open and enjoyed. The Bible reminds us in Luke 2:17-20 that after Christmas is a good time to reflect on what we have just seen and heard. The events are significant and the text above gives us three ways we can celebrate the birth of Christ going forward.

Shepherds Spread the Word
Once the Shepherds had seen the baby lying in the manger, *"they spread the word"*. Our job as Christians is to do exactly the same thing. We are not supposed to keep this news to just ourselves. We need to let others know the magnificent and life-changing impact that the birth of Christ will have on their lives as well.

Mary Pondered
Secondly, *Mary decided to "treasure up all these things in her heart and ponder them"*. To ponder something means "to consider something carefully for a long time". The news that Christ is the Savior to the world is something we can allow to dwell in our hearts and minds deliberately.

Praising and Glorifying
Finally we read that the shepherds returned *"praising and glorifying God"*. We can praise and glorify God by spending more time in prayer, by committing to reading His Word daily and by emulating His son Jesus Christ in thought, word and deed.

One Minute Reflection
How will you proclaim, ponder or praise Christ today?

"We consider Christmas as the encounter, the great encounter, the historical encounter, the decisive encounter, between God and mankind. He who has faith knows this truly; let him rejoice."
(Pope Paul VI)